D0131355

THE
SOUTHERN
TIGER

Santiago's main avenue, Alameda, in 1963. For decades, the city's commuters made do with an informal private bus system, plagued by high costs and inconsistent service.

Alameda Street in 2011—transformed into a modern avenue just a stone's throw from the Santiago Stock Exchange. A public Transantiago bus system and a modern metro both line the corridor.

THE SOUTHERN TIGER

Chile's Fight for a Democratic
and Prosperous Future

RICARDO LAGOS

WITH BLAKE HOUNSHELL AND ELIZABETH DICKINSON

FOREWORD BY BILL CLINTON

palgrave
macmillan

First published in 2012 by PALGRAVE MACMILLAN® in the United States—a
division of St. Martin's Press LLC, 175 Fifth Avenue, New York, NY 10010.

Where this book is distributed in the UK, Europe and the rest of the world, this
is by Palgrave Macmillan, a division of Macmillan Publishers Limited, registered
in England, company number 785998, of Houndmills, Basingstoke, Hampshire
RG21 6XS.

Palgrave Macmillan is the global academic imprint of the above companies and
has companies and representatives throughout the world.

Palgrave® and Macmillan® are registered trademarks in the United States, the
United Kingdom, Europe and other countries.

ISBN: 978-0-230-33816-6

Library of Congress Cataloging-in-Publication Data

The southern tiger : Chile's fight for a democratic and prosperous future / by
Richard Lagos.
    p.   cm.
Includes index.
ISBN 978-0-230-33816-6
    1. Chile—Politics and government—1988–   2. Chile—Economic
conditions—1988–   3. Chile—Social conditions—1970–   I. Title.

F3101.3L34   2012
983.06'6—dc23

                                                                        2011028278

A catalogue record of the book is available from the British Library.

Design by Letra Libre, Inc.

First edition: January 2012

10   9   8   7   6   5   4   3   2   1

Printed in the United States of America.

To the Chilean people, who made this journey possible.

CONTENTS

Foreword by President Bill Clinton   x

Acknowledgments   xiii

ONE   The Finger   1

TWO   After the Coup   15

THREE   Fall of the Chicago Boys   39

FOUR   Prisoner of the State   69

FIVE   Interregnum   105

SIX   The Morning After   122

SEVEN   Pinochet's Ghost   146

EIGHT   The Chilean Way   172

NINE   Bush, Saddam, and Me   200

             Epilogue   242

Index   255

On April 25, 1988, Ricardo Lagos became the first Chilean to publicly denounce the dictatorship on live television. "I am speaking for 15 years of silence!" he proclaimed, wagging his finger at then-President Augusto Pinochet.

RAQUEL CORREA: Your Party for Democracy favors a "No" vote, and you believe that "No" will win. Many people in this country are wondering: What would happen the night of a "No" vote?

RICARDO LAGOS: It would be the beginning of the end of the dictatorship. And more importantly—I believe essentially—at that moment, the country will have stopped General Pinochet, who would otherwise stay in power for 25 years. General Pinochet has not been honest with this country. First he said . . . first *you* said, General Pinochet, [that] you had goals but no deadlines. Then, General Pinochet, you had a timeline and imposed the constitution of 1980. I will remind you, General Pinochet, that you said on the day of the 1980 plebiscite, "President Pinochet would not be a candidate in 1989."

The camera is focusing, I hope. [Camera focuses on a newspaper clipping from 1980, reporting a speech in which Pinochet promises not to stand as a candidate in 1989.]

And now you would have the country pass through another eight years . . . with torture, assassinations, with the violation of human rights. . . . To me, it is inadmissible that a Chilean would have such ambitions to power, to be so bold as to stay for 25 years in power!! . . . Others have never been [so ambitious] sir, and you will have to answer . . .

RAQUEL CORREA: Ricardo, those who are gathered here tonight . . .

LAGOS: . . . and you will have to answer, between "Yes" and "No."

CORREA: Ricardo! What the country wants to know . . .

LAGOS: . . . and you will be summoned [to answer] for what you did. . . . Raquel, you must excuse me; I am speaking for 15 years of silence!

FOREWORD

Wlen I met my friend Ricardo Lagos at a Third Way conference in June 2000, he was just beginning his Presidency, and
I was nearing the end of mine. We discussed, among other
things, how Chile could become the cornerstone of the free-trade area we were
building in our hemisphere, something I had been working on with his predecessor Eduardo Frei Ruiz-Tagle, a Christian Democrat.

President Lagos, however, was a Socialist—the first Socialist President of
Chile since the deposed Salvador Allende—and although his party was not
generally thought of as enthusiastic proponents of free trade, the new President had already proven himself to be anything but a typical politician. The
same man who witnessed the Freedom Rides 50 years ago as a university student in North Carolina knew that inequality—particularly institutionalized
inequality—doesn't disappear simply by the election of people with good intentions but rigid ideologies.

Ten years earlier he'd been appointed Chile's Education Minister in the
first post-Pinochet government, after playing a key role in the landmark plebiscite that resulted in the General's ouster after 70 years of despotic rule. It
would have been simple, perhaps even expected, for Education Minister Lagos to demand top-down reforms and cultivate the support of the powerful
teachers' union. There was no money in the budget for reforms—in one of its
last acts, the *junta* had privatized much of Chile's educational system—and he
could have spent his term simply disputing the inequalities of the dysfunctional
system he'd inherited. Instead, in homage to his country's Nobel-winning poet
Pablo Neruda, Minister Lagos built small libraries, using what little money

was available through the government coffers and donations from the World Bank. He asked the teachers to become innovators; in essence, to take control of their own destinies and devise programs to raise the standards for the most troubled schools.

Four years later, as Minister of Public Works, he came up with a plan to finance highway improvements that, for a Socialist, was a Nixon-going-to-China moment: he proposed to finance it with private tolls. Through collaborations with the business sector, Chile's roads would be able to support the commerce and travel a growing country demanded. Global trade, he was to argue later as President, was the key to Chile's future. Only through world markets would Chile's historical inequalities be addressed; and through diversification and global trade, Chile's over-reliance on world copper prices could be lessened.

At this point one might wonder exactly what kind of Socialist Ricardo Lagos was. But the truth is that free-trade agreements like the one President Lagos engineered between the United States and Chile, begun under my administration and signed under George W. Bush's, only offer the *opportunity* for expanding markets; the hard work is in developing on-the-ground, sustainable solutions to produce goods that can be marketed abroad. This is also true with healthcare; rights on paper don't necessarily mean anything in practice. Chile had traditionally guaranteed healthcare to all of its citizens, but the infrastructure couldn't live up to it, and so disparities in medical care between the well-off and the desperately poor were extreme.

As I spend my post-Presidency addressing the tragic inequalities that persist in the world—the vast gulf between those who can rely on the benefits of development and the other half who subsist on less than two dollars a day—I see the tremendous difference leaders can make when they address how to make necessary changes, rather than simply how much to spend on a project or where the money will come from. Often these solutions come about through partnerships between government and the private sector, with the help of non-governmental organizations to fill in the gaps. It's crucial to concentrate on the *how,* instead of the *how much,* especially during times of economic hardship like we're facing now.

President Lagos took over the helm during an economic recession—the Asian financial collapse had just occurred—and unemployment in Chile, like much of South America, was threatening double digits. He immediately began a jobs program that relied heavily on infrastructure improvements, so that the benefits, such as improved highways, would remain when the economy recovered. His administration came up with a specific plan to fight homelessness by building small, innovative homes that could expand with a growing family and clustered them in communities with good schools and law enforcement. It was never just about how much something would cost, but how it could be achieved given the resources and political realities at hand.

My friend Ricardo has never slowed in his efforts to fight the persistent inequalities in Chile and around the world. His particular mix of optimism and ingenuity pervade this book, and even readers familiar with the story of Chile's re-emergence from its darkest chapter will discover something new about its revitalization and the role of this extraordinary statesman. Even when imprisoned by the junta, his grace and optimism never faded, his courage was steadfast, and, more importantly, his vision for a better country did not waver. His is a remarkable story, and, like Chile's, it's not over yet.

—President Bill Clinton

ACKNOWLEDGMENTS

Not so long ago, my country did something extraordinary: We defeated tyranny with peace. Against all odds, the people of Chile believed that democracy could be restored to their military state. And using nothing more than a ballot box, they proved it to the world.

This is the story of that moment, when the force of history turned its glance toward our quiet country on the edge of the Southern Hemisphere. This is the story of a people who believed in the power of democracy—one that is just, equal, respectful, and grounded in the truth. The people have always been the true authors of Chile's future. And as such, I owe them the most profound thanks for everything that is written in these pages.

On that long, sometimes difficult journey, there were so many men and women who worked with all the force of their spirits. They were the political organizers, the local city leaders, and the local supporters. Each believed in his or her own way that democracy was possible. The list of those to whom I owe my appreciation is long and filled with memories.

This story is also that of a man who was a minister and a president—a man who had the pleasure to work and collaborate with and lead the incredible Chilean people. At each step, when I was one of the leaders of the opposition, then later president of a party, then minister of education and of public works, and then president, I incurred a great debt to the service of so many colleagues. You have taught me a great deal with your work, dedication, and spirit—and there are far too many of you to name individually.

There is so much about a presidency—so many promises, plans, debates, and compromises—that you wish you could have done, or done better. The responsibility for those unfinished projects and unrealized dreams ultimately lies with me. But the successes belong to all those who worked beside me. As ministers and secretaries, as ambassadors and directors, as parliamentarians or public servants, each and every one should feel ownership of the successes that we achieved.

To the "second floor" (as the press likes to call those members of government who work on the second floor of the presidential palace, La Moneda) and to the thousands of regional and local leaders stretching the length of Chile, you have my thanks. Many of the ideas that follow in these pages were enriched by my contact with these invaluable colleagues. I hope that many of them will feel represented in these words. If they do, then I will know I have succeeded: I have written a portrait of our collective voyage these last four decades in Chile.

I also owe words of thanks to those involved in the writing of this book: to Angélica Alzamora, my secretary, who has transcribed countless tapes, and certainly to my editors Elizabeth Dickinson and Blake Hounshell for all of the many conversations and discussions that led us to the final manuscript. Whatever eloquence of English language that this book may contain can be attributed to their professionalism.

I must also thank Moisés Naim, my friend of so many years, for pushing me to write a book of the sort that these pages now contain—not a scholarly memoir, or a detailed account of my life, but rather a look back at the broad strokes and big ideas that have shaped my life.

Last but certainly not least, I must thank those closest to me, my companion and wife in all these years, Luisa, my children—Ricardo, Ximena, Hernán, Alejandro, and Panchita—and our entire family, which has grown as we've welcomed grandchildren. It is ultimately because of them that this incredible journey was possible in the first place. Thank you!

ONE

THE FINGER

On the cool night of April 25, 1988, General Augusto Pinochet sat in the basement of his home, a low-slung bungalow set back from a quiet street in a wealthy part of Santiago, where he resided as president of the ruling junta in Chile. He was watching a television program on the giant screen that adorned his wall. That evening, Raquel Correa, an incisive journalist of slim but commanding stature, was set to interview various officials from Chile's registered political parties. Correa had an aura about her that seemed to emanate impartiality, and her weekly interviews in *El Mercurio*, Chile's biggest newspaper, were extremely popular. She was the only one who dared to ask tough questions of the generals who ruled us.

On the other side of Santiago, in the television studio, I was preparing intensely. I had been rehearsing this appearance for weeks. I had sought advice about what to wear, how to look, and how to speak on camera. Now it was show time. I was tense but focused as I sat down at the long oval table that separated me and the other three guests from the journalists questioning us. As the show began, I guessed—I was almost certain, in fact—that Pinochet would be watching. And I was planning to speak directly to him.

Everything had to go perfectly that night. It was the first chance for my party, the Party for Democracy (PPD is the acronym in Spanish), to persuade a mass television audience to set aside its fears and vote. At that time, Chile was still a wounded nation. Since military rule had been forced upon the country 15 years earlier, we had seen too many horrors to count. The 1973 coup had been our September 11, as Pinochet and the other members of what became the military junta besieged and bombed the presidential palace, La Moneda, violently ousting the previous Socialist government. Thousands were rounded up that day and brought to Santiago's main stadium, where most were tortured and many killed. Many of them were my close friends. The military regime that followed built an internal intelligence service so sinister that after it assassinated dissidents, it used helicopters to dump their bodies into the sea. The state was accountable to no one but Pinochet. Its reach extended to every corner of Chile, and even beyond. Pinochet targeted a handful of exiled enemies in terrorist attacks—a sniper in Rome, a car bomb in Argentina, and another in Washington, D.C.

By 1988, the junta was no longer murdering dissidents. It didn't have to. To live in Chile at that time was to live in fear—not abject terror, but the low-lying, constant stress of peril that puts a person always on edge. If you were a young man in Santiago, you could be grabbed by the military at any time and asked to prove that you were loyal to the regime. As a businessman or an intellectual, your work could be monitored, and strangers seemed to know a bit too much about you for comfort. There were rumors of cameras in the voting booth, watching to see which box you ticked. What was true or not about the regime's presence in Chileans' lives was almost irrelevant; fear made everyone a believer.

That night was our best chance to change the dynamic. After 15 years, we finally had a window to defeat the dictatorship nonviolently, and Pinochet himself had given it to us. Eight years earlier, in 1980, the general had forced through a constitution calling for a plebiscite, the results of which would decide whether the junta's candidate (whom everyone knew would be Pinochet) would remain in office for another eight years. Pinochet assumed he'd be able to win the plebiscite easily—the confidence of a man accustomed to having things his way. But those of us in the opposition wanted to make a real contest of it. Our task was to convince Chileans to register to vote, so that when the plebiscite took place, Chile would reject another eight years of dictatorship.

First, however, we had to conquer the fears of an entire country. And that's where Correa's television program came in. We had to persuade the nation that change was actually possible after the years of stagnant military rule since Pinochet had ousted Salvador Allende 15 years earlier. The political situation was far from a rosy "transition to democracy," as Pinochet had dubbed his last eight years. Still, we could use the opening he had given us, however small, to win. Unlike the previous plebiscite, which ushered in Pinochet's 1980 constitution, this one would be fair. Why? Because we were going to ensure that each polling station was packed with our observers. We would watch to guarantee a free and secret vote, the results of which we could tally independently and transmit to our central computer system. And, unlike in 1980, there was going to be an electoral register; we were going to get people to sign up en masse. We calculated that to win beyond any shadow of a doubt, we would need 8 million registered voters to mark their ballots "No" across the country's 35,000 polling stations. To get them to do that, first we would need to prove to Chileans that their votes would matter.

This was a tall order for a program meant to last just 45 minutes (plus 15 minutes of commercials)—and the interview would not just be us in the PPD. Correa and her colleagues were playing host to all the country's registered political parties. And while that included our fellow reformers in the Christian Democratic Party, represented by its president, Patricio Aylwin, it meant that the conservative National Renewal Party and the National Vanguard, the progovernment parties, were also there. Each party would be represented by four officials and would respond to the questions posed by three journalists.

Several weeks earlier, we in the party had decided on the three colleagues who would join me in the interview. First would be one of our vice presidents, Armando Jaramillo, a conservative man with an imposing voice that made his every comment sound like a fatherly instruction. He was a well-heeled land owner, and one of the few people in our party who could truly claim to be from the old aristocracy. He certainly looked the part, wearing his finest three-piece suit and sporting a particularly gaudy ring with a large stone in the center, of which he was quite fond. (I asked him to take it off for the interview—a suggestion he declined.) But he was also an avid believer in human rights. His strength was precisely in that balance; many conservatives supported Pinochet, but few had, like Armando, retained their democratic convictions.

From the other side of the spectrum came our secretary-general, Jorge Schaulsohn, a thin man who was just out of the university. A radical, Jorge had distinguished himself as a student leader who fought mercilessly against the dictatorship. At 37, he was still young and filled with fire. The fourth party member at the television table was Carolina Tohá, a slim university student who looked more comfortable in her usual bohemian wardrobe than in the pressed white shirt that she wore that day. Carolina was the daughter of José Tohá, who had been minister of the interior in Allende's government. She knew more intimately than any of us what it meant to live under Pinochet; her father had been sent to a brutal prison camp after the coup and later "committed suicide" in police custody. But Carolina wasn't angry; she just wanted things to change.

That night, as we sat closely packed together under the high ceilings of the television studio, we were all in agreement about what we needed to do.

Traveling through Chile in the dry southern summer was no pleasure tour. When we arrived in the northern town of La Serena on December 18, 1987, months before the television show, we were tired amid a whirlwind of speeches, frustrations, jubilation, and hope. The town of 150,000 people, more than 300 miles north of the capital, bustled with the low-key intensity of a mid-sized rural hub. By the end of 1987, my colleagues—Aylwin, of the Christian Democratic Party, and Luis Fernando Luengo, a representative of other forces on the left—and I had trod across the region, our suits coated with dry dust and our throats parched from speaking. We had been on the road for months in the heat of summer, visiting every city and town in the dry zone where it almost never rained, even in the winter. La Serena was our stop on the way to the even smaller town of Ovalle, after which we would conclude our journey in Illapel, traveling on bumpy, unpaved roads.

But calling Chileans to register for the upcoming vote wasn't just grueling because of the sun beating down on our faces. Most were skeptical; many more were fearful; and some were downright hostile, claiming that participating in the vote would be equivalent to playing by the dictator's rules. Those in the latter camp had adopted the slogan "Registration is treason." Even Luengo doubted that registration would work, but he joined us to show solidarity against Pinochet.

The venue waiting for us in La Serena was modest, a movie theater holding about 300 people. Around 20 or 30 of them were shouting at us, calling us traitors for registering voters for Pinochet's democratic charade. They didn't need to scream for us to get the message; La Serena was, like much of Chile, a hard sell. Nevertheless, we set up to speak on an elevated wood stage framed by red velvet curtains. The microphone was troublesome, being a handheld, so we couldn't use notes. It was a warm day outside, but the cool shade inside the theater meant that I was not uncomfortable in my necktie.

As I was preparing to begin, a woman from the press handed me a cable, already taken from the envelope. The all-capital letters on the white paper, pasted onto a yellow backing, read: "Arica, urgent." It was from Pinochet; he had given a speech in Arica, a city in the extreme north of the country, threatening us for making "little waves" against his government. "There is some 'Lagos' somewhere," he had said. "We know all your steps."

It was the first time Pinochet had ever referred to me in person, and it was exhilarating. So unusual was it that a dictator would address you by name that I knew I had to have done something to get his attention. I felt no fear. Rather, it was rewarding, during a difficult time, to know that at least my opponent had noticed I was fighting.

Many of my colleagues suspected that Pinochet had mentioned me because he found it useful to have a leftist adversary like myself, a long-time member of the Socialist Party, on whom he could blame unrest or discontent. But I had another theory. For months, I had been speaking on the radio, calling for people to register to vote. A year earlier, at a time when the press was under siege, I was asked to interview for a short spot on television. I knew, however, that they would edit my response if I said what I wanted to. They would use only a small clip of my longer answer, choosing my least confrontational words. So I asked the reporter how much time I had to answer; I would give her a quote of exactly the correct length so that she would have no choice but to use it in its entirety. Nervously, she consulted with other members of the television station and finally agreed to give me 30 seconds—on the condition that I not name names (nor utter the words "dictator" or "dictatorship").

I knew how to get around it. For Chileans, there was only one "Captain General"—Bernardo O'Higgins, who fought for Chile's independence from Spain—but Pinochet had recently given himself the same title. That's how I would refer to him. Speaking of the junta leader sarcastically as the Captain General would remind my countrymen that Pinochet had co-opted Chile's once-democratic history in every way—even in name.

Whatever the reason for Pinochet's warning, in La Serena it had none of the intended effects. I turned directly from the cable to Aylwin, asking, "Let me speak first to calm the people." He agreed, and I was introduced to the small but fierce crowd, which had begun shouting the moment I told them they should register to vote.

"I beg you," I said. "Be silent. I am going to read you a cable that has just arrived, to which I must respond." A brief measure of calm allowed me to recount what Pinochet had said.

In that impassioned moment, it occurred to me to speak directly to Pinochet, as if he could hear me from that distant post. "I am speaking to you, General Pinochet," my voice raged. "All the way from La Serena, I am replying. We will continue our fight to defeat you in the plebiscite!"

The crowd leapt to its feet in applause. I was as surprised as anyone. When I addressed Pinochet directly by name, the effect was tremendous. That wasn't something you did in Chile in 1987, and the same people who had angrily shouted, "Registration is treason!" were now suddenly swept up in the moment.

It was a formula I repeated, to the same result each time, in every town and countryside stop we visited. Of course, the people watching us in those visits were very few. They were the true believers, some of whom had been there 15 years ago when the Socialist Party I then represented was ousted. But they were hardly militants, and they were still afraid. Speaking directly to Pinochet helped them see a way forward. If only the Captain General had known what an inspiration his threatening cable would become.

Just a week before the television program in April, one of Pinochet's supporters asked me what I would do when I spoke on Correa's show. We were gathered at a radio station, one of the few, rare forums left where one could express views of every political stripe. "I will tell Correa some of the same things that are said here," I replied to the man, alluding to the need for democracy and an electoral transition. A good friend turned to us and grinned. "I know what you are going to do, Ricardo," he said. "You will look at the camera and speak directly to General Pinochet."

We all laughed. But in fact, that is precisely what I was planning to do. For the two weeks before the program, my three colleagues and I had been planning and practicing our approach. In a small, haphazard studio close to where we lived and worked in the old neighborhood of Providencia, we had re-created the entire set of the program—from the oval table that would separate ourselves from the journalists to the layout of the chairs and cameras. We arranged for three well-known journalists, two women and one man, from opposition newspapers to play the role of the interviewers, and they proved far tougher interrogators than the real television journalists would be. With each run-through, we four sat across the table, imagining that it was the night of the program. Getting it perfect was the least we could do for the thousands of Chileans who had already taken the risk to register and the many more we hoped would do so. We needed to allay the fears of millions, explaining why we were so confident that our path of nonviolence could defeat a dictator. And we had to do it in a way that everyone in Chile would understand.

The interview would be divided into three parts: first a discussion of our general party platform, then our economic position, and lastly, the referendum. The segment on the referendum was critical, but the first two were also extremely important; we would have to convince the audience that we had a plan to rebuild Chile. After a decade and a half under Pinochet's rule, many had a difficult time imagining anything else. How, they wondered, could a country so accustomed to dictatorship, so beaten down by inequality and economic stagnation, become a vibrant democracy once again?

The trick was to appeal to Chilean tradition. Chile, a country far from the center of global power and surrounded by the Andes mountains, didn't have the same natural wealth—the gold or silver—of other countries in the Spanish empire in Latin America. But we had always had at least a semblance of democracy. We achieved independence with only minor instability, and we were able to consolidate the institutions necessary to peacefully elect president after president. We wanted to remind Chileans that Pinochet was an aberration, a black mark on their proud, democratic history.

I always compared our situation to the devastation of Europe following World War II, when countries needed to simultaneously reconstruct their infrastructure and their very souls. Coalition governments, like those of General Charles De Gaulle in France and Alcide De Gasperi in Italy, would need to integrate everyone from the far right to the communists under one roof. These examples of national unity seemed like a good model for Chile, we told the viewers, whom we knew held among them vastly different opinions about how to govern the country.

One thing all of the opposition factions could agree on was how greatly the country had suffered under Pinochet. Chileans had paid dearly during the financial crisis of 1982, when prices rose drastically even as the economy shrank by more than 20 percent. We had seen purchasing power drop and social protection fall from its already modest levels of the 1960s and 1970s. The resulting poverty was devastating. Pensions lost 10 percent of their value when Pinochet resorted to deep budget cuts to balance the budget. The minimum wage hardly deserved its name. If you wandered the streets of Santiago, you couldn't help but notice countless men and women begging on the streets, and their ranks were growing. So too were the number of sellers hawking fruit and small goods on every corner and sidewalk. Even the way people dressed was changing; around that time, Chile began importing used clothes because so many could not afford new ones. Even if the dictatorship would never admit it, people knew all this; they saw the misery unfolding before them every day.

What they didn't know was that they also had the courage to fight back. Part three of the program, during which we would discuss the referendum, was our time to prove that. We planned to use the same direct approach that had won us so many supporters on the road. But we also planned to remind Chileans that the last time they had a chance to vote, in the 1980 plebiscite meant to ratify the constitution, they were robbed. There had been no electoral registers, no voting lists, and no real choices other than Pinochet's. This time didn't have to be that way, but it would be unless Chile rose above its fears.

On the morning before the television program, I left the office for a brief walk. While I was gone, a fellow member of the Party for Democracy stopped by to see me. He was from the city council in Ñuñoa, the district in Santiago where I had grown up. When he arrived in my office, which looked more like a law firm than the headquarters of a grassroots revolution, my secretary greeted him, telling him I was out. "Let me leave this for him," he told her, handing over a small newspaper clipping with a letter attached. "I imagine it might be useful for his appearance on television tonight." (I learned many years later that the letter had come from a historian who became one of my speech writers in Santiago. He never admitted to being its author until I stumbled upon his note in my archive years later.)

The clipping was small, perhaps just a few inches across, recounting a minor speech that Pinochet had given back in 1980, around the time of the new constitution. But it was precisely the evidence we needed. From the beginning of his dictatorship, Pinochet had said that there were goals, but no timetables or deadlines for transitioning to democracy. There was a job to do, he explained, refusing to put limits on what he had deemed a necessary "dictatorial period." Then came 1980, when the new constitution mandated a period of presidential transition set to last between 8 and 16 years. At first, Pinochet had planned to give himself that 16-year mandate without interruption. But the minister of the interior and the lawyers advising him warned that putting such a long term in print would be an international embarrassment. So Pinochet cunningly instituted an 8-year period in which he would rule with the junta. Thereafter, a plebiscite would be held for voters to say "Yes" or "No" to the junta's chosen candidate for president, whose identity was to be determined later. Pinochet had clearly promised in the 1980 speech that he would not stand for office again in 1988. By now it was clear that stepping down—a minor promise among the hundreds of broken pledges he had made over the past 15 years—was never his intention. He had lied then and was lying now. The clipping became an integral part of our plan.

We arrived at the studio tense but ready, knowing we had prepared, but understanding that a live program meant there was no margin for error. In those final moments, our focus switched from facts and arguments to image and presentation. It was not just our words but our demeanor, our placement, and our very looks that would need to be exactly right. We were perfectly shaven, made up, and clothed in our best.

I sat down, surveying the scene that so closely resembled our practice replication. "Of all these cameras," I asked the producer, a man named Gonzalo Beltrán, "which one will be facing me?" He pointed to one of the few facing the stage, "This is it."

"Also, sir, I want to be sure of something," I went on. "Normally, I should speak to the journalist, I know. But if I want at any time to turn and speak to the audience, will the camera turn away from me?" He looked puzzled, but answered nonetheless. "I could not turn the camera away if you were facing it," he said, explaining that such a move would look very bad on live television. That camera was my window straight to Pinochet's television screen.

We followed the Christian Democrats in the program. The first and second parts went smoothly. The discussion of the economy in particular brought me into my element. I had spent much of my time in recent years immersed in the topic, and I knew that the figures I had at the tip of my tongue were damning.

During the commercial break that would lead into part three, Beltrán, the producer, turned to us. "We went over our time limit on the first and second parts, so we will have to reduce the third from 15 minutes to just 9," he said. I felt panic rise. It would suddenly be very difficult to both address Pinochet and explain why the previous plebiscite was flawed. I begged them not to shorten the segment, but there was nothing we could do. My mind surged with adrenaline and apprehension. My biggest fear was that I would be interrupted—that the journalists would not allow me to say everything I needed to say.

That is precisely what happened. When the cameras started rolling, I began like a sprinter, jumping up from the starting line to get straight to the point. "It is the beginning of the end of the dictatorship," I told Correa, whose practiced television smile gradually vanished as I spoke. I kept going. The camera focused in on the newspaper clipping, and I explained the lies and injustices that so many years of dictatorship had wrought. I began speaking to Pinochet directly, my arm extended out, my finger pointed straight to Pinochet. I told him his ambitions to power outstripped any past leader of Chile . . .

And Correa could stand it no more. She interrupted me, breaking my concentration. Years later, she told me she had feared for the very existence of the television station in that moment. Surely, after my impertinent comments, it would be shut down the next day. She had to stop me from going further to save what little freedom the dictatorship had given them.

As Correa tried to talk over me, my thoughts flew back to December 2, 1983, the day that the first protest against the dictatorship was held in the port city of Valparaíso. Perhaps 10,000 or 15,000 youth, lawyers, human rights activists, political party members, and dock workers all gathered in a soccer field outside the city. I had just assumed the presidency of the Democratic Alliance, the first incarnation of the same group of opposition parties leading the fight today. With our newly unified coalition behind me, I was feeling bold. "I speak for 10 years of silence!" I shouted into the crowd.

Until the television show, that had been the last time my emotions and the stakes ran so high. So what I said next came out naturally. "Excuse me, Raquel, but I am speaking for 15 years of silence!" I said angrily, cutting her off. For those 15 years, it had been impossible to interrupt a television program in that way. It had been impossible to interrupt the march of dictatorship. It had been impossible to interrupt the message Pinochet wanted to send—of a Chile making great strides toward economic prosperity and democracy. Speaking those words was, in a way, a means of ending the period of repression. And we were doing it without violence.

I have been on television countless times in the years thereafter, but never have I felt so much tension as that night. The very credibility of our political strategy—something many Chileans doubted—was at stake. If I failed to persuade them, we might be stuck with Pinochet forever.

After the program, I finally took a deep breath. I was still worried about the time that was cut, and I turned to Correa to explain my irritation. We had not been able to denounce the farce of the 1980 plebiscite, nor were we able to explain that this time around we would be vigilant and guard the polls with our own observers.

The journalist looked at me, trying to cool my displeasure. "Ricardo, you don't know what has happened," she said in measured tone. "There will be a true revolution with what you have said tonight." I was preoccupied with my complaints, and her words didn't sink in. I insisted that we had not been able to say all that we had wanted. We had prepared a cocktail of messages for the end of the program, none of which was heard.

But we did not linger. About 50 of our friends from the PPD who had helped us prepare for the program were waiting for us at Jaramillo's home. It was a beautiful French-style house with several floors and an enormous dining and living area, which we knew would be stuffed with people. Quickly, we gathered our things and made our way out of the studio, stepping into the night. No sooner did we fling open the studio doors than we were met by shouts and applause. An enthusiastic crowd of 100 or so had already gathered to meet us. Surely, they did the same every night when the program ended, I thought. Of course, the opposite was true; never before and never again would they leave their houses in the night to cheer.

In many parts of Chile, people spilled into the streets to celebrate, clamoring with excitement and anxiety, unable to resist the urge to speak with neighbors about what had just happened—and what would certainly occur next. When we arrived at Jaramillo's home, the mood was exhilarating, and a new sense of optimism—one that we hadn't felt in years—filled the room. The country had been taken by surprise by what we had said—even our own supporters, and yes, even Pinochet.

We were almost certain that Pinochet would be watching the program, and this was shortly confirmed. Newspapers reported how the dictator, watching in his home, had risen to his feet in anger. His first reaction was to order one of his generals to deploy tanks to the streets. "Of course, my general, but for what?" the loyal soldier had replied. When his rage calmed, Pinochet must have realized his folly. No tanks were ever seen that night.

The day after the speech, however, urgent meetings were taking place in La Moneda. Our television appearance had inspired a near panic. The minister of the interior went on television and explained that the government had gathered to determine how to respond to my denouncement. "We will take care of you, Mr. Lagos," he said, looking at me as if in reply to my on-camera confrontation with Pinochet.

Pinochet's supporters and the right-leaning press whipped up anger against me. Suddenly, there was a real choice to be made, and it was polarizing the country. Some, including Admiral José Toribio Merino, a top member of the junta, insisted that my televised attack would play into Pinochet's hands and help him win the Yes vote. Such rage and insanity, he reasoned, would do nothing but discredit the opposition. I responded that, if this were the case, perhaps the government should replay the famous interview—a suggestion that was, of course, dismissed.

What I saw on the streets the day after April 25 washed away any lingering fear of my message being lost. That day, on my morning commute along a pedestrian route in the center of Santiago, people began to approach me, reaching toward me for a handshake or applauding me for what I had done. When I at last arrived at my office, another rush came forward to congratulate me. I was beginning to realize the gravity of what had just happened.

Before returning home that day, Aylwin and I took a trip to Curicó, a city south of Santiago, where we planned to continue registering voters. It was one of the cities in Aylwin's district, where until 1973 he had been a senator representing the Christian Democrats. I expected his name to draw a respectable crowd to the modest, paint-chipped theater, but I never imagined the crowds that surged forward to greet us. "Do you see that the television program has changed the spirit of many people?" Aylwin turned to me, saying. "Congratulations for last night!"

Yet we were still living in Pinochet's Chile; so far it was only the mood that had changed. Even a child could see that. My daughter Francisca, just 12 at the time, stayed up that night waiting for me to return from Curicó, refusing to sleep until I had arrived. She had heard the interior minister's words. She had watched the journalists speculate openly about my fate. Like them, she was convinced that it was only a matter of time before I was arrested. It had happened once before, just two years earlier. Back then, they had come for me in the night—and when Francisca woke the next morning, I was gone. This time, she would stay awake and alert so I couldn't be whisked away. She asked me late that night when I got back from Curicó, "What will happen to you?"

Without a doubt, the television program marked a clear before and after in Chile—before, our victory looked impossible, and afterward, it became possible. Not only did people continue approaching me on the streets, but I received invitation upon invitation to travel throughout the country, calling for people to vote No. Something had changed. Chile was shedding its fear.

I had accidentally become—both in the minds of Chileans and of Pinochet himself—the nemesis of a dictator. I'm certain that Pinochet realized it, and of course, he didn't stay silent. Just a few months after the show, on June 9, I was traveling the countryside when he lashed out. "I say to those bad Chileans who insult us on television because they know we are in a democracy and we are not going to do anything to them: Be careful, because patience has a limit and this limit can be felt." He added, "As we approach the plebiscite we are going to show this minority, which shouts and vociferates . . . we are going to wipe them off the map." He called me a "bandit," using only my middle name, Froilán, to identify me.

But in many ways, he was too late. To understand the impact of the television program was to understand everything it had shattered—the fear, the anguish, and the deep danger of reprisal that had kept Chileans quiet and submissive for too long. Maybe Pinochet's biggest mistake was not arresting me after the program. For years, critics had fled abroad or been exiled by the state, their names added to a long list of citizens who woke up one morning and were no longer residents of Chile. I expected the same might happen to me if we went too far. But that was the genius of the No campaign: We walked so close to the line of what was tolerable that we obliterated its existence altogether.

More than 20 years later, one of Chile's most notable journalists, Alejandro Guillier, came to see me at my office at my foundation. On the wall there hangs a picture from that April 25 night, when I wagged my finger at Pinochet. Looking at the photo, Guillier turned to me. "I remember it as if it were today," he said, marveling at two decades passed. "My children, who had not wanted to register, decided to do so after seeing the program. That program changed their minds," he told me, adding, "and I told my wife, 'Today, we saw who dares to confront the dictator.' Until then, the opposition had not had the courage."

TWO

AFTER THE COUP

In January 1961, I boarded a bus in Durham, North Carolina, on my way to Duke University, where I was about to become a student. It was my first time in the United States. Just 22 years old at the time, I had seen poverty and I knew what inequality meant. I knew how the lower-class *campamentos* neighborhoods in Chile were packed full with humanity, and the water, electricity, and even food were never enough. But I had never seen what awaited me on that bus: the most overt segregation. The blacks were seated at the back of the bus and the whites in the front. In the moment, I didn't know where I fit in. I suppose I am white, so I awkwardly shuffled into my place.

My country, Chile, had taught me about injustice—about oppression, repression, and the daily dignity of struggling to survive. But it was a bus in Durham and the American South that taught me how difficult it is to break with the past—something I would spend the rest of my life working on. A few weeks after my awkward introduction to North Carolina, "freedom riders" began a months-long bus-riding campaign that would eventually overturn the Jim Crow laws. But even as the rules officially changed, some people's behavior didn't. I decided, some time later, to sit in an empty seat at the back of the bus. But the moment I sat down next to a black man, he got up and moved away.

I never knew if he was frightened or annoyed by what I had done. It took another decade, a mass movement of political pressure, and profound leadership before that situation would change.

I realized something then—viscerally—but not yet in a way that I could have expressed. I had known it the first time I picked up an economics textbook. I knew it when I saw change come from within the United States and within other countries as they frayed at the end of the Cold War. My life was going to be about making change—putting things straight back home in Chile, where crushing poverty was an affront to so many people's dignity. It would be about liberty—of the sort my black peers didn't have in Durham, my impoverished countrymen couldn't dream of back home, and all of Chile lacked after 1973 under a military dictator. It would be about restoring what we had lost.

What I didn't know then is that I would have to fight Chile's history not with my thoughts—my academic degree—but with the very whole of my being. I would have to become a politician.

M y mother never wanted me to be president. Of a university? Maybe. But of Chile? That job was too dangerous.

President Jose Manuel Balmaceda's mother must have thought so too—and that was who my mother remembered as the source of her fears. In the late nineteenth century, he unwittingly led the country into a civil war, a blunder he paid for with his life, choosing suicide over defeat. Another president, Salvador Allende, would meet the same fate 82 years later. No, this was not a job for Ricardo Lagos, nor was politics at all—until there was no other way to bring Chile back from the brink.

But my mother's apprehension was not just born of fear; it was practical. She had become a single parent when I was just eight years old, and from that moment forward, she took it upon herself to make sure I was prepared for a life better than hers had been. My parents were raised in rural Chile: my father, Froilán Lagos, from Chillán, almost 250 miles to the south of Santiago, where he had been a farmer. He sold his land and bought a plot near the capital. My mother's parents owned land in Rengo, but it was not enough to support their large family, and after the crisis that accompanied the 1891 civil war—the same one that killed Balmaceda—my grandparents were forced to move to Santiago.

My mother, Emma Escobar Morales, took her arrival in the city as an opportunity. She became a concert pianist and teacher. Education had opened the door to her for a middle-class life, and she was determined that it do the same for me. My father's death only reinforced her convictions. His illness must have exhausted her with worry and loss, but she wasted not a moment in making sure that I understood my duties in life. I was to study—to walk through every open door that offered itself.

She was right that I would have to work to maintain even a middle-class lifestyle. Chile in those days was typical of Latin America in the 1950s—pleasant enough for those who could afford to live well, and dreadful for those falling behind. The city was filled with buildings in the French and British architectural styles; Santiago was a colonial masterpiece of churches and European-style parks. But most neighborhoods were far from developed. In the rural areas, many of the few who attended school went without shoes, solid roofs, or even food in their stomachs. Even in Santiago, education had only begun to rectify the city's social stratification, and as my mother knew, it was far from given that even that would be enough.

In 1949, at age 11, I entered the National Institute, the most prestigious public high school in Chile, well prepared by my mother's work ethic and by the years she paid for me to attend a private school close to home. It was here that it all sunk in—just how privileged I was to eat, study, and be well while others were suffering. Santiago's income-segregated neighborhoods were all represented in those classrooms; I could see the various shades of poverty and wealth.

I was drawn to that inequality and, more specifically, driven to eliminate it. So it was no wonder that, when I entered the University of Chile in 1955, I was fascinated by the left-wing ideas of politicians and public intellectuals like the late Pedro Aguirre Cerda, a former president of Chile whose slogan was "bread, roof, and shelter." Just like that, I had unknowingly entered the world of politics for the first time, joining the students' left-leaning Radical Party.

It wasn't just our own poverty that loomed large over those early debates. Underlying every discussion were the international politics of the Cold War. Chile, we all knew, fell under the U.S. sphere of influence in what was then very much a bipolar world. Not only did Washington's military and political arms extend all over Latin America at the time, but its economic

ideas were dominant throughout the region. We learned about that reality
from all the people in the university who were close to the seat of political
power in Santiago; the faculty included many professors with active public
lives, be they members of parliament, of the judiciary, or even future government ministers. But rather than taking our US connections for granted,
we began asking questions—particularly after 1957, with the Soviet Union
launched Sputnik. We knew the Soviet Union was a place where the kind of
political freedoms that we had in Chile didn't exist, but it intrigued us that
another country may have found a path to prosperity—enough to challenge
the United States.

One question led to another, and soon we found ourselves immersed in
yet another debate—a far more amplified and profound one—around the system of democracy that had existed in Chile for much of the country's history.
Conservative, Christian Democratic, and socialist ideas competed for political
and intellectual space every day. In hallways and cafes, my friends and I argued
over seemingly every policy initiative to emerge from the populist government
of Carlos Ibáñez. We even chose classes based on whether they would give us
the chance to talk about current events.

Economics was an especially passionate topic of discussion. Before the
Great Depression, Chile's economy was already at the mercy of the export
price of its two commodities, copper and nitrates. But in the 1930s, things
got worse—much worse. The country's international currency reserves disappeared overnight, and we grew yet more reliant on imports for practically
every part of daily life. The prices of our exports continued to crash, and the
trade deficit grew accordingly. That same story played out over and over again
across Latin America. And Chile, like so many of its peer countries, decided to
close its markets to the world in hopes that protectionism would foster the rise
of domestic industry. The idea sounded fine enough, but it required massive
injections of capital from the already bankrupt state.

The human side of this emerged in profound ways. Santiago's bursting
populaciones callempas—settlements that had sprung up, mushroom-like, as
rural migrants came to the city looking for work—were growing too fast. (Indeed, by 1970, one in every three Chileans lived in Santiago.) Those on the right
often blamed this on the poor themselves. But I always believed that, in many
ways, the system was rigged against them. Education was the best way to break

Chile's long trend of inequality. Only a third of Chileans attended high school back then, and education was only required for six years. If not better prepared, how could the lower class ever rise above unskilled jobs in back-breaking labor?

I entered law school, but with poverty all around me and inflation in Chile hovering at 85 percent, it was economics that truly fired my imagination. I found work in the economics department of Alberto Baltra, who had been a minister of the economy in the 1940s. I went to conferences, read every economics book I could get my hands on, and learned all that I could to feel like I could be part of the solution. The intense public debate about Chile's economy inspired me to participate in student forums, and in my fourth year, I was elected president of the student center of the law school—my first "public office."

I hoped to go to Britain to continue my studies. But I soon learned that scholarships there were very modest and I would need help financing this next step. So I turned to the United States, where I applied to a number of schools. Several universities accepted me, but the tuition was still too high. Baltra knew a professor at Duke University, Robert S. Smith, who taught economics with a focus on Latin America. Smith helped me obtain a scholarship, and I entered the school in 1961. I arrived at the Raleigh-Durham airport that year ready to pursue my master's in economics.

I brought my wife, a beautiful woman named Carmen Weber, who I had met not long before. It had happened one day when I was visiting a friend. Two sisters were also there in his house, and before we knew it, there was one for each of us. I immediately fell in love with Carmen's dark, curly hair and fair skin, and then with her exuberant personality. I asked her to come with me to Durham. We married in Santiago, followed by a honeymoon trip to Mexico City, conveniently located on the way to America.

I arrived in the United States amid a divided world. It had been 16 years since the end of World War II, and from the moment the Berlin Wall went up, the battle lines were drawn. On one side were the capitalists, led by America and the West. The communists in the Soviet Union were joined by China.

But I was from a part of the world where a third group of countries was emerging—one that captivated our imaginations more than Washington or Moscow ever could. Colonization was coming to the end, and new leaders were sprouting up indigenously, rather than being planted artificially to serve the geopolitics of the time. India had Jawaharlal Nehru and its moral conscience, Mahatma Gandhi. There was Gamal Abdel Nasser in Egypt, who came to power after throwing out the monarchy. We witnessed the force of Yugoslavia's Marshal Tito, a communist whose every breath was nonetheless taken with the intention of ending his country's subjugation by the Soviets. Together, those three leaders had decided at the Bandung Conference in 1955 that they wanted to belong to neither the capitalist "first" world nor the "second" communist one. This new generation of leaders decided their "Third World" would no longer be told what to do by the two hegemonic blocks that dominated the global system. Chile could certainly relate. Every time our discussions turned to Latin America, it seemed, it was actually a debate about the relative merits of the United States and the Soviet Union.

My guides in this intellectual journey, my professors, were each exceptional in different ways. Calvin B. Hoover had first-hand experience in the Soviet world, a fact that made him very influential in Washington. Joseph J. Spengler was a first-rate economic historian. At first, I found his class was, at best, a little disorganized. He enjoyed coming to class with 10 or 15 books piled up on his arms, and he would talk at will about any or all of them during the lecture. Yet chaotic as it seemed at the time, I was quick to realize that he was simply enthusiastic about all the books he carried—and indeed, the reading list from the class was superb.

One professor who became something of a mentor figure to me was William P. Yohe, a young scholar in his thirties. Outside of class, we would have long discussions about politics and economics, and most importantly, about how economics was being put into practice in Latin America. Yohe taught the economics of John Maynard Keynes, which was the dominant orthodoxy of the time. But by then, several key criticisms of Keynes's work had emerged. I heard one very pointed criticism at a lecture given at the university by Milton Friedman, who later became a close advisor of Pinochet's economic team along with the "Chicago Boys," young Chilean economists who were fervent believers in Friedman's free-market philosophy. Friedman's most important criticism of Keynes was essentially that monetary policy—managing the money supply and interest rates—was more effective in running economies than fiscal policy, or government taxing and spending. But in 1960, everyone was still

pretty much a Keynesian. We thought that if we understood Keynesian economics, the world would never return to the economic depression that had
engulfed it in 1929. The next time would be different; we would know how to
manipulate the variables that determined a country's economic performance.

I also took courses on development economics from Stephen Enke, and
here, too, the feeling was that social scientists like us understood how to "solve"
the problem of underdevelopment through the proper application of our craft.
Walt Rostow, a professor at the Massachusetts Institute of Technology who
wrote the influential 1960 book *The Stages of Economic Growth* and later became
a top advisor to John F. Kennedy and his successor Lyndon Johnson, argued that
countries modernize in five major steps. A country that invested in education,
a stable banking sector and currency, and a few promising economic sectors
would thrive. The result would be a virtuous circle in which savings would grow
while the level of investment continued to rise. When a country reached this
crucial juncture, it was said to have economically "taken off"—and from then
on, nothing could stop it from becoming part of the developed world.

Economic growth was not the only problem we believed we had solved.
For the blight of social inequality, there were also "solutions." We saw that the
gap between rich and poor in the United States had narrowed tremendously
since the 1930s thanks to President Franklin Delano Roosevelt's New Deal. It
was based on this historical example, among others, that Simón Kuznets published his famous article, "Economic Growth and Income Inequality," demonstrating that, although sustained economic growth would increase inequality
at first, in the long term, it would reduce it, as the working class benefited
from a booming economy. The cycle of savings and investment would boost
incomes. Kuznets believed that periods of growth would be followed by industrialization, and with them unions and organized labor, demanding higher
salaries and other worker-friendly policies.

All this left us with the empowering sensation that we knew how to induce
growth, and more importantly, the right kind of growth. It seemed as if we
had all the tools needed to lead the world: a series of equations and bench-
marks that depended on variables we knew inside and out. And on top of that,
the political scientist Seymour Lipset suggested that when life improved for
the masses, the natural result would be their political empowerment. They
would demand democracy. With our knowledge of the economy, we could not

only grow jobs and businesses but also pluralistic political systems. What more could we possibly want?

There was one task no textbook could have ever prepared me for: being a father. In 1962, my first son, Ricardo, was born. It was an incredible feeling, taking my son home from Duke Hospital, which we did on a snowy winter night that February.

My professors proposed an enticing idea: You've come this far to get a master's degree. Why not study for a doctorate as well? It would take just two years, which I could spend almost entirely in Chile, and I could hardly say no. I returned home to Santiago in March 1963, eager to begin my research, and by 1966, I was back at Duke presenting my dissertation to the faculty. I became a "doctor" of economics that same year.

Upon my return to Chile, I was offered a faculty post at the University of Chile. I was thrilled. To become a professor was a dream fulfilled, and I planned to spend my days researching and teaching. Carmen had gone home the December before, by then pregnant with our second child, Ximena, who was born the month I returned. We moved into a beautiful house in Santiago's Providencia neighborhood owned by my mother-in-law. It was an older building in a quiet area, and far nicer a place than I could have afforded at the time. It was the future I had envisioned for myself—as my mother also had all those years ago. I split my time between the law school and the economics department.

I also grew active in campus politics, and in 1969, I became the university's chancellor. The most important part of the university's election, however, had little to do with politics or even economics. I had divorced Carmen, and in 1969, I met Luisa Durán de la Fuente, my future wife, while attending a party that followed university elections for dean of the law school (a post for which I was campaigning but didn't get). When the party began, dancing soon followed, and a pair of eyes caught mine from across the room. It was Luisa, then a student. After I met her that night, we walked through the campus talking together. We discussed the election, among other things (good news: she was planning to vote for me). We married a few years later, in March 1971.

The new house that we rented became our home, not only for the two of us but also for the two children that each of us brought from previous marriages. "I want your children to know that they will have a bedroom in our house," Luisa told me. And they always did.

S alvador Allende, the fiery socialist president whom Augusto Pinochet would eventually oust, was a hard act to follow at the podium. I should know because that's how I met him in 1954, as a young university student.

On June 27 of that year, Guatemala's democratically elected president, Jacobo Árbenz Guzmán, fell victim to Cold War politics in a coup orchestrated in part by the United States. Many of us were outraged, Allende and another future president, Eduardo Frei, included. As for me, I had something of a personal connection: My aunt was married to Chile's outgoing ambassador to the country. I had met many of the Guatemalans who had fled to Santiago.

One evening shortly after the coup, another former Guatemalan president, Juan José Arevalo, came to Chile to speak at a dinner. I was asked to say a few words, and so was Allende, whose speech would have to come last so that he could first attend a vote in the Congress, where he was a member. In a last-minute change of plans, however, Allende went first, just before me. His impassioned words left a lump in my stomach as I took my own turn.

I must have done all right, though, for Allende stayed in touch. And slowly but surely, I came to know him as a politician, an intellectual, and a man. He was a wonderful human being—not to mention charming and well-dressed. Allende was the kind of man who could simultaneously win your affection on the first handshake and then later impress you with how serious a thinker he was, deeply concerned with alleviating social injustice. He had written about public health policies and had been a minister in the government of President Pedro Aguirre Cerda, a Radical Party leader who led Chile from 1938 to 1941.

By the time Allende ran for president in 1964, it was only natural that I should work in his "central planning office"—a sort of think tank to develop the policies we would enact should he be elected. I had been writing and speaking extensively about politics since I returned to Chile to do my Ph.D. research, so here was a chance to put words into action. We proposed an ambitious agenda that included land reform, nationalizing the copper mines, and transferring banks to the public sector.

Chile in 1963, however, wasn't yet ready for Allende. We were approaching the end of the presidency of Jorge Alessandri, a conservative. As his term came to an end, Eduardo Frei Montalva, leader of the Christian Democratic movement, captivated Chile with his promise of a "Revolution in Liberty," a platform that was clearly sympathetic to the United States and contrary to the growing regional influence of Cuba's Fidel Castro. The following year, Frei was elected president, although Allende finished with a respectable 39 percent of the vote.

Six years later, Allende finally had his chance. His Popular Action Front party convinced the Radical Party and others from the center to form a Popular Unity coalition capable of winning a majority. Allende was elected by a very slim margin over the conservative candidate, Alessandri, who had sought to return to power. (In Chile, presidents may be elected more than once, but not for two consecutive terms.)

I was never officially part of Allende's government, although I acted as an advisor and emissary on several occasions. About a year after his election, I became secretary-general of the Latin American Faculty of Social Sciences (FLACSO), an international organization based in Santiago whose mission was to train social scientists in the region. (My colleagues there included great minds like future Brazilian president Fernando Henrique Cardoso and future São Paulo mayor José Serra.) Because of our work, Allende's foreign minister, Clodomiro Almeyda, had asked me in August 1971 to become Chile's delegate to the U.N. Human Rights Commission. Upon my return from New York, Almeyda asked me to serve once again, this time as part of the country's delegation to the U.N. General Assembly, which was to take place the following month.

During that year's assembly (thanks to Chile's vote, among others), the People's Republic of China was elected the sole representative of China, displacing Taiwan from the United Nations. Ironically, even as U.S. president Richard Nixon and his aide Henry Kissinger were fretting about the rise of socialism in Chile—which they saw exemplified in Allende—communist China not only entered the United Nations but became a permanent member of the Security Council. (It was also during that session that I first met George H. W. Bush, the U.S. representative to the United Nations at the time.)

I also took part in the debate of the General Assembly's Economic and Social Commission while I was there, and in my speech on behalf of the Chilean delegation, I summarized economic advances made in the first year of the

Allende government. Then I moved to a broader, even more pertinent topic: Nixon's stunning August 15 decision to remove the gold standard that had been established at Bretton Woods after World War II. Nixon made this unilateral move after De Gaulle had chosen to exchange dollars for gold, depleting the gold reserves held at Fort Knox. I recall it because it was the removal of this gold standard that allowed the United States to begin accruing such a huge trade deficit—the same one that bears so heavily upon its debt figures today. During Nixon's time, countries could exchange a pound of gold for $35, when they had a favorable trade balance. As of this writing, a pound of gold costs well over $1,700.

Halfway through his administration, Allende called me directly, this time to ask if I would be his ambassador to the Soviet Union. I was taken aback by the offer and explained that I didn't have the necessary preparation or experience. But he insisted. "To have a person from academia, independent of any political party, is more important," he said. I finally agreed but never made it to Moscow.

Allende's election was an opportunity for socialists like myself, but not everyone was celebrating. In Washington, the advent of a "Marxist" government was seen as a disaster, heralding a red tide sweeping across Latin America. And the CIA under Nixon sought desperately to prevent Allende from ever taking office. The first cable to Washington from U.S. Ambassador Edward Korry left no room for nuance: "Chile voted calmly to have a Marxist-Leninist state—the first nation in the world to make this choice freely and knowingly," he wrote. "Dr. Salvador Allende proved the wisdom of Soviet policy in Latin America."

What was happening in Chile, though, wasn't really a story of Soviet influence or of the triumph of communism. With economic growth still lagging behind political development, new sectors of the population were demanding to see their incomes rise. And their voices were becoming louder and louder, even as growth seemed slower and slower. The urgent desire to find a solution, be it through Frei's Revolution in Liberty or through the more radical sort of reforms proposed by Allende, was ultimately what caused Chile's democracy to collapse; nothing could satisfy the people quickly enough.

In the first year of Allende's six-year term, the pressure from below weighed heavily upon him, and he did all in his power to meet the country's growing social demands. The economy was churning along at a healthy 8 percent, and life was beautiful. But it was also unsustainable. Allende was pumping money into the system as fast as it could be absorbed, and indeed, idle capacity and unemployment disappeared. Yet other things soon disappeared too: foreign currency, government reserves, and stability. Writing in journals and speaking with colleagues, I warned that the government could not keep goosing the economy without causing every politician's worst nightmare: runaway inflation.

Unfortunately, this is exactly what happened in the second year of Allende's term. Chile's currency, the peso, spun out of control. The difficulties compounded each month. By its third year, Allende's government had to resort to rationing goods and services. Some of this was the result of business owners hoarding their stocks, eager to do political damage to Allende's already frayed credibility (sure enough, just days after the coup, supermarket shelves were stocked again, as if by a miracle). But there's no question the Allende government mismanaged things.

By 1973, there wasn't a household in Chile that wasn't either fervently in favor of Allende or against him. The country was deeply divided. In parliamentary elections that took place that year, Allende's coalition won just 44 percent of the vote. And so the Chilean political system became a precariously balanced contest between an opposition that claimed 56 percent of the electorate and a president whose party commanded less than half of the votes. There seemed to be no way out of the resulting deadlock. The increasingly frantic opposition in Congress needed a two-thirds majority to remove Allende, and the votes simply were not there. At the same time, Allende needed a simple majority to implement his campaign promises—a majority he didn't have. The result was a debilitating political stalemate. Allende could only govern using his veto, and that's precisely what he did.

I was in the shower when I heard the news. "Ricardo: It's the coup!" Luisa's alarmed voice came blaring over the sound of the flowing water. At 8 A.M., September 11, 1973, *Radio Nacional* had announced the military take-over. It was what we had feared for months—and now it had finally happened. All of us had seen it coming, even Allende.

Everyone knew that Chile's polarized politics couldn't remain stable for long. But we would only learn later that, behind the scenes, powerful forces well beyond our control were also working around the clock to ensure that Allende would fall. Not only had the Nixon administration tried and failed to prevent his inauguration, but the U.S. Congress moved swiftly to enact crushing sanctions against his government once in office. Ironically, for all his disdain for socialism, Nixon was petrified that Allende might succeed in office, winning popular support for his social policies. Determined not to let that happen, the American president instructed his CIA director, Richard Helms, to "make the economy scream."

Meanwhile, the intelligence agency stoked opposition in the military and in the press. Prior to Allende's inauguration, the CIA forged contacts with military officers they believed would be sympathetic to the idea of fomenting a coup, pre-empting the election of a socialist president. The coup attempt, authorized by Nixon himself, didn't work then, but it did create a web of sympathetic military officers with whom the U.S. government would continue to liaise. Throughout the 1960s, the CIA had also poured funds into the right-leaning newspaper El Mercurio. When the paper was at risk of going under in 1971, the Nixon administration bailed it out with a $700,000 grant, conditioned "on the understanding that El Mercurio will launch an intensive public attack on the Allende government's efforts to force them out of business," according to a secret CIA memorandum signed September 30 of that year. All told, between 1970 and 1973, the U.S. government, working through the CIA, spent $3.5 million to foster and encourage opposition to Allende.

By November 1972, Allende was worried. Sensing that something was stirring in the military, he named the army's commander in chief, General Carlos Prats, as his interior minister, and he gave cabinet posts to two other senior military officers. He hoped to head off the staunchly anti-communist and increasingly anti-Allende sentiment in the upper ranks. In June 1973, a tank regiment in Santiago led a brief uprising that General Prats swiftly put down. But the momentum was by then irreversible. This first coup attempt only sowed the seeds of the second when Prats, a stalwart defender of the constitution, was forced by more radical commanders to resign his post on August 23. It was Prats who fatefully recommended that Pinochet, whom he saw as loyal and staunchly democratic, succeed him as army chief.

As rumors of a new coup attempt swirled, Allende made a last-ditch attempt to save his presidency by appealing to the centrist Christian Democrats and asking Santiago's Roman Catholic cardinal, Raúl Silva Henríquez, to mediate talks in a stalled Congress. The Christian Democrats, however, had no interest in compromising; for months previously, the CIA had worked intensely to secure the party's backing for a coup.

Allende was searching for a political solution to a political crisis. But when the military officers learned that the president was planning to call a plebiscite on his policies on Wednesday, September 12, they planned their coup for the day before—September 11. In a secret meeting earlier that month, the commanders of the military chose Pinochet, the Army commander, as the head of their junta, and set the plot in motion. The CIA knew about the meeting; the agency also knew exactly when the coup was scheduled to begin.

And so it was. With the break of dawn on that day, as I was getting ready for work, tanks filled the streets. Our children came home half an hour after the news began to unfold; school was closed.

"This is going to be terrible," I told my aunt Leontina a few hours later when I saw her at my mother's house. "Allende will not leave the palace." I knew he was going to die in La Moneda.

By mid-morning, the air force's British-made Hawker Hunter jets were bombarding the presidential palace. I heard them myself—the sound of democracy dying—from my office in the neighborhood of Providencia. The palace was just two miles away.

Picking up Luisa along the way, I rushed immediately from work to my mother's house, but found that she wasn't there. And after an anxious search for her whereabouts (she had gone to the beachside town of Quintero, just north of Santiago), Luisa and I then hurried to her parents' house in the upper-class suburb of La Reina; our children were already there, waiting for us. Luisa's father, Hernan Durán, was a well-known doctor who had worked for the United Nations and was a prominent Allende supporter.

We weren't the only ones who sought refuge at the Duráns' beautiful, large home. Alicia Soto, the wife of one of Allende's personal doctors, Oscar Soto, arrived soon after we did. Oscar was in La Moneda with the president, who, as I expected, had decided to stay and fight.

Our ears were glued to the radio. We paced back and forth. We listened, in pain, as Allende's last address was broadcast. "Surely this will be the last opportunity for me to address you," he began. "These are my last words, and I am certain that my sacrifice will not be in vain, I am certain that, at the very least, it will be a moral lesson that will punish felony, cowardice, and treason." By 1:30 P.M., tanks were attacking the palace from the square outside as the aerial raid on the palace continued. Then the news came, in a 2:30 P.M. phone call from Soto to his wife, that Allende had committed suicide.

We know now what happened in those last few, painful moments. Allende ordered the rank and file to leave—to save themselves from the military's palace takeover. He walked with them backward, hands on his head, toward a side door. But Allende never walked out that door. He had forgotten something, he said, and had to go back upstairs. On the second floor, he sat down on a boxy, red velvet sofa in a small room just immediately off the stairwell. The AK-47 rifle was pointed at his chin. And he fired. As his body fell backward, the arm of the sofa collapsed with him. (It remains on the floor of the palace today, exactly where Allende's last moments left it.) He was too proud to be taken alive.

By midday, there was a blackout of all information, save that coming from the military. Radio Magallanes, the station that had broadcast Allende's dramatic final speech to the nation that morning, had been shut down at 10:30 A.M. The four leaders of the junta appeared on television that night to address the country. There would be a rotating presidency—and Pinochet would hold the first term.

The junta leaders' voices were terrifying to us, as a household filled with mostly members of the socialist and other left-wing parties. Air Force General Gustavo Leigh vowed to "eradicate the Marxist cancer from our fatherland, until the last consequences." It was hard to believe that this was happening in our own country. We didn't have to imagine the new Chile, however; we were in it. And if the coup had been painful to watch, what followed was even more difficult.

Having secured the presidential palace, the military's next target was the Chilean people. On the day of the coup, every leftist, student activist, suspicious civil servant, and Allende supporter the soldiers could find was rounded up in the back of the military trucks scouring the city. Man, woman, young, old—it didn't matter. People were crammed into vehicles and then thrown ominously into the national stadium, whose bleachers were quickly filling with frightened prisoners. The military was taking over all of Chile—not just the government or a few blocks in downtown Santiago. The junta was a way of life, and being from the left—or sometimes just being at the wrong place at the wrong time—would not be tolerated. About 100 leftists were shot there on the spot; hundreds more were tortured.

Many thousands also began to flee. Running to embassies, looking for ways out—they were desperate for amnesty somewhere. Hundreds were holed up in foreign embassies until the government finally let them leave.

Carlos Prats was one of them. The former general immediately left for Buenos Aires, knowing that his life was at stake. He understood what the military was up to, as he told me later. "When you take military action, you are thinking about your objectives," he calmly explained when I saw him in Argentina. "If you want to control a country in 20 days, there will be a certain number of deaths. If you want to gain control in 10 days, there will be 10 times as many deaths. And if you want to gain control in 5 days, there will be 30 times the deaths. If it's 48 hours, as in fact happened in Chile that day, there will be 100 times the deaths."

That's exactly what was happening. In addition to the initial roundups, the military began calling people to present themselves before the Military Academy. As a prominent academic and a socialist with close ties to the Allende government, I was clearly in danger. My plan, if summoned, was always to go and present myself, even though Luisa warned me not to be so foolish. "There will be no judge there, and they will send you straight to prison," she said.

They never called me. But many of my friends were summoned, and they naively appeared, believing they would leave the next day. A good number of them disappeared. I first heard about where they had been taken when a *Wall Street Journal* correspondent I had met at the United Nations in 1971 arrived in Chile to cover the coup. He called me one day to ask if I knew about Dawson

Island. I didn't. "It is an island far away in the Straights of Magellan, at the end of the world, practically uninhabited," he told me. "It is there that the junta is taking them."

I struggled to believe it, but I knew it must be true. I had to tell the wives of some of the missing senior officials that their husbands had been sent there, with little more information. The island, the International Red Cross later revealed, was an extremely harsh place near Cape Horn where about 100 prisoners were living in appalling conditions. There was forced labor and little to eat. There was torture and isolation. Many years later as president, I found myself on a Navy ship full of high-ranking officers, along with several tourist agencies exploring new opportunities for travel to Chile's beautiful southern archipelago. We passed by Dawson Island, and shivers ran down my spine. And the junta transformed hundreds of other locations in Chile into similarly horrid places of torture.

The coup shattered countless lives and dreams. Our desire to build a more just, equal society, something that many believed required a rapid shift to the left, had come to fruition—only to be crushed with equal haste by the junta that took power after the coup. It was the beginning of a black period in Chile's history, rife with depraved and systemic violations of human rights, with torture and repression. None of us could have imagined that all this would be possible in our small but civilized nation, so proud of its democratic traditions.

The breakdown of Chile's democracy reverberated throughout the world. But in Washington, officials were celebrating. On September 13, the United States decided on the policy going forward—which was by then already a foregone conclusion: "The U.S. Government wishes to make clear its desire to cooperate with the military Junta and to assist in any appropriate way," a classified White House cable read. And assist it did. In less than a month's time, Washington had granted Pinochet's new regime $24 million of aid to purchase wheat, effectively ending the shortages of the Allende era. The Inter-American Development Bank also began loans again, pouring in $237.8 million between 1973 and 1976.

Many years later, after I had served my term as president, I agreed to take part in a seminar in Berlin at which Nixon's national security advisor, Henry

Kissinger, would be present. As now-declassified CIA and White House cables make clear, preventing a socialist Chile had been Kissinger's obsession, and he developed close ties to Pinochet.

When Kissinger entered the room that day, he approached me immediately. Without any introduction, he told me, "President Lagos, I want you to know that I had nothing to do with the coup d'état." It struck me as bizarre— the way in which he made such an unsolicited effort to impress this upon me.

"And what about the human rights violations that took place under Pinochet?" I wondered. Thousands of memories came flooding forward in my mind: of the numerous congressional hearings in which Kissinger had spoken out against Allende's election, and then the way his government had financed newspapers and unions that opposed him. And worst of all, I was reminded of the way he worked with Pinochet once the junta was in power. I remembered the 1976 speech he gave at the Organization of American States, Latin America's main diplomatic forum, telling Pinochet to improve his human rights record (and I remembered the transcript of their private meeting beforehand, in which he told the dictator, wink wink, not to worry). I found it revealing that Kissinger had been so eager to explain his role in what had taken place— information for which I had never asked.

It is difficult to describe how abruptly mindsets changed in Chile after the coup. When I needed to go and speak with officials at the Foreign Ministry— where just a few days earlier they would have greeted me with respect as Mr. Ambassador (reflecting my designation as ambassador to the Soviet Union)— suddenly it was as if no one knew my name. Who is this dangerous person demanding to speak with the minister?

In the coup's aftermath, I began to realize, like so many others did, that it would be impossible for me to stay in Chile. Anyone with the slightest socialist sympathies was considered suspect. Even books that *criticized* Marxism were banned—for having the word Marxism in the title—and the universities were being purged of leftists. A highly placed relative assured me that, for the moment, no one was looking for me. But there would undoubtedly be a time in the future, I thought, when my ties to Allende would lead to trouble.

Equally in peril, however, was my organization, FLACSO. As an international organization legally beyond the junta's control, it was clear that we were not welcome under this regime. Our only office was in Santiago, but efforts were underway to establish other branches throughout Latin America. There was no better time to speed our exit. So I began negotiating with the new government.

Typical for the junta, which had militarized everything, my counterpart in the discussions was a colonel who headed the War College and was the Chilean government's designated representative to FLACSO. The discussions were tense, but we eventually agreed that the organization's secretariat would move to another country in the region. FLACSO had three academic bodies: the school of sociology, the school of political science, and the institute of social science research. The first two would leave Chile, but the last institution would remain in the country, and only 13 or 14 researchers, who would need to be approved and credited by the Chilean government, could remain.

In February, my family left for Buenos Aires, where the secretariat would now be. Our oldest child, Ricardo, was just 11 years old, and on the twenty-first of that month, he turned 12. That night, we went with the children and a few other friends from Chile to a restaurant to wish him a happy birthday. We were not very happy at all, though, with such trying times. No one was sure how long Chile would remain under military rule.

Still, I considered myself fortunate to have my family together. I was never exiled in the formal sense, but I knew that it would be difficult to move back to Chile for a long time. (I certainly couldn't have guessed that I wouldn't permanently be returning home for more than four years.) I did visit on occasion during those years, and each time, I learned more about the daily horror of life under the junta. I remember meeting Moy de Tohá, whose husband José was still imprisoned in Santiago after a stretch on Dawson Island. She gave me a letter for General Prats who, like me, was living in Buenos Aires at the time. Prats wasn't sure he could help. "I am nothing in this country," he said when I gave him the letter, but nonetheless told me he would see what he could do for José and got in touch with Argentina's ruling general, Juan Perón. But it was too late. A few days later, I received word that José had "committed suicide" in his cell, apparently by hanging. To this day, I don't believe José would have done himself in that way. A Chilean judge is currently investigating the case.

Prats was also a target, and he knew it. "Tell General Prats that we know they are looking to assassinate him, and he must leave Buenos Aires," a friend of mine told me in Santiago. But when I relayed the information, Prats looked at me calmly and said, "What can I do? I'm asking for a passport because all I came here with was my identity card. Without that, you know that I cannot leave Argentina."

The phone rang at 7 A.M., and Luisa rolled over to pick up the receiver. It was September 30, 1974, and I had just moved back to Chapel Hill, North Carolina, to take a visiting professor post after my term with FLACSO expired, and we were still exhausted from settling in. The voice on the line was Federico Gil, the professor who had invited me there, and the early hour of his call told us right away that something was wrong.

"They've just said on the radio that last night General Prats and his wife were assassinated," he said. A car bomb, attached to the underside of his vehicle, had gone off the day before as they were driving through the city. It was clearly Pinochet's work.

I remained quiet on the line, dumbfounded. I couldn't believe it. We had left Buenos Aires just over a month ago and had become friends with Prats and his wife. I thought about their youngest daughter, who had been with them in Argentina and would now grow up without parents. A few days earlier, I had sent Prats a letter to tell him that we had arrived safely and were beginning to settle in. I had sent him a few books that I thought would interest him in his work, and I hadn't heard back from him yet.

"We'll still get a letter from Prats," I told Luisa—and we did, just a few days later. He was finishing his memoirs, he had written, and hoped that he could send me a draft for my feedback very soon. Of course, I never received it.

I may have been back in the United States, but we never forgot the military junta, our friends in exile, the countless disappeared, and the many more in prison. America seemed like another world to us. Out of Latin America's chaos, we had suddenly arrived in an idyllic place. I felt so lucky to be there, but at the same time guilty knowing that so many were suffering at home.

We did what little we could from abroad, and that included setting up a scholarship program for fleeing academics to take up posts at the Latin American Social Sciences Council.

In fact, we had been working to help academics head abroad from the moment the junta seized control. On September 12, Cardoso, then director of the Brazilian Center of Planning (CEBRAP), called me from Brazil. "I know they will have a lot of difficulty getting out," he said of the scholars, "so I am sending you money." More than $5,000 arrived from São Paulo at a time when the plane fare from Chile to Buenos Aires was a mere $50. With the money, I orchestrated the exit of more than 100 Chileans, who left Santiago for an "international seminar" in Argentina. They left with the excuse that they would be gone just days—but of course, they never came back. They went into exile abroad. They were just a few of the as many as 200,000 Chileans who left the country during the Pinochet years.

Luisa's family was among them. Her brother Hernán went to Grenoble, France; another brother, Pedro, with the help of the embassy of Honduras, went to Lima and later to France; a third brother went directly to Lagos, Nigeria, where his father got a job at the World Health Organization following a brief period in Geneva. We all met on one occasion in Geneva, while I was traveling there to raise money for FLACSO. What a strange family reunion it was—the Chilean diaspora in miniature.

In my academic life at Chapel Hill, where our existence was very comfortable, the searing wound of Chile was also constantly on my mind. In April 1975, I led a week-long seminar that allowed me to organize one of the first gatherings of Chilean opposition figures and intellectuals abroad. It was the first meeting in which Christian Democrats and socialists were in the room with one another, face to face, since the coup. After tacitly supporting the military takeover at first, the Christian Democrats had by then come to see things our way; democracy had to be restored.

Just a year after taking on my visiting professor post, I was on the job market again, and the Latin American Institute of the University of Texas at Austin offered me a spot. Our bags were practically packed when UNESCO called. They wanted me to move back to Buenos Aires to work in a program that would boost post-graduate studies in Latin America, particularly in Argentina, Brazil, and Mexico. I leapt at the chance to be next door to home and to travel throughout the region. During those three years, my friends and family joked, the place you were most likely to run into me was at the airport.

In 1978, I finally saw an opportunity to return home to Chile. I would be working for the Regional Program for Employment in Latin America and the

Caribbean (PREALC), a branch of the International Labor Organization that had been established in Chile in the 1960s. The director, Victor Tokman, invited me to come, joining their research on "self-employment"—an important topic given that many people in Latin America didn't have a formal job but still needed to find ways to earn a living.

It was not so easy to pick up and leave by then, however. Our children were grown, and they had also grown accustomed to the relatively cosmopolitan life that Buenos Aires had to offer. Our children also knew that I had been offered the chance to work for the United Nations in New York or Paris (they preferred the latter). They knew Chile only through a few vacations in the summers and had found Santiago far too modest and provincial. But I had no doubts. I knew I'd have diplomatic protection, and the post would give me a platform without being too overtly political. We decided to go back.

Luisa left first to look for schools for our younger children. We had arrived in Argentina with four children and now there was a fifth: Francisca was born in Buenos Aires in 1975. Her birth brought together our marriage. I have always said that I have three children, Luisa has three children, and together we have five.

That March, I celebrated my fortieth birthday in Buenos Aires with only one Chilean friend. "When you return to Chile," he told me, "you will feel compelled to fight against the dictator—even if you don't know how."

M y return to Chile was also a return to the subjects that had motivated me to study from day one: poverty, unemployment, and all the things that had made Latin America one of the world's most unequal regions.

By the end of the 1970s, population growth was still very high in Latin America, and the flow of rural migrants to urban areas boosted the supply of labor even as the supply of jobs fell. The only insurance against unemployment was employment on the margins—a sort of underemployment. There were countless of these "self-employed" workers in the informal sector who scratched out a living selling food by the side of the road, parking cars, picking up trash to resell or recycle, or owning small shops. All of these were jobs that contributed little to a country's productivity and came with very low incomes.

International institutions like the International Monetary Fund (IMF) weren't helping. For every crisis, no matter the sort, the IMF advised the region to tighten its belt. But with each tightening, social welfare and infrastructure programs were the first to be affected. As a result, every fiscal adjustment mandated by the international finance institutions led to an increase in unemployment. So, in most cases, when we visited a country and met the minister of labor, we soon found that it was the minister of finance and the head of the central bank who had the real explaining to do.

PREALC was a great place to begin thinking about a new economic philosophy for our region. Long before American economists like Joseph Stiglitz started critiquing what became known in the 1990s as the "Washington Consensus"—the reigning economic doctrine of the time—an unorthodox way of thinking was taking shape in Latin America. Washington's view extolled low tariffs and fiscal austerity, downplaying the importance of government investment in the economy. But we had our doubts. For those five years, between 1978 and 1983, I was immersed in the consequences—the collateral damage— of the economic policies that had been prescribed for the region. It was not easy to recommend alternatives, but it was also clear that mandating budget cuts in a region that was growing so slowly would, in most cases, yield little more than a rise in unemployment.

Developing an alternative economic narrative was important not just for its own sake, but also for the political credibility of the opposition in Chile, with which I was rapidly become more involved. Pinochet's implicit message to Chileans was always that, although a dictator, he could run an economy far better than Allende's socialists. Many Chileans had bad memories of those years of Allende's economic mismanagement and weren't sure whether they could trust the left to run the country.

We were set upon proving them wrong. And some of the best ideas about how to do so came from think tanks. Alejandro Foxley, a future finance minister, was producing much of the best research critiquing Pinochet's economic policies and the intense "shock therapy" that was all the rage at the time. PREALC also tried to think outside the box, led by the insights and disposition of Fernando Faynzilber and his colleagues of the Economic Commission for Latin America and the Caribbean Countries. What began to emerge was not just a new theory, but a new way to think about what was considered to be the dominant economic ideology of the time. Instead of painful belt-tightening, we urged Latin American countries to develop their infrastructure and improve their public works.

By 1983, five years after I returned to Santiago, Pinochet began making our case for us. A decade into the dictatorship, the Chilean economy abruptly collapsed.

THREE

FALL OF THE CHICAGO BOYS

Some 5,000 miles north of Santiago, on the sleepy University of Chicago campus, a young economist named Milton Friedman was beginning to make his career. It was the 1960s, more than two decades since the end of the Great Depression, and memories of the Keynesian fervor inspired by Franklin Delano Roosevelt's New Deal had all but disappeared. What remained of it, Friedman aimed to put to rest with his work. As he laid out in academic papers, magazine columns, and his influential 1962 manifesto *Capitalism and Freedom,* the postwar world would be a time for open markets and deregulation. Underdeveloped countries could catch up—but only if they tightened their belts and shocked their economies into compliance. The antidote to communism was economic liberalism, and Friedman was the prescribing doctor.

As it turned out, the University of Chicago—whose neoliberal thinking Friedman had come to define—ran one of the most successful academic exchange programs in the world, swapping students with the Catholic University in Chile. Another of the Chicago professors, Arnold Harberger, journeyed south each year to recruit the best of our economics students, persuading them to come pursue graduate studies in Illinois. Harberger lectured on the Catholic University campus during what was Chicago's steaming summer and Santiago's crisp winter. As the temperatures dropped, students would fill the lecture halls on the stone-windowed campus, located just minutes from the center of power, La Moneda.

As each year of the 1960s ticked by, the lectures and the attending students grew less and less fond of the governments occupying the presidential palace just a few blocks down the road. When the conservative President Jorge Alessandri was in office, the young economists scorned his over-active government intervention. The Christian Democrat, President Eduardo Frei Montalva, was even less popular; and Salvador Allende's socialist revolution was downright despised. By the time of the coup, the economics department at Catholic University had become a hotbed of anti-socialist thought.

Pinochet became a convert to the new faith. His coup was not just an obliteration of Chile's democracy; it would prove an all-out war on the ideological direction the country had taken under his predecessors. Economics were the general's primary weapon, having taken on that portfolio from the minute he came to office. Where there had been labor activists, Pinochet arrested their leaders. Where there had been state corporations, Pinochet privatized. Where import markets had been closed, Pinochet opened the flood gates. And the ideological war on the Allende period was only the cover story. The truth was simply pragmatic: When the world began closing its doors to Pinochet, in protest against the atrocities committed by his regime, free-market neoliberalism came to his rescue. Pinochet brought on the "Chicago Boys"—an elite group of about two dozen Chileans who had gone to learn the Chicago way and who by then were just old enough to be returning home. Armed with private investors ready to pour in their capital, what need had Pinochet of Western governments' aid?

The Chicago Boys leapt at the chance to put their theories into practice. For some years, the young scholars had been putting together an economic plan known simply as "the brick" for its mighty 500 pages. It was a document about undoing more than doing: rolling back state intervention, cutting the civil service, stripping the budget—basically turning Chile into a neoliberal economic paradise. Now, Pinochet was offering the Chicago Boys the enticing prospect of putting their brick into practice, without the usual frustrations of a democratic state pushing back against the most painful reforms. It was a blank check to redesign the Chilean economy. All they had to do was give Pinochet a way out of his growing international isolation.

The Chicago Boys more than delivered. Just two short years after the coup, word of Pinochet's ambition to turn his country into the Southern Hemisphere's first free-market experiment had traveled right back up to Chicago, inspiring Friedman himself to visit the country in March 1975. Shock therapy was what Chile's economy needed, Friedman proclaimed. "The fact is," he said, "Chile is a very sick country, and the sick cannot expect to recover without cost."

The press went wild. The economic right grew even more ascendant when the long-time dean of the Catholic University economic faculty, Sergio de Castro, became the economic minister in April 1975 and finance minister a year and a half later. He was far and away the most powerful minister of finance the country has ever had. His word was essentially the law.

The reforms were already underway when de Castro came and picked up the pace. Companies that had been nationalized under Allende's government were returned to private hands (although 20 of the most lucrative industries—including mining and energy—remained under state control). Thirty to 40 percent of the land that Allende had expropriated for redistribution was sold. Then in 1978, José Piñera, an ally of the Chicago Boys, was recruited to the Ministry of Labor, which Pinochet urged him to "modernize." Labor legislation was put in line with the other neoliberal reforms; pensions and health care were privatized.

De Castro was granted unquestioned authority because he gave Pinochet exactly what he wanted. A new map of the Chilean economy was being drawn, and with it came an entirely new bourgeoisie, Pinochet's newest and strongest constituency. The transformation took place practically overnight, and unsurprisingly, Pinochet's friends—the well-connected businessmen close to the government—found themselves profiting most.

In addition to pleasing this growing swathe of supporters at home, economic reforms were succeeding at neutralizing Pinochet's growing number of critics abroad. Soon after the junta seized power, the general entered into a despicable security alliance with a number of other countries in the region. Under a covert agreement known as Operation Condor, various governments agreed to collaborate to assassinate one another's most irritating exiles. It was under this alliance that Pinochet killed General Carlos Prats, the former head of the Army, in Argentina. Operation Condor also targeted Bernardo Leighton, an exiled former Christian Democrat vice president, in Rome.

Then in 1976, Pinochet went too far. He set his secret police upon Allende's former defense minister, Orlando Letelier, who was assassinated when a bomb attached to his car blew up in Washington, D.C. The explosion, on Embassy Row in the American capital's Dupont Circle neighborhood, sent shockwaves straight to the White House. It wasn't long before the CIA suspected Pinochet's secret police. Jimmy Carter, who had been elected president that year vowing to boost U.S. support for human rights, was furious, as were many in Congress.

The uproar over the Letelier plot shined a harsh international spotlight on the human rights abuses for which Pinochet was already infamous at home. The sanctions against his regime were piling up, threatening to stop the flow of goods and credit. But just as Pinochet had hoped, the Chicago Boys' open markets offered him a lifeline. Private investment flowed in, evading the sanctions. Wall Street is always fast to hear rumors of easy money—and the Chile buzz was no exception. De Castro's shock therapy had already proven to the markets that Chile was serious about implementing reform. Now, analysts were predicting a complete takeoff. For the most optimistic, Chile looked poised to become the next Korea or Taiwan—a Latin tiger.

Before long, his wayward allies, Britain and the United States, changed governments, and Pinochet's fortunes turned around. Margaret Thatcher and Ronald Reagan swept into office with popular mandates to downsize the state and stand up to international communism, and they were ideologically sympathetic to what many in the West were calling the "Chilean miracle." (Later, Thatcher hailed Pinochet's "positive legacy" and credited him with overcoming the "chaotic collectivism" of the Allende years and turning Chile into "the model economy of Latin America.")

That "miracle" could never have happened in a democracy. The Chicago Boys' policies created enormous hardship for millions of Chileans—about half the country, in fact. Textile markets opened abruptly to overseas competition, and 145,000 of the industry's 175,000 Chilean workers were unemployed overnight. De Castro took a buzz saw to the state, reducing the number of public employees from 700,000 to 550,000. Labor organizations, which had reached the pinnacle of their influence under Allende, were obliterated by arrests, detentions, and just plain fear.

Pinochet grappled with the resulting social strife with the hard hand of a dictator. He viewed the economy as a near-sacred domain and shot down dissent whenever it cropped up. In 1978, General Leigh, the head of the Air Force and always Pinochet's most formidable rival within the junta, began to criticize de Castro's shock therapy and the extraordinary authority his Finance Ministry had amassed. Pinochet would have none of it. Within months, Leigh had "resigned," ending the careers of a dozen other loyal generals with him. Pinochet's consolidation of power was complete.

But the truth is that whatever opposition Pinochet faced didn't matter much in those days. One after another, he swept his liabilities away. Knowing that his record on human rights was his Achilles' heel, in 1978, Pinochet declared an amnesty for all the junta's political crimes—with the notable exception of the Letelier affair, for which the general was making simultaneous diplomatic amends. He renamed his secret police from the Dirección de Inteligencia Nacional (DINA) to the Central Nacional de Informaciones (CNI) in 1977 to signal their supposed reform, and he extradited one of the principal agents of the Letelier crime, a radical anti-communist American named Michael Townley, to the United States. Pinochet knew he had to make amends with a furious Carter administration.

As one final precaution, he fought back against a U.N. declaration decrying Chile's human rights violations. In a bid to prove that the people were behind him, in January 1978, Pinochet called a domestic "plebiscite" on the international decree. At the ballot box, you could mark a sentence favoring the "independence of Chile" or "the intervention of a foreign power in the internal affairs of Chile." This was Pinochet's idea of democracy—and, of course, he won. Emblematic of just how confident he had become, after the votes were counted, Pinochet declared that he saw no need for further elections or consultations for at least the next decade.

It was to this environment that I returned to Chile on April 29, 1978, with the feeling of Pinochet's triumph and omnipotence still lingering heavily in the air.

Four and a half years after the coup, Chile's political landscape was bleak. There were practically no organized parties aside from those propping up Pinochet's state. The Christian Democrats, who had survived the coup at first, were now withering. The Socialist Party had essentially disappeared, its leading cadres exiled, assassinated, or imprisoned. The same was true of the Communist Party and the leftist forces that had supported Allende. There was essentially no one left to oppose Pinochet.

How, I wondered, could we possibly fight the dictator? With all semblance of opposition obliterated, who was left to do battle? Pinochet had consolidated every advantage and pre-empted every threat. He had found an eloquent solution to his legitimacy problems in the Chicago Boys, even winning applause abroad. How could we possibly overcome all that? We couldn't, I remember thinking, although we would have to try.

Pinochet quickly broke his promise not to call any more elections for the coming decade. Now was the perfect time, he must have reasoned, to legitimate his government once and for all. He had just won the plebiscite in 1978, the economy was growing at a record pace, and the opposition had practically ceased to exist. He would draft a new constitution and crown himself the "elected" president. With the economy booming and his authority assured, how could he possibly lose?

All the groundwork was already in place. Several years earlier, Pinochet had formed a constitutional commission under the direction of former President Jorge Alessandri. Their work was nearly complete, so he planned to call a plebiscite to ratify the draft—once it had been approved by the junta. (Alessandri ended up resigning over the matter, after almost none of his ideas made it into the final document.)

In no uncertain terms, the new constitution was a bid to solidify the dictatorship's authoritarianism. It would finally liberate the junta from any threat of civilian power. Parties deemed to be leaning toward socialism or communism would be forbidden. The president could never dismiss military commanders in chief (like Pinochet) without a vote from the country's Security Council—a body half made up of military men. The draft disempowered the Congress, moving the body an hour and a half away from Santiago to the port city of Valparaíso, where it remains today. Representatives could not introduce new spending, only cut from the president's wish list. On top of it all, amendments to this new constitution would have to pass through impossible hurdles.

By August 1980, all this had been in the works for months. But Pinochet called the plebiscite just 30 days in advance, to the surprise of everyone in

Chile. His voice boomed over the national and radio television stations: Ominously, the vote would be held on September 11.

So there we were, just a month away from a vote that would rewrite Chile's history, and there was little we could do. There were few voices by then who could truly fight back. Ex-president Eduardo Frei Montalva tried to lead a "No" campaign but to little avail; the way the elections were organized made opposition moot. The junta had promised back in 1978 to create full voting registers before future elections to ensure a fair ballot. Now, with just 30 days to organize, that would be impossible. So on the seventh anniversary of the coup, Chileans went dutifully to the polls, their right-hand index fingers dyed with ink to show they had voted. Electoral officials made a small cut in each voter's national identity papers so that every person could have only one vote—and so that it would be obvious who had failed to show up.

It goes without saying that Pinochet "won" the plebiscite with a solid 67 percent of the vote. But the fact that a third of the population voted "No" even under such desperate conditions—when many still feared exile and disappearances happened seemingly every day—was something of a triumph. No matter to Pinochet; he seized the victory as absolute and began to rule with more of a "mandate" than ever before. The newly constitutionalized president even accelerated the reconstruction of La Moneda, home to Chile's presidents dating back to 1840, vowing to occupy it from the day he assumed power "legally" on March 11, 1981. That's exactly what he did.

It is surely one of history's great ironies that Augusto Pinochet's strongest moment would precipitate his eventual downfall. For in that painfully tyrannical constitution, we found the nascent shred of democracy—just what we needed to bring down the dictatorship. It took years for it to become clear that we could use the loophole as an escape hatch. But looking back, perhaps it was Pinochet's strength that made our position plausible to a society torn at the seams; since the general himself had endorsed a transition—not out of fear but with all his might—our push for change was also legitimate, if perhaps slightly insane. History easily could have turned the other way had we chosen to fight with something other than a paper and pen.

Half a decade after the Chicago Boys transformed Chile's economy, and just when Pinochet was settling in, the signs were apparent: This thing was about to collapse. The "bricks" that de Castro had used to build his fortress were made of sand. The Chicago Boys had pushed the economy to the brink, luring in creditors at any cost to keep the easy money flowing. Then, in 1980, a global recession hit, and the bubble couldn't last. It began to pop in 1981, when a sugar plant went bankrupt and sent small shockwaves through a weak system. Next came devaluation; copper prices were falling too fast and imports, especially of oil, rising too steeply. I feared the worst. Banks would fail and the government would have to step in. Loans would come due, foreign credit would dry up, and the easy cash would go away. I saw a terrible financial crisis coming closer each day.

So I did what most economists did not back then: I said something. In an interview with *Cosas* magazine, a sort of Chilean version of *Life* or *Vanity Fair,* I predicted a big crash. In text laid between photos of the latest fashionable wardrobes and local socialite gossip, I laid my thesis bare: Chileans were living on foreign loans, with savings rates too low at home. The country's currency would have to slide, making loans in dollars unbearably expensive. Banks would go bust. It would be a meltdown.

The seemingly odd placement of my economic interview in *Cosas*'s lifestyle pages actually brought me more local publicity than academics like myself can usually expect. In fact, my warnings made it all the way up to La Moneda. "Silly Lagos" was essentially the reply from an economic team there. The Chicago Boys believed they were invulnerable. The state would never have to intervene, they replied. This was a matter for private banks.

But then my worst fears came true. By April 1982, not long after the article was published, de Castro resigned as the economy imploded. By June, Pinochet had devaluated the currency—a move he made so quickly that no one even had time to make a run on the banks for dollars. The price of copper plummeted even as the cost of gasoline rose. Lenders defaulted and banks folded. Then, just 24 hours after the new finance minister from Catholic University, Rolf Lüders, assured investors that there was no need for a bailout, the state was forced to guarantee all of Chile's commercial loans. Firms with debt denominated in dollars defaulted. In the end, almost a quarter of the capital in Chile's banks was lost, and seven banks and one investment firm had to be bailed out. After that, many of the Chicago Boys remained in the government, but with their most extreme ambitions greatly curtailed.

The Chicago Boys had liberalized markets without any checks at all. Regulation was spotty or missing entirely, which meant that the bank default wasn't just messy—it was disastrous. The gains during the good times had benefitted the emerging rich class. Now, the losses hit everyone. A country slowly getting used to modest growth saw its economy shrinking—and fast.

In 1982, the Chilean economy contracted by 15 percent. And whereas the public could be battered into submission before, people were now up in arms and ready to protest. The middle and working classes watched their money prop up the banks even as their own jobs disappeared.

I had seen all of this coming because I had spent the last three years watching. In 1979, just after I returned to Chile, I approached a colleague, an eminent but rather iconoclastic social scientist named Enzo Faletto, with the idea of opening a modest research center to ponder questions about Chile's future. Faletto was a socialist like myself and something of a dreamer, famous at the time for *Dependency and Development in Latin America,* a book he had written with Fernando Henrique Cardoso, a sociologist and the future president of Brazil. A great thinker, Faletto could have been a powerful man in Chile on many occasions, but he always shunned the spotlight. During Allende's administration, when most other socialists were close to the action, Faletto was content to study the most obscure of subjects: Chilean social structure in the nineteenth century as seen through the eyes of great novels. When I was elected president of Chile years later, Faletto practically bid me farewell, saying, "I'll see you when you are no longer president." It took a joint invitation from both myself and Brazilian President Fernando Cardoso to convince him to finally come to dinner at La Moneda.

But at our small think tank, Faletto was in his element. Together, we began to build up a small group of other thinkers like ourselves—Eduardo Ortiz, Eduardo Trabucco, Rodrigo Alvayay, and Heraldo Muñoz. We called the institute "Vector," Latin for "to lead," at the suggestion of our new president, a former Allende minister named Luis Matte Valdés, or "Lucho." He came from a very old, wealthy Chilean family—one in which he was clearly the black sheep, especially after being harassed by the military after the coup.

The name "Vector" fit our simple goal: to chart a new course for socialism, in turn creating a set of ideas and concepts powerful enough to combat those of the Chicago Boys. The opposition had been decimated, and with most of the socialists exiled, dispersed, or balkanized, any and all intellectual resistance to Pinochet had met the same fate. We had to undo the damage. We had to deconstruct the tale of intellectual grandeur and enlightened democracy that Pinochet had woven for himself. The junta had been adamant about having "goals and no deadlines." It pretended to be the creator of "protected democracy" built on the premise that the public didn't know how to choose best for itself. What made matters even more difficult was that it wasn't just Chileans who had bought Pinochet's story; it was the world. Beginning in the 1980s, when Thatcher came to power in Britain and Reagan in the United States, neoliberals the world over were looking to the example of what Chile had done, granting a sort of legitimacy and even prestige to Pinochet for his tyrannical experiment.

We had to look elsewhere for new models. And we found some hope in Europe—from the Mediterranean governments of France, Italy, Portugal, and Spain—all of which were turning left while simultaneously becoming more democratic. Our connection to Europe was more than just coincidental. Many of the local communist and socialist leaders coming of age in Europe had found their calling after watching the fate of Allende's administration in Chile.

The task before us was nothing less than redefining our country's socialist thought. How should we configure the financial system? Where does privatization end and state control begin? Where should the market be free and where should regulation be imposed? The answer to every question started with the simple premise of democracy. No matter how diverse our individual visions were, all of them fit within a truly democratic structure that saw the obliteration of Pinochet's peculiar "democratic" system.

As we equipped ourselves for the coming battle of ideas, we realized our great need for soldiers—in this case, academics, the hundreds or even thousands of Chileans who had gone abroad to study, work, and think in the safety of voluntary exile. It was time for them to come home.

Help came through an old friend, Dudley Seers, a distinguished development economist from London who showed up at my doorstep a mere 10 days after I arrived back in Chile. He wanted to help repatriate the Chilean students who had fled to the safety of Britain to get their post-graduate degrees. There were plenty to pick from. At the time of the coup, Britain's minister of cooperation and development, Judith Hart, had just been granted funding for an aid project benefiting the Chilean economy. When Pinochet took over, she repurposed the money to help Chileans who were in trouble with the dictatorship travel to Britain for school. Hundreds of students left Chile this way. And now, five years later, many of those students were finishing up.

With the help of several of the academics abroad, we built a list of names of possible repatriation candidates and began approaching them one by one. Doubts and skepticism were common; many worried about what life would be like if they returned to Chile, since merely belonging to the left was enough to brand them an enemy of the state. For each student we approached, we had to investigate whether he or she was "clean" enough to re-enter the country. It wasn't as easy as checking a list of exiles; that list wasn't public, and many of those who were harassed were never on it anyway. Often, the only way to find out whether you were disallowed was to go to the Chilean consulate for a passport renewal. Those who found an "L" at the end of their passport stamp were permanently exiled. That was how you learned you couldn't go home.

For those who were clean, the next step was to find positions for them to occupy back in Chile. The British government had offered to pay their wages for one or two years upon their repatriation, which helped facilitate an otherwise difficult task. Some were physicians who wanted to practice medicine, so we worked to renew their local licenses. Others opened small shops, and still more went to work at non-governmental organizations.

Reconstructing socialist thought also meant spreading it to students still within Chile. So we began to offer "classes" on Monday evenings, from 6 to 8.30 P.M. (in Chile dinner is late, about 9 P.M.) for a group of economics students from the University of Chile. I recruited many of the attendees through professors I knew. And in those few weekly hours, we tried to teach our new pupils that our reading of economics was not crazy. We looked deeply into the economic history of Chile, demonstrating that the country's prosperity did not go hand in hand with the ideological fundamentalism of the Chicago Boys. The poor didn't have to suffer for investors to do well.

Students couldn't get this kind of instruction at the university, where, thanks to the military, they were obliged to swallow neoliberal economic doctrine, no questions asked. Those who dared to think otherwise were expelled.

We gave them reading lists that included books the University of Chile had long ago effectively banned. So our classes had to be held in secret.

One day, I ran into one of my clandestine students, a young lady named Alejandra Mizzala, at the U.N. office where I still worked during the day. She had come for a conference, and when I passed her in the hallway, I tried to say hello. She said nothing, passing quickly as if she didn't recognize me. Struck by her silence, I asked in the next class what had happened—had she not seen me in time? "Mr. Lagos, there is no way that I can admit to having known you before that conference. If I am interrogated tomorrow, and I say that we were acquaintances before then . . . well, you must understand that your lectures are clandestine."

She was right. Our ideas, while in the political center today, were nothing less than toxic back then. I espoused them increasingly openly—which made me a dangerous character for students to know.

Of course, our ideas were toxic to the military not only because of its ideology but because Vector's whole purpose was to imagine a Chile without Pinochet. In no uncertain terms, we were opening a debate about how to unseat the dictatorship.

Debating was one thing; doing it was quite another matter. We had seen just how difficult concrete action was a mere two days after I returned to Chile, as Luisa and I were still settling into our old house in Santiago's Ñuñoa neighborhood and long before our furniture had arrived back from Argentina. On May 1, 1978—Labor Day—we met up with Faletto, who had learned of a workers' protest to be held that day. When we arrived at the site of the demonstration, we found only an awkward agglomeration of a few people who, like ourselves, were waiting for something to happen. Well-dressed men with the mannerisms of Pinochet's secret police also combed the area, and we tried to stroll innocently for a bit. Nothing happened, and we left.

Later that night, we learned that there had indeed been a protest—just not where we had been. So tenuous were the contacts between workers at the time that the location had been transmitted incorrectly. Across town, a modest-sized group had turned out, but the demonstration ended violently, broken up by the police with water cannons and tear gas.

As we tried to keep up with the few demonstrations taking place against Pinochet, we grew closer to the union leaders who were beginning to emerge in opposition. Through their powerful characters and constituencies, a social movement was beginning to organize itself. Such contacts would prove increasingly vital after the economic crash—when people were at last ready to take to the streets.

I t was November 1978, and I had arrived in Mexico City on a U.N. project with a jam-packed schedule. The hours ahead promised meetings, research, and diplomatic courtesies. But there was one visit that I had to make on top of it all: You couldn't pass through Mexico in those days without visiting the widow of Salvador Allende.

Tencha Allende had fled to Mexico after the coup, and years later, she was still mourning the loss of both her husband and her country. Although she had left Chile, her mind and spirit were still there. She knew everything that was going on, reading voraciously and speaking with every exile who passed through.

"You arrived in Mexico two days ago and only call me today?" She spoke as if giving orders, somehow still retaining the charm of a woman who has been the first lady of a state. She commanded me to meet her for lunch on Saturday at her small apartment, neat and well-decorated but modest. Our agenda was already set: A split had recently opened within the Socialist Party, one that would come to define it over the next decade. She wanted to hear all the details.

Six months earlier, the Socialist Party had held a secret meeting in East Berlin (although for safety's sake, it was publically announced to have taken place in Algeria). The party's leadership had transferred hands, from the more liberal Carlos Altamirano to Clodomiro Almeyda, Allende's more militant foreign minister. The change widened a growing rift within the party over how to approach the dictatorship. There were two questions at hand: how to fight, and with whom. On the latter question, Almeyda favored an alliance with the leftist Communist Party; Altamirano preferred to reach out to the center right-leaning Christian Democrats. As for our resistance, Altamirano's faction favored a non-violent, democratic transition, but others, including Almeyda's supporters, believed in using "all means of resistance" against the dictator—a euphemism many communists had also begun using to justify violent methods.

To me, embracing violence meant certain defeat. If the Chilean people were already frightened as a result of the regime's repression, imagine what would happen if the opposition used weapons against a military that was heavily armed and fiercely loyal to Pinochet. And even if it succeeded, overthrowing a dictator with force would deal a deathblow to any hopes of creating a peaceful democracy thereafter. Violence yields only violence, and that's exactly what we were hoping to end. Still, it didn't seem so clear cut to everyone. And the schism within the Socialist Party was emblematic of a larger divide within Chilean society as a whole.

I recounted all this to Tencha, expressing my lament that the party was split. Surely, if we were hoping to fight back against Pinochet at all, a divided party would make that impossible. The Socialist Party was by then a very fragile organization. The last thing we needed was more damage—this time of our own making.

"And what about you?" she asked me. "What's your position?"

"Well," I began to reply, "Many of us at Vector refuse to take a side. Dividing the party would be a profound error. We want to find a platform that can be accepted by all."

Tencha quickly replied, "Ah-hah! So you are like the Swiss—always neutral in the conflicts that have polarized humanity for the last 200 years." As simple as that, we were dubbed "The Swiss."

With Tencha's blessing, we "Swiss" became the unexpected moderators in an attempt, in early 1983, to unify the Socialist Party. We set up a Permanent Committee for Socialist Unity, the CPU, through which to negotiate. The factions at the table that February spanned the distance between Almeyda and Altamirano. The latter group, believing that their representatives should be based in Chile, had elected Ricardo Nuñez as the secretary-general. Other splinter groups also formed.

The socialists, it soon became clear, were traumatized. The animosity, fear, and resentment that permeated negotiations were not surprising. Allende's term, then his suicide, and the subsequent torture, disappearance, and death of so many had stunned us all, and it was difficult to look across the room and not blame one another. To many sitting there, those who had abandoned Allende were traitors. To others, the party's leftward drift before the coup had gone too far. If Pinochet had done one thing effectively, it was encourage the opposition to cannibalize itself.

Amid the rancor, Vector was neutral ground. Since we didn't take sides, we didn't lose participants before they even arrived. We never said that the Socialist Party was fractured; it could have easily become a self-fulfilling prophecy. The CPU made quick progress, and by September of that year, we felt united enough to create a single Socialist Party Central Committee. Most everyone wanted the Swiss to be represented there—an odd idea since our only position had been, well, no position at all. While other factions had constituencies of hundreds, we were just seven people—academics, really—who had been able to negotiate without taking sides. Thus far in the CPU, we had been represented by two people at a time. Now, there was talk of having a Central Committee of 60 members, 10 from each of the six distinct political groups.

The problem was, we didn't *have* 10 people—let alone 10 who could participate. We were seven, but Faletto, with typical reclusiveness, refused to participate, try as we might to convince him. So we proposed just six members: Heraldo Muñoz, Eduardo Ortiz, Eduardo Trabucco, Rodrigo Alvayay, Jaime Ahumada, and me. The whole committee had to shrink in size to conform; just 36 people sat there in the end.

I hadn't realized up to that point just how paranoid the various CPU factions had become. When we all met for the first time, my Swiss colleagues and I quickly realized that the other groups referred to one another by aliases. They were clandestine in all their meeting minutes and official documentation, just in case they fell into the wrong hands. "You'll have to have names too," they told us, a thought we found amusing at best and ridiculous at least. I exemplified the absurdity by forgetting mine over and over again. Mid-meeting, I would regularly fail to respond to my alias until someone else nudged me. To this day, I cannot remember the name.

But it was striking to see. Here were some of Chilean socialism's boldest, most accomplished men, and they were afraid—or at least extraordinarily careful. We all knew that what we were doing was risky. But we saw no other options. Nascent protests were beginning to show that people—everyday, hard-working people—were ready to take risks. And if they could, we must.

The Socialist Party announced its reunification in a press conference on September 4, the traditional date on which Chile elected its presidents. Embarrassingly, however, we soon realized that not all the cracks in our party were sealed. Almeyda's representatives in Chile, Akin Soto and Julio Stuardo, had moved too quickly toward reconciliation for the taste of their constituencies in both Chile and Berlin. Almeyda declined to sign the document of unity and refused to authorize his representatives to do so either. Many of his followers parted ways and followed Soto's and Stuardo's compromise. But in practice, Almeyda's faction remained on the outside. It would stay this way until December 1988, when Pinochet had been defeated and the question of how best to fight him was no longer relevant.

By the beginning of 1983, the economic crisis had produced an entirely new landscape in Chile, particularly among the country's working class. When you walked through lower-class neighborhoods, the poverty was staggering. The ranks of unemployed had exploded. While the official unemployment rate hovered around 15 percent, most historians now believe that unemployment reached as high as a quarter of the population, and countless more toiled in a hand-to-mouth struggle for daily survival. Where there were once a handful of beggars, now there were scores. Tens of thousands of Chileans were desperate—and they were getting no help from a government that believed social justice would trickle down.

On top of those daily struggles, Pinochet inflicted upon the working class an injustice that it simply couldn't overlook. Pinochet had begun going after labor leaders—the few brave souls who had dared to talk back. One leader in particular had caught the junta's attention in late 1978—a strong-voiced, 50-something man named Tucapel Jiménez, who had been working to unite the various labor unions, just as we had done with the socialists.

Jiménez was particularly dangerous because he wasn't a radical; he was a social democrat. He had been opposed to Allende. Now, his pragmatic, depolarized politics were attracting followers. It suddenly looked possible to bring together two of the factions of the trade unions that had until then been rivals within the Coordinadora Nacional Sindical. His work was hard. But that was exactly why Jiménez was so important—and so dangerous.

That is also why he didn't last long. On February 27, 1982, as Chile's summer holiday was winding down, I got word of Jiménez's disappearance. Two days later, he was found with his throat slit. No one had to explain. Everyone knew what the justice system would later reveal: that a former member of Pinochet's CNI had orchestrated the assassination. Jiménez's death set back the unification of the trade unions quite a bit. The movement lost not only a dominant figure but also the international contacts he had made—for example, with the U.S. AFL-CIO and with trade unions in Brussels.

Still, Pinochet couldn't stop the wave of discontent that the economic collapse had created. Whatever social contract he had predicated on economic growth was now shattered; his legitimacy, however contrived, was gone. A year after Jiménez died, social discontent was everywhere. In May 1983, a group of several Christian Democrats, socialists, democrats from one of the right-wing parties, and members of the Radical Party all appeared together to release what they called a "Democratic Manifesto," calling for the government to make amends with the country through the ballot box. Earlier, a group of jurists had banded together to create the Group of 24—an organization aiming to reimagine the constitutional makeup of Chile.

Then there were the protests. Into the void left by Jiménez's murder stepped Rodolfo Seguel, a new union leader from the Christian Democrats. As president of the copper trade union, one of the most powerful in the country, he decided to call a general strike on May 11, 1983—the first in more than a decade.

Seguel's strategy was met with skepticism at first. Calling for a general strike would be difficult; people would be afraid. They risked losing their jobs if they failed to show up at work—and in hard economic times, no one could justify that. So Seguel started small. He called for a national protest involving acts of simple, banal disobedience that would add up to real dissent. Parents would not take their children to school. Copper workers would walk to the mines instead of taking the bus; then they would refuse to eat lunch. It would be a day of subtle signals. Until that night.

Just before 8 P.M. that evening, I was driving home to the condo we had just moved into in a residential area called La Reina. It was smaller than our old house in Ñuñoa, but it had one key feature: it was safer. The condos were set back from the road, tucked away behind a long pebble driveway guarded by a gate. We knew our neighbors, many of whom also worked for the United Nations or other international organizations.

The clock was ticking toward 8 P.M. as I approached home that night, and I could feel my nerves on edge, tightening my shoulders and pushing adrenaline through my veins. We already knew that our new neighbors were the type of people who would protest. But we never dreamed the demonstrations would reach the magnitude that they did.

At first, we heard the sound of just a few people banging pots, a gesture meant to symbolize their plight: The pots were empty, with nothing—not even potatoes or grains—to eat. Within minutes, the entire sky filled with that deafening sound. People flooded into the streets, liberated by the simple idea of participating in something forbidden: a protest. These were taxi drivers, restaurant staff, office managers, and construction workers. They were ordinary Chileans. And they were overwhelmed with joy and relief. For many, this was the first time that even close friends learned that they were both against Pinochet. Talking about politics had become taboo; just about the only safe subject, by that time, in fact, was soccer. So flooding into the streets that night was like realizing you had shared a secret all along. "Y va caer!" filled the night sky. Step down! They didn't even need to say the dictator's name.

Pinochet was as surprised as anyone at our success. He didn't crack down on the first protest; it was too big and too sudden. He did follow up, however. Just 48 hours after the banging had ended, the general suspended broadcasts from Radio Cooperativa, the station used by the Christian Democrats, fearing that it would exaggerate the extent of the protests. Pinochet must have known that the demonstrations wouldn't stop there, and that Radio Cooperativa was the beacon used to organize them.

The retribution went further, and as was so often the case under Pinochet, it was the poor who suffered the most. On May 14, the president mobilized the military garrison in Santiago for the first time. Brigades of soldiers flooded into the city's most crowded neighborhoods, demanding that people leave their houses. Everyone, from teenagers to 60-year-olds, was called out onto the streets at 5 o'clock in the morning. The military moved them to football fields or other public places, where soldiers subjected them to a "review." Were they loyal to the regime? Pinochet inflicted upon the most humble of men a complete humiliation—to be treated like common criminals in their very homes.

But Seguel didn't give up. Instead, he and other union leaders called another protest, this one for June 14. Instead of just Santiago, this time Seguel sought to include all of Chile. And if the first demonstration was a surprise, the second found us all prepared. An angry speech Pinochet gave in the north that day did little to deter the crowds, nor did police barricades set up to block off certain neighborhoods. No, this time, people came ready. They shouted above the security forces. They brought megaphones and speaker systems to amplify their voices.

It was too much for Pinochet. Seguel and other union leaders were arrested, and the government accused many political party officials of aiding the protests. Before the third protest could take place, three Christian Democrats, including the party president, Gabriel Valdés, were also detained, rendering them incapable of coordinating the next protest. But the plan backfired, provoking protestors to demonstrate even more forcefully—now not just for economic reasons but political ones as well. Several were killed when the police mobilized to quash that third, large demonstration.

Still, no amount of force could stamp out the very real impact the demonstrations were beginning to have. When Valdés was released from prison shortly after the third protest, he galvanized the opposition against Pinochet. He writes in his memoirs that the policeman holding him in detention told him he would be taking the afternoon of the protest off; he had asked for the leave so that he could take part in the demonstration.

The conditions were ripe to create a real, coherent opposition among the five major parties that opposed Pinochet. But if unifying the socialists was difficult, creating a coalition including the Christian Democrats, liberals, radicals, Social Democrats, and socialists would be far more complicated. On August 15, 1983, we formed the Democratic Alliance (AD)—the first real challenge to Pinochet. Our founding document, "Bases del Diálogo para un Gran Acuerdo Nacional" (Principles of Dialogue for a Grand National Accord), laid out our raison d'être: to denounce the dictatorship of Pinochet, to establish a provisional government, and to call a constitutional assembly to rewrite our future.

Bringing everyone on board with that basic platform had come with relative ease, but one issue in particular remained fraught: who else to include. The socialists thought it vital to reach out to the Communist Party, the other clear group in the opposition. But it wasn't as easy as that. Many communists at that time were still calling for "all means of resistance" to be used against

Pinochet. Bringing the relatively right-leaning Christian Democrats into a coalition with the far left, moreover, was a hard sell. It would be another five years before we could finally all agree to come together to say no to Pinochet.

The AD was organized as a coalition of diverse parties, and leadership would rotate among us all. Each month would see a new president, from a different party each time. The Christian Democrats under Gabriel Valdés held the first presidency in October, followed by Enrique Silva Cimma, president of the radicals, the following month. I had known Silva Cimma for years—he had been my professor and later colleague at the university and continued to be a wise, mentor-like figure in my academic life.

During Silva Cimma's term, the AD organized its first real public gathering. Such an event required the regime's approval, and so we made our case to the authorities. We were granted permission—but the Pinochet government played what it thought was a nasty trick on us. Sure, we could hold an event, but it would have to be in Parque O'Higgins, a massive stretch of land in central Santiago's core whose size Pinochet picked so as to dwarf our own ranks by comparison. It would have been easy, he must have reasoned, for us to pack a small neighborhood green of the sort that Santiago is famous for. In Parque O'Higgins, we would look like a family picnic.

How wrong he was. More than 50,000 people came that day. So large was the number of attendees that the noise from our microphone couldn't canvas the entire field. The crowd was excited as Silva Cimma took the podium and patient upon realizing that he had carried 44 pages with him to the microphone and planned on reading each and every one. I knew Silva Cimma well by then, and I had always found him incredibly thoughtful and intelligent. His speech was this way, too, perfectly capturing our priorities for a post-Pinochet Chile. It was long—but it didn't bother the crowd, by then still euphoric at the thought of being together and united in our opposition.

The launch of my own political career in the AD was even more lively. By December, it was the Socialist Party's turn to take over the presidency. But who would take the job? Here we were in a coalition of parties that were decades and decades old, filled with cadres of competent and organized politicians. And the socialists? Our most prominent leaders were all abroad or dead. Those remaining could scarcely do anything publically. I was among the most well known—not only as an economist but also as someone who had been in intellectual opposition to the coup. So I got the nod from the Central Committee of the Socialist Party.

Building on the Parque O'Higgins event, we called a demonstration in Chile's second largest town, Valparaíso. It would become the site of my first real speech against Pinochet. Like the last event, we were welcomed in Valparaíso, this time in a large football field filled with more people than we had ever imagined would come. When it was my turn to speak, the words came naturally—and forcefully—to an effect that caught everyone by surprise. I spoke about our history, reminding the crowd that their country had once been known the world over as a strong democracy. The last 10 years, however, were an anti-history of Chile, in which our true past—our true legacy—was displaced. Framed this way, it was only logical that we, the AD, were the true heirs to the Chilean political tradition. With the force of history behind us, Pinochet had nothing.

I stepped back from the roaring applause, and I still remember the look of surprise on the faces of Valdés and Silva Cimma. Here was this professor energizing the crowd like a well-rehearsed campaigner. It was the first time I realized that maybe I could be a good speaker after all.

A few days later, the AD received an international boost when we were invited to the presidential inauguration of Argentine president Raúl Alfonsín. It was the end of the dictatorship in our neighboring country—an event that gave us hope for our own future at home. I remember the event as surreal. There we were breaking all norms of protocol, chatting openly with the European and Latin American presidents from our front-row seats in the Salon Blanco of the Casa Rosada, Argentina's White House, even as Pinochet's delegation was relegated to the far, far, back of the attending crowd.

Before this flurry of political activity as the AD's rotating head, I had to step down from my position within the United Nations, since politician and diplomat are incompatible roles. Resigning had occurred to me many times during my service, but actually doing so felt like jumping into the abyss. I would have to find another way to provide for my family. It was hard to take that step—to sit down with Luisa and my children, Ricardo at 21, Ximena 20, Hernán 18, Alejandro 16, and Panchita, the youngest, just 8—and tell them that I was going to dedicate myself to fighting the dictatorship with no certainty about when or from where the next paycheck would arrive.

That was a moment I won't easily forget. Everyone understood what I was trying to say. There were no guarantees, all of a sudden, about the future. But my party—my country—had already suffered through the torture, disappearance, and death of many of its members. Exile or assassination had never befallen me. After so much luck in such terrible times, how could I ignore a call so great?

When I returned from Argentina, the AD had ample momentum, but I was fast realizing that we were missing two things: a coherent political organization and more concrete goals. If the transition was going to be based on democracy and ideas, we needed more of both.

I started with the latter, trying to put parameters on what we wanted to accomplish. I called a conference, "Chile: The Grand Themes of the Reconstruction," in La Comedia theater, a symbolic place for its unusual satire of Pinochet's regime. There, for the first time, we delved into the nuts and bolts of how an opposition-led Chile would be run. We knew that our success would depend not only on our resistance to the dictator but our ability to replace him after he was gone. We needed a plan for infrastructure, for politics, and for an economy that would strike a balance between growth and social cohesion. What that conference produced was the closest thing to a plan that anyone had imagined since September 11, 1973.

Just as important were our efforts to transform the AD from a loose coalition into a coherent political force. That meant traveling around the country, reviving small shreds of the party that had once existed but had long since faded away. We met in backyards and high school basketball courts, attracting sometimes a handful of people, sometimes barely anyone at all. We sought out socialists as well as members of other AD parties, with whom we always expressed our openness to work. We relied on the generosity of local people in whose homes we stayed and whose food we ate. Our methods were equally simple: go, meet, discuss, convince.

I learned some of my most fundamental political skills on the road. When we met local politicians, I was certain to note the key concerns and complaints they raised. I took down their names and trained my brain to remember details about them. Then, when we spoke to local crowds, I would explain how each of those grievances, worries, and concerns fit perfectly in line with the solutions the AD was proposing. Democracy was the natural progression of Chile's history, and framing individual, personal concerns in those terms had a powerful effect. Slowly, indefatigably, we added lists of cities and towns to our national network. This grassroots core was what would make us a real political force with which Pinochet would have to contend.

The dictator knew what we were up to, and he didn't like it one bit. In 1984, he made a rather canny attempt to pre-empt our opposition: He offered to negotiate with us. Pinochet sent his interior minister, Sergio Onofre Jarpa, to hold regular discussions with the AD. Pinochet never intended to give in or even to negotiate basic terms. His goal was to confuse us. He wanted the protests to stop; he wanted the opposition to do what it had done for the last 10 years—fall apart. On top of it, he wanted to look as if he were doing something to appease our concerns—and frame us as the uncooperative ones. I declined to participate in the conversations for that very reason. Besides, I knew that I would be excluded by the government, which could not talk with a "socialist." Valdés went on our behalf instead, and in the first and second meetings, he put forth our three demands: the resignation of General Pinochet, a transitional government, and a constitutional assembly.

You might imagine how the minister to a dictator responded to our demanding that his boss resign. Jarpa was unyielding—and, of course, how could he not be? In one particularly tense moment, Valdés tried to give Jarpa a copy of our demands in writing. Jarpa refused to accept, protesting that he would sooner leave the room than hold such a provocative document in his hands.

On the night of March 25, 1985, I stopped at the Santiago Cathedral on my way home, ascending the stairs to the second floor where I could find the Vicariate de la Solidaridad. The Vicariate, as we called it, was an initiative run by the Catholic Church for victims of the junta—it was the voice for those without a voice, as its founding cardinal put it. The Vicariate was where your parents or your wife or your children went after you didn't come home from work or school. It was where the disappeared were mourned and their cases, finally, investigated. It was the last refuge for a society with no safety nets.

I arrived that night as I often did during those times, to check in, to get up to speed, and to show my support for the work the Vicariate was doing. But this was no ordinary night. Just days earlier, three teachers had been kidnapped right in front of their high school. The incident had caused more than the usual stir for its disturbing brazenness. How could you seize a teacher in front of the very children he had been teaching?

The mood in the Vicariate was already gloomy. But then, around 9 P.M., the father and mother of one of the teachers, José Manuel Parada, arrived. They were two well-known actors, Roberto Parada and Maria Maluenda. The father's commanding baritone was unmistakable; any Chilean would have recognized it. I was there in another room when they came, but I can still hear his voice in my ears: the "No" of Roberto Parada. It was a cry, a scream, a primordial call for some sort of supernatural justice. It crossed the walls of the Vicariate; it penetrated deep through our skin and sat there, lingering. They had told him what had happened to his son. He'd been found, together with the two other teachers, throats slit—all.

José Manuel Parada's case was what the Vicariate had been created for. Immediately after the coup, the church had formed a predecessor organization called the Committee for Peace, a federation of Catholics, Lutherans, Protestants, Jews—everyone. But it was disbanded at the order of the government just a year later. So the cardinal of Santiago at the time, Raúl Silva Henríquez, established the Vicariate by decree. It met on the second floor of the Santiago Cathedral, with a small, inconspicuous entrance that allowed you to enter directly without first moving through the church.

In the Vicariate, Silva Henríquez near single-handedly built the most important human rights organization in Chile. The doors were open to everyone, not just Catholics. It had the resources to help families in distress; Silva Henríquez was a prolific fundraiser and traveled to Germany and Belgium often. The fact that the Vicariate was Catholic in an overwhelmingly Catholic country added to the feeling of sanctuary. Churches became centers of public organization—the one place where we knew we could always turn. When I traveled the country for the AD, most of my meetings took place with the help of bishops, priests, and monsignors. Although a non-believer myself, I knew the Catholic Church was saving Chile's soul.

It was also the one place Pinochet could never penetrate, although he often tried. When Silva Henríquez retired in 1984, many in La Moneda rejoiced. By then he had become known to them as the "Red Cardinal," an allusion to his supposed "communist" sympathies; surely his successor wouldn't be such a problem. And indeed, the new bishop, Francisco Fresno, certainly looked sympathetic to the regime at first; he was a conservative man from the sleepy neighborhood of La Serena with not nearly so fiery a temperament.

But Fresno turned out to be no easier to crack. One of his first acts, in August 1985, was to try and reconcile Pinochet with the opposition through a "national accord"—an agreement already signed onto by the AD and the right-leaning party led by Jarpa, who by that time had resigned from the ministry. Fresno took it to Pinochet, who was obliged to meet the religious leader. But Pinochet kept saying no, and on Christmas in 1985, he made things even more clear. The new cardinal had gone to wish Pinochet a merry Christmas and hand him the text of the accord. "Let's turn the page, Cardinal," Pinochet replied instead, hinting that it should never be brought up again. Fresno was forced to give up. But Pinochet also gave up trying to win over the Church.

By 1984 and 1985, the Church wasn't the only place where Pinochet started losing. Parallel institutions were popping up in the opposition, competing with the junta's traditionally uncontested political space. In addition to the existing labor unions, new organizations were forming, from the outspoken Women for Democracy to the student democracy groups that started proliferating on campuses. Neighborhoods created collectives, as did different economic sectors, pushing for better wages and working conditions, improved health care, and the restoration of pensions.

The press was also meekly expanding beyond the fawning coverage to which Pinochet had grown accustomed. The dictator-friendly *El Mercurio* (the same paper that was once funded by the CIA to oppose Allende's rule) and *La Tercera* were now joined by a modest cadre of opposition papers. Daily newspapers got around prohibitions on reporting on the opposition by referring to us as the parties that "didn't exist." Each of us individually was known by our respective descriptors. Valdés became "the ex-chancellor," for the position he had served under former President Eduardo Frei Montalva. Silva Cimma was the "ex-comptroller." I was known simply as "the economist." One magazine,

Análisis, even began to release a series of video debates between various party leaders.

Slowly but surely, these small changes were having an impact. If nothing else, people got to know who the opposition *was.* I was recognized more, often in the odd ways that dictate how one must behave under an autocrat—with a wink and a nod that acknowledges you share a secret. One weekend, my family was visiting El Quisco, a beach near Santiago where my in-laws had a small house. I ran a quick errand to the pharmacy and was greeted with surprise. "I know you! I saw you somewhere," the pharmacist said immediately. "Ah yes, I know! You look like someone named Lagos." Then his voice grew quieter: "I saw you in a video from *Análisis.*"

Chile's "opening," however, was really quite accidental. In fact, Pinochet was trying to do the opposite. He called a state of emergency in late 1984 and tried to crack down on the new organizations threatening his rule. Some did have to shut down, but by then, it was too late. The people of Chile were accustomed to leading clandestine lives and holding secret conversations. Organized and motivated, we knew that we could keep it up as long as we needed. And indeed, by the end of 1985, despite the state of emergency, Chile's civil society was more vibrant than ever before.

That's not to say that it was easy. I and surely many others were being closely watched. Pinochet's secret police had broken into my offices just after I took over the rotating presidency of the AD in November 1984. They entered while I was out, going through my files and inspecting our meeting space. When I arrived on my second-floor office on Serrano Street that day, just off the main avenue in Santiago, I found one of the officers still there. The man approached me, speaking in a harsh tone. He knew what I was up to, he said angrily, and the repercussions of messing up would be grave, especially for my family.

I was furious and replied angrily. When the man finally left, descending the staircase and moving toward the door, he ran into a pack of journalists coming to see me. Innocently, they asked him where my offices were. "Mr. Lagos?—He's finished," the man replied.

Finished is how Pinochet wanted all of us. He saw his omnipotence fading but was in many ways powerless to stop it. Even the movie *Gandhi,* which was released that year, had a huge impact. I can still hear the applause echoing from the movie theater at the moment the audience realized that pacifism had worked. (Pinochet was, of course, less thrilled with the example, and he suggested the film be banned.)

People could also laugh about the dictatorship in those days, knowing that comedy was among the best ways to criticize. That was the premise behind much of the work at La Comedia Theater in Santiago. The scripts were clearly written with Pinochet in mind. A family goes to watch a soccer match, where they are met by a guard. "You have to obey me," he says sullenly. "When I say clap, you clap—when I say stand, you stand." As the teams come in, the family stands in applause. "No! That's the wrong team!" the guard shouts. The game progresses, and the guard hands the family blindfolds. "You don't see what's going on? Don't worry, I will tell you what's happening in the field." The now-blind family hears the scoring of a goal—"Goal goal gooooooooal," shouts the crowd. "Nothing happened," the guard insists. That was Pinochet's Chile.

Something else important changed in 1985: the U.S. position. Pinochet's insistence on maintaining power was increasingly becoming inconvenient for Washington. Now, in Reagan's second term, administration officials were beginning to realize that while propping up the dictator may have been helpful in the short run, long-run support would prove hazardous.

I traveled to the United States that year to take part in a seminar at the Woodrow Wilson Center for Scholars, along with the two future presidents of Uruguay, Jorge Batlle and Luis Alberto Lacalle. The three of us spoke of returning democracy to the so-called southern cone region of South America. During that trip, I held a long meeting with Elliot Abrams, then the assistant secretary of state for inter-American affairs. He struck me as a committed right-winger, but he listened carefully to our case and was candid in his reply. He supported democracy, but he was concerned about the Communist Party and where they would come down on the matter. I knew exactly how to reply: When Allende was elected, the communists were about 10 or 15 percent of the votes; now they were a mere five, I told him. Engaging them would be the key because to abandon or separate them out would provoke them toward violence, a position toward which they were already inclined.

By the time I left, having also spoken to two key senators, Richard Lugar and Christopher Dodd, I felt as if I understood the U.S. position. Chile should transition to democracy—but not too fast, for any rapid change could jeopardize stability. By Washington's standards, these were torrential winds of change, and to be sure, they were felt by Pinochet's representatives and diplomats as well.

Perhaps the clearest sign of all this was the ambassador that Secretary of State George Shultz named to Chile in 1985. Harry G. Barnes, Jr. was a career diplomat who had just left an assignment in India, where he had won praise for his ability to engage all sides of an equally tense political debate. Shultz judged him a perfect candidate for Chile. Just weeks after Barnes had received his credentials and was settled in Santiago, he approached us for a meeting with the AD—something his cautious predecessor had never done. Thus began a series of regular meetings, rotating among our various offices in the city center. Over time, I came to see him as a decisive man and an ally of the opposition. The government, meanwhile, considered declaring him persona non grata on more than one occasion.

Then Pinochet made a mistake—a huge mistake—that turned the tides of U.S. relations permanently against his regime. On July 2, 1986, almost a year after Barnes arrived in Chile, a young 19-year-old student named Rodrigo Rojas de Negri was snatched from the street for photographing a protest. Pinochet's goons soaked him and his companion, 22-year-old Carmen Quintana, with gas, lit them on fire, wrapped them in a blanket, and threw them in the back of a military truck. The pair were discovered, alive but barely, near Quilicura, an area in the outskirts of Santiago. Rojas lived for just three days after that, and Quintana survived only after three operations.

The military had done equally awful things countless times before. But Rojas, the son of a former Communist Party activist, was a U.S. resident and had returned to Santiago just weeks before. The military denied everything—denied that the act was committed by soldiers—but the CIA identified the vehicle as belonging to a military man, and the agency's local office wrote to Washington.

As a gesture of protest, Ambassador Barnes and his wife went to Rojas's funeral with the boy's mother, Verónica de Negri, who had arrived from the United States just five days earlier. A thousand people attended the funeral, which ended in tear gas being unleashed on the crowds, the U.S. ambassador included.

It was another huge mistake by the regime. Secretary Abrams appeared on ABC News that night to say how concerned the Reagan administration was. "I used my appearance yesterday on ABC's Nightline to stress our commitment to eventual free elections in Chile . . . sooner rather than later," he wrote in a memo to Shultz. "But more than verbal volleys will be required to get Pinochet to agree to leave, or to persuade the Army to persuade him."

And so came 1986, which I'll always see as the decisive year. It was apparent by then that our protests and political organizing alone were not going to force Pinochet's resignation, so we would have to move forward another way. But there was still one final debate to be had among ourselves: whether to use that narrow window in the constitution—the 1988 plebiscite—or turn to violent resistance. While the AD clearly preferred the former, a strong constituency had emerged for the latter. The Communist Party and the radical Socialist Party faction led by Clodomiro Almeyda had united to create the Popular Democratic Movement (MDP) with the goal of fighting back.

We began to meet with the MDP, just as we had always done with the communists before. I held several such conversations, always secretly and never with the organization's top leadership. The night before our meeting, or sometimes the day of, I would receive word about a clandestine location. I would arrive, wait for my secret negotiating partner, and then begin—all without names or specifics.

It was important to remain in contact with the MDP. We had always hoped that we could talk them back from the edge. But they never understood that fighting against the dictatorship would be a disaster—suicide. Not only would we fail, but violence would give Pinochet exactly what he wanted: another pretext to double down on repression.

On August 11, 1986, we saw where the MDP stood when a massive stockpile of arms was discovered 400 miles north of Santiago. The cache, hidden in an abandoned mining site near a beach, held some 50 tons of weapons—everything from M16s rifles to Soviet RPG–7 rockets to hand grenades. Under the cover of a mining firm, the armed wing of the Communist Party had brought the weapons to Chile by sea on Cuban boats, knowing that the land route through Bolivia and Peru would be too perilous.

Chileans were taken aback. Imagining all those arms being unleashed on the country was too much—especially for a population already scarred from years under Pinochet's military state. People wanted a way out, to be sure, but not *that* way. Anything but that way. Almost overnight, the "violent option" ceased to exist in the eyes of the Chilean public. But it didn't yet cease to exist for many who had supported it. In fact, it merely accelerated other plans for resistance.

Just a month later, on Sunday, September 7, the would-be assassins struck. Pinochet often spent weekends at his second home in El Melocotón, about 50 miles from Santiago near the Andes Mountains. And on this particular Sunday afternoon, the assassins were waiting along the road nearby when his convoy passed. There were three identical Mercedes in the motorcade, and the militants had managed to find out which one held Pinochet. When their rocket struck, it went up through the roof, damaging the convoy but leaving the dictator untouched. Five guards died in the ensuing firefight, but Pinochet's armored car managed to escape while his assailants fled.

The assassination attempt shocked and enraged Pinochet, and the consequences of that rage were tragic. That same night, orders were given to detain all known leftists who opposed Pinochet. And on that list was my name.

FOUR

PRISONER OF
THE STATE

"Lagos, they've come for you." The words pierced the crisp September night air, jolting me awake. My son Alejandro's voice drew closer, calling me as he and his brothers always did: just Lagos, not Father or Papa. I rolled over in bed to face the door, turning on the bedside lamp. As my eyes adjusted to the light, there was no mistaking the images hovering over the bed. They were policemen. Their tall figures lurched over me and Luisa, automatic rifles pointing in all directions.

"What are you doing here?" I demanded, my blood rising. My eyes were now fixed on the one who seemed to be their leader. I asked them to show me a warrant.

"We are from the Policía de Investigaciones, and we have come for you," he replied stiffly. "Get up and follow us."

It was surreal enough to be the stuff of dreams. But by now I was fully awake. So we had reached this point? Someone had tried to assassinate the dictator, and he had in turn viewed it as an excuse to do anything—to round up anyone he disliked?

"I'm going to call my lawyer," I said, and rose resolutely, moving from my bed on the side closest to the door to the opposite corner, where the phone sat on a small table.

"Call whomever you want—but you'll still have to follow us," the officer replied impassively. "Don't worry, Mr. Lagos, we are professionals."

Great. So I was being arrested by "professionals."

"Well then identify yourselves," I demanded.

"Sir, follow us."

I was determined to make that call first. With Luisa looking on from the opposite corner of the room, now standing also, I dialed a lawyer friend and told him what was happening. "They *say* they are from the Policía de Investigaciones," I told him, pointing out that they had refused to show me any identification. The lawyer couldn't do much. He promised to make some calls, and just like that, there was nothing more to say. We hung up.

I got dressed and looked around the room again at the half-dozen men, as ready to go as one could be. "Bring warm clothes. It's very cold in the prison at the Policía," one officer said. It was September, and although the Southern Hemisphere spring was beginning, on cool, dry nights like these—it was by now 2:30 in the morning—temperatures could drop to near freezing. I reached for my leather jacket and we were off.

The commotion had awoken the rest of my sons by now, and the entire family was looking on, peering out of their doorways with eyes on the hallway that I would have to pass through to leave. The only one who had managed to remain asleep was Panchita, by then just 10 years old. I sighed with a bit of relief that she would not see her father disappear into the night with the band of "professionals." I asked the rest of my family to remain calm. There was little anyone could do aside from follow orders. And for the moment, my order was to walk from my bedroom and down the short hallway that led straight to the door. My family stayed inside, helplessly, as we passed into the night, me and the professionals.

The next part was more difficult. Our small house in La Reina was at the end of a vine-covered path tracing the way past a dozen or so similar homes. From there, the sidewalk led out onto a long, narrow parking lot and driveway that extended from our row of houses down 200 yards to the gate of the complex. The police cars were parked at the far end. The walk from the safety of my door to the uncertainty of their vehicles lasted for what seemed like hours, my feet crunching in the gravel over and over again as if in slow motion. I had time—too much time—to think about exactly what was happening to me. They must have been sweeping up everyone in the aftermath of the assassination. But how could they justify my detention? Surely they knew that I had nothing to do with the attack. My position within the Socialist Party had, if anything, been the opposite: I had worked tirelessly to dissuade those who would prefer a "violent option." Then again, I knew Pinochet didn't need reasons. These were the games he played.

When we finally arrived at the cars, the officer turned to me as if to reassure me. "You see? We are from Investigaciones. See our vehicles?" The logos looked the part. But I remained unconvinced. "You know better than anyone that these days, it would be very easy to disguise your vehicles to look like someone else's. How can I be sure that you are from Investigaciones if you refuse to show me your credentials?"

My skepticism didn't matter. What was happening now was a procedure: I was ordered to be arrested, they were going to arrest me, and nothing could or would change that. We got in the car, where I was squeezed into a cramped middle seat, one "professional" on each side of me. Perhaps it wouldn't have been so crowded if not for the weapons they all wielded, half pointed inside at me and the other half extended from the window, as if to give off as foreboding an air as they could. A second police car followed ours.

The drive to Investigaciones, about three miles away, went fast on the curfew-emptied streets. We drove furiously, whipping around the abandoned avenues. The car soon pulled into the back entrance of the police station, where I was taken inside the building. At least by now it was clear that the professionals hadn't been lying about at least one thing: They really did seem to be from Investigaciones.

The professionals didn't waste time. Within a few minutes of my arrival, they were interrogating me. I was plopped down in a room with just two chairs, one for me and one for a man behind a typewriter, who began asking me questions.

"Señor Lagos, can you explain to me how you spent this Sunday?" Indeed I could.

The streets of Los Dominicos were bustling when we arrived late in the morning on Sunday. The houses, painted in their unconventional shades of yellow, blue, and red, reflected the spring sun. Window shutters flapped in the wind, their colors contrasting with even brighter tones. We had gotten up early that Sunday to visit the neighborhood, Santiago's closest approximation to Paris's famous 14th Arrondissement. Our task was to buy a set of bedside tables from the artisans who worked there. We encountered no acquaintants, except briefly the wife of the Spanish ambassador, Alicia de Solano, whose husband was traveling. We exchanged a few words and were on our way.

When we arrived home from Los Dominicos around 2 P.M., we were met by the terrible news that our dog Teodoro had been hit by a car, and he was in poor shape. We got straight back into the car and drove him to the veterinarian at a nearby pet hospital. They could fix up his broken leg, the vet said, but Teodoro needed to stay for observation.

After a few more errands, we returned home to have tea at around 5:30 P.M. And it was there, with my mother, that we learned of the assassination attempt. The television was broadcasting the breaking news, and we all sat down to watch, slightly dumbfounded. I had a lump in my stomach thinking about who might have taken this violent route.

At around 8:30 P.M., my son Hernán, who had gone to play rugby, returned home complaining of an injury. He suspected a sprain and wanted to go to the Clínica Alemana, where we ended up staying until 11 P.M.

By the time we got home, what a day it had been. My brother-in-law, Pedro, came by to join us, and together we sat, eyes fixed on the television. The next day, I was supposed to travel to Uruguay to advise the country's minister of labor, but I wasn't thinking about my early flight and we stayed up late, watching the news. Anyway, my bag was packed and I was set to rise early. I finally lay down to sleep, thoughts about the assassination still playing out in my head.

None of this made for a very helpful alibi. Had anyone else seen me in Los Dominicos? Well, only the Spanish ambassador's wife. The police officer explained, a bit exasperated, that he could hardly summon a diplomat as a witness. What about in the afternoon? The officer stopped typing, again looking at me directly in hopes of a more promising reply. But I had only seen my mother, I told him, and of course such a close relative could not prove my innocence. (Even the story of Teodoro was being inscribed into the history of Pinochet's near-death experience, as the officer demanded the name and location of the clinic. And sure enough, the next day, the police showed up at the clinic demanding confirmation: "Where is the dog Teodoro?") My saving grace was Hernán's trip to the doctor's office, which not only provided a witness but also proved that I couldn't have been at the scene in El Melocotón, as I wouldn't have been able to make it back to Santiago in time to reach the clinic.

It was 3:30 or 4:00 A.M. by the time the officer finished recording my statement. He pulled the paper from the typewriter and handed it to me to sign. I asked permission to call Luisa, and he took me to a phone.

Luisa answered my call on the first ring, so I knew she was still awake. Telling your wife to go to sleep after you've been arrested is a bit unhelpful, of course, but I told her exactly that. The next day, she would have to start working to alert everyone we knew about my detention, particularly our international friends.

And so I made the final stage of my journey to my new home, a prison block around the side of the building. The small holding area was secured by a floor-to-ceiling set of steel bars, set off from the hallway by several stairs. Once inside the first gate, I could see rows of individual cells, perhaps 25 on that level and another 25 immediately above, all overlooking a central area no bigger than an average dining room. They put me into a cell on the left, four or five in from the entrance.

It was dark inside that small cell of less than 100 square feet, and it was soon filled with nearly a dozen people who kept arriving that night. A small hole was carved into the ground with an angled concrete rim around it. This was our not-so-private latrine—one of the many means by which, I quickly learned, one's human dignity was slowly taken away in detention.

I was among the first to occupy the cell that night. They must have swept me up from my home first, so I claimed the most luxurious corner of that barren cell—a concrete slab extending a few feet out and up from the wall. I could sleep on my side there if I faced a certain direction. But as soon as I was settled, trying to find some measure of rest, the door would open and close with a rusty creak to let more fellow prisoners arrive. First came Germán Correa, an official in Almeyda's wing of the Socialist Party. Guillermo Sherping, a leader of communist professors, followed. Another from the left, Father Rafael

Marotto, and several others were brought inside. And one arrived who was announced only as Señor Araneda.

"Who are you?" I asked him, trying to determine what might have landed him there.

"Anytime something happens, or there is a protest, they come and arrest me. I have not done anything—but there is another man with the same name. It always takes them a few days to figure out that I am not who they think I am," he shrugged. "My being here again this time is no surprise."

We slumped into our corners and tried to sleep, I in my one-side-possible position and Señor Araneda crouched in a sitting squat. For weeks after I finally left prison, that left hip where I had lain on the concrete was terribly sore.

Pinochet was furious, and the rage was contagious, infecting his secret police, the CNI. They ripped through the city, picking up everyone, trying to pin blame on anyone, eager to exact pain upon all corners of the opposition. It wouldn't be for days that the extent of the purge really began to emerge, when *La Nación* newspaper published a list of those who had been arrested.

But they had made a mistake with my detention. I was supposed to have been picked up—not by the "professionals," but by Pinochet's CNI henchmen. In fact, I was supposed to have died that night. My obituary should have read like that of the journalist José Carrasco, who had once been the international editor of the opposition publication *Análisis*. I noticed right away that he hadn't been swept up by Investigaciones; he wasn't there in the prison with us. Instead, Pinochet's men had taken him, and they killed him not long thereafter with 13 shots to his head.

In my case, something incredible happened instead. Right after the assassination, one of those who saw the hit list at the Policía de Investigaciones knew me—a former student by the name of Henríquez who had taken a class from me on the economic history of Chile.

Henríquez knew that there was really just one thing he could do to prevent the worst: get to me first, before the secret police could. So I was the first to be picked up—and not a moment too soon. On the way to the prison, we had been stopped briefly, and I'd never known what had happened. It had been the CNI, demanding that I be handed over. By some twist of fate, I was not.

Carrasco was not so lucky. After taking me to Investigaciones, the same police officers had gone to look for him. But when they arrived at his home, he was already gone. Carrasco would have lived if he had been taken by Investigaciones, as I had been.

It was only two decades later that I learned all this, during an investigation into what happened that night. It was a terrible feeling to know that my name had been on the list, just like Carrasco, just like so many others. The night he was taken, Carrasco had just returned from Buenos Aires. What if he had simply stayed just one more day? Would he still be living? Fate never seems as random and unjust as in the hands of a dictator. I suddenly understood what the agents from the Policía de Investigaciones had said to me: They *were* professionals. I was going to live.

M y first night of sleep in prison lasted less than an hour. By 6:30 A.M., we were awake, called to line up for attendance. It would become a daily ritual through which the guards were able to verify that no one had escaped. After all our names were read out, the guards passed out meager pieces of bread and cups of tea for breakfast. We were stuffed back into our crowded cells.

My first look around in the daylight revealed that the prison was filling up fast, stocked not only with political prisoners like myself, but also petty criminals. In my cell, we were still practically introducing ourselves when, around 9 A.M., a guard came looking for me. "Lagos, come with me."

Finally! I thought to myself. They must have resolved everything. From my statement, it was obvious that I had nothing to do with the assassination attempt. I left the cell hoping that it would be for good.

It is amazing how foolishly optimistic the human spirit can be. I was not about to be dismissed; far from it. Instead, the guard led me down the flight of concrete stairs and around the corner, into a small office with a window looking out onto the street. It was a well-decorated room, for a police station, with a cabinet on one wall, a long meeting table in another nook, and a handsome, large desk facing the door. The guard introduced me to a man who said he was the officer responsible for public relations.

I wasn't there to see the media man; they had brought me here because there was an official from the U.S. Embassy who was asking to see me, a man named Douglas Tomkins. Clearly these quarters would be a far less embarrassing meeting spot than my cell. "Wait here," they told me, and left the room. I could hear noises from the street in the silence they left behind.

Tomkins entered and sat down with me, a concerned but ever-diplomatic look on his face. He had come at his ambassador's instruction, he explained, and wanted to verify that I was in good health. Washington was very concerned about my predicament, he assured me. I told him all that had happened, how I had been detained, and reiterated that I had nothing to do with the assassination attempt. He listened attentively and then left.

No sooner had I been returned to my cell then I was pulled out again and taken back to the same office, where another visitor was apparently awaiting. It was Patricio Aylwin, then the vice president of the Chilean Bar Association, and Alejandro Hales, a former minister of President Frei Montalva. We exchanged greetings, and the conversation quickly drifted toward politics. What effect would all this have on those who had preferred a violent solution to the end of dictatorship? Hopefully they would finally give up; it was we, in prison, who were paying the price.

These visits were the first signs of the work that Luisa was doing tirelessly behind the scenes. She had called every friend we knew. She phoned human rights organizations. She visited international ambassadors personally, and she called our friends back in the United States. Word spread fast in a world that was by now well accustomed to hearing of Pinochet's abuses. Sometime after my release, we even received a photograph of a young university student, a girl, clutching a sign that demanded my release.

I received a third visit just hours later, this one outside. Around midday, the guards came to my cell yet again, opening the rusty door with a creak, and asking that I follow them down the stairs and out the back door of the prison, into the modest back gate and parking lot where police cars usually entered. From the outside, I remember thinking that this building looked exactly as I would have imagined a prison should—the tall, gated entrance enclosing us entirely within the compound, even as officers came and went.

When we got outside, the iron gate to the compound lifted. And there, on the other side, was my mother, seated on a bench.

She stood immediately and rushed to embrace me. Her leather jacket was wrapped tightly around her to keep her warm in the cool air. She had just turned 90 that year, but the way she leapt up from her seat, you would have thought her far younger.

"Resist," was the first word she said into my ear as we were embracing. "Don't become weak. Everyone is concerned about you." Then she continued, "This will be long and difficult; you must also be ready for that."

As my mother offered me such courageous words, however, all I could think about was how dangerous it certainly was for her to be there with me. "How did you get here?" I asked.

"Ah! Well," she smiled slightly, "since they did not let me come in the front door, I came here. I walked in, and they told me that I had to go. But I looked back at the man. 'I am going to sit on this bench until I see my son,' I told him. 'If you want, you can drag me out. But it will take all your force. I am going to defend myself. Until the moment I see my son, I'm not budging.'"

Perhaps taken aback, the officer had finally told her to wait outside on that bench. And an hour and a half later, I appeared. "Now that I've seen you, I can go," she said. "I'm glad that you are all right."

Even more visitors came that afternoon, and I met them all in the office of public relations. In fact, so often did I meet visitors there that by the time I left prison, I felt as if the office was practically mine.

On the third or fourth day in that room, after one of my visitors had just gone, the office door opened and several people walked in with pro-Pinochet placards. There had been an organized rally that day in support of the dictator, who was trying to drum up support in increasingly hard times. The moment the men walked in, they threw the placards in the trash. "This is where these signs belong," one of them scoffed with a half-laugh.

I watched dumbfounded, knowing that they hadn't yet seen me. It was one of those moments when you wish you could disappear into the background. It wasn't long, however, before the officers turned my way. Clearly embarrassed, they fumbled to explain. "It's just that we are obligated to go to these sorts of things," one of them muttered sheepishly.

Aside from the relative luxury of having visitors, my life over the coming days became increasingly hard. I spent much of my time pacing in the cell, moving back and forth as much as the small space allowed. I stayed sane by the simple coincidence that the cell allowed for five steps across the longest possible diagonal. As a child studying in my mother's home, I had realized that an odd number of steps meant that I could alternate which direction I pivoted to turn around—a trick that prevented me from getting motion sickness. Had the cell been just four or six steps long, the back and forth would have been nauseating. My cellmates laughed. "Trying to stretch your legs?" They gave me a gentle ribbing, but of course they understood as well: You cling to any routine you can when everything else has been taken.

They fed us terribly and I was hungry much of the time. In the morning, it was a meager meal of tea and bread. Then came the *porotos*—the bean dish that is traditionally served at the end of any working Chilean's meal to top off whatever hunger might still linger. For us, however, those boiled beans were our entire meal, more like a ration, really. The *porotos* were lunch and sometimes dinner as well. Soups were a treat. But everything we ate was some shade of brown.

I was also interrogated several more times by the Policía de Investigaciones in the coming days, adding yet another ritual to the monotonous jail life. Each time, they asked me what I had been doing that day—that famous Sunday when Pinochet was almost killed. And each time, I told them the same story.

One day, however, the usual dance changed. The guards led me to a new room for the interrogation, this one with no windows and just one table with two chairs. Two men entered, neither of whom I had seen before. One sat across from me, and the other stood behind his colleague, pacing.

The sitting officer commenced, but with each question, the standing man grew more and more visibly tense. "I've had enough of this, leave this to me," he told his colleague at one point. He turned to me: "Now, you are going to respond to me directly because we are going to ask our questions *differently*," he said, using *tu*, the familiar form of "you" in Spanish.

"I know how you extract information," I replied.

And so it began. His questions seemed less important than the threatening gestures his arms made, as if he were about to reach across the table and hit me. Unless, of course, I answered, and then the first investigator— the calm, courteous one—would continue from there. I had no doubt they were from the CNI, Pinochet's secret police, and they were playing good cop, bad cop.

You might say the difference between bravery and stupidity is the outcome, and what I did next was one or the other. "Sir!" I said sharply, offended by the bad cop's presumption of informality. "Who authorized you to address yourself to me like this, using the 'tu'?"

Silence. I waited for something, a punch, anything. "I told you that this one is a *caballero*," the good cop said of me. A gentleman. "Imagine him treating us like this."

It's hard to believe this was enough to end their routine, but so taken aback by my reply were the two men that they returned to their "traditional" methods of grilling me on the ins and outs of my story. It was the closest I ever came to experiencing Pinochet's secret police. And after we finished, I finally had mug shots taken. I still have them.

One afternoon while I was pacing, a man came by the cell and caught my eye as I was walking toward the door. It was General Ernesto Baeza, the head of the Policía de Investigaciones at the time, a thin, angular man clothed in civilian garb. The general recognized me, as we had seen one another before at various embassy functions across town, and quickly approached my cell and extended his hand through the bars. "Mr. Lagos, I hope you will remember me."

Still shaking my hand, Baeza peered by me and into the cell, by now crowded with men. "It's not right for you to be held like this," he said, turning his welcoming smile into an eyebrows-lowered frown. He promised to see if there was anything that he could do.

Something I was always keen to avoid, however, was separating myself in any way from my fellow prisoners. Nothing levels the playing field like prison, and I wanted to keep it that way. If I had visitors, others should have that right as well. If Baeza was able to move me, I told him, he would have to move all of my cellmates as well.

Baeza returned a bit later and called me aside, taking me out of the cell with the guards' help. There were two rooms nearby, he told me, each designed to hold just two detainees. I began to protest. "If I am moved, it must be everyone," I told him. "Everyone needs better conditions." But Baeza insisted. "Mr. Lagos, they simply won't hold everyone," he replied.

He was right; the cells were tiny. Still, they were an enormous upgrade, and all of us moved out of our cell and into new quarters. One of the rooms had a real bathroom, something I've never been so happy to see. With that small shred of privacy, we regained a bit of our dignity. It felt like a five-star hotel in comparison, even though we still had to take turns sleeping in the four beds that we now shared among ten people.

That move was only the first relocation, and the next came on Friday. An Italian delegation came to see me that day, after having spoken with Baeza, and they informed me that they had pressed for my relocation to an even better place. Where, they weren't sure. I and 16 other prisoners would be moved right away.

The next day, Saturday, we had the first look at our new quarters, which I later learned were those used by the Carabineros, one of Chile's several police forces, when they were working on special shifts in Santiago and needed to rest for the night. To us, they were spectacular. The place was exceptionally nice, given that we were prisoners of the state. There was a gym, a basketball court, and space enough for easily 100 or 150. There were bathrooms—regular bathrooms!—that seemed extraordinary, even though they lacked hot water. We were elated, realizing that we had not forgotten what it meant to be human.

We were even more surprised when the captain of that commissariat, Lionel Acuña, came to greet us the next morning, a sort of diplomatic honor that we would never have expected. Calling us all out to listen, he addressed us without emotion. "I understand the circumstances in which you have all come here. It is a decision of the government that I do not discuss or question; I respect it. My obligation is to take care of you," he said—the words of an obedient officer.

There was a notable improvement in the quality of our lives. We were allowed to read books and magazines and write to our families. Soon, visiting hours were established and life in the commissariat acquired a routine. Early in the morning, we rose to breakfast, followed by walks or jogs, since the quarters had a gym. We then retired to do what we pleased, be it reading or conversation. The books we read had to be approved by the captain, but there was never a problem. I read *Marco Polo* and a memoir by Enrique Bernstein, an influential official at the Ministry of Foreign Affairs. Captain Acuña saw me reading the latter book and asked me to lend him the copy when I had finished.

We had lunch and dinner, and since we were allowed visitors, they often brought us pastries or other small treats. Even visiting hours were a bit flexible, both in time of day and in the company that we were allowed to keep.

I remember once receiving a correspondent from the Barcelona newspaper *Vanguardia,* who had asked for an interview. I imagine that no one in Chile saw the article, because if they had, it could surely have caused problems for me to be speaking with a foreign paper. Giving interviews to local journalists would have been similarly forbidden.

We got to know one another intimately; there was little else we could do. We joked, laughed, and established a sort of understanding that only close, prolonged proximity can produce. I never saw some of them again, but at the time, we were best friends.

One detainee I became particularly close with was Guillermo Sherping, a communist who was on the board of the teachers' union. A physical education teacher, Sherping happened to be an instructor in *la cueca,* the national dance. And so to prepare ourselves for September 18, Chile's national day, we requested a few cassettes and availed ourselves of Guillermo's expertise.

La cueca is not easy to learn. I had never in my life had the urge to do so, but I figured I would never again have such a good opportunity. Despite my initial optimism, however, I soon watched shamefully as each of my cellmates improved, becoming noticeably better each day. I, meanwhile, was a dancing disaster. My feet didn't move in time; my body didn't spin with grace. And my frustration made matters even worse. There is nothing less graceful than an irritated artist.

To this day, I am rather inept at dancing—a shortcoming I unfortunately passed on to my son Ricardo. Years later, at an independence-day celebration organized by then President Michelle Bachelet, Ricardo tried to show off his *cueca* skills, and soon thereafter, the country erupted into a debate about what kind of dance, exactly, Ricardo had been trying to do. Well, he had tried to dance just about everything—except *la cueca.* (He has since progressed quite a bit, he says. But that will be a question for history to answer.)

Between these few distractions, however, was the serious business of being in prison and all that it entailed. The day after the national holiday, I was informed that I would be taken to a military prosecutor who was investigating the botched assassination attempt. I rose early and was led to a vehicle meant specifically for carrying criminals in custody. Our car was joined by a larger convoy for the quick journey across town to 120 Galvez Street, where the prosecutor's office had been set up.

A military prosecutor named Joaquín Earlbaum was waiting to receive me. About 40 years old, the lawyer spoke calmly, but his questions were pointed and direct—not a breath wasted on an inefficient word. Our conversation, however, was far from tranquil, not least because his phone rang every few moments, and each time he would rise to take the call in a nearby enclosure. I couldn't help but wonder if there was something afoot.

When he finally came back and sat down with me, I began my well-rehearsed explanation of the assassination Sunday and of my life—the political positions I had held—explaining that to associate me with the violent campaign would be a profound error; I had devoted my time and energy to arguing against it.

He didn't let me finish, his face unconvinced. What about the interview I had given to *Newsweek* on August 18, 1986? What did I mean when I predicted, "The violence is going to get worse. Pinochet has declared war"? I had been referring to what the dictator had himself said, I explained. Pinochet vowed to stay in office after 1989, and he had no plans to renounce his power. What about the arms that were found in Carrizal? The prosecutor continued, hitting all the pressure points that could conceivably have linked me to the violent campaign. What about the assassination attempt?

It was immediately clear that the prosecutor was trying to create a narrative in which I was the intellectual author of the crimes of the left. To me, there was no greater insult, and I soon grew indignant as he pushed on. The pitch of our voices rose quickly, first one then the other, up a level, then another, and another. I wasn't about to back down. Since December 1983, when I left my U.N. job, I had adamantly opposed not only Pinochet, but all those who sought a violent path to unseat him.

The tension was broken with a sudden ring of the prosecutor's phone—yet again. He rose without a word and walked back to his private alcove. I sat back in my chair after he left, only then noticing that I had been inching forward and forward, leaning into the conversation.

Just as my back hit the chair, my glance fell and I noticed that there, sitting open in front of me, was my case file. I peered over the table and began to read it—looking at the letters upside down in hopes that the prosecutor wouldn't return and see me doing so.

The page that was open was my profile, a basic set of typewriter-written particulars along with my picture. But I noticed that my address was listed as 630 Oxford Street, a house that I had briefly rented long ago—back in 1968, when I was in the process of divorcing Carmen. Then, I remembered that a former law school professor of my son, Ricardo, had been living there. And so something began to make sense: Beginning in 1984, that professor began to receive notes—death threats addressed to one Ricardo Lagos. Knowing that I had once lived in the house, he would give the letters to my son, who would in turn pass them along to me. But I had never thought much of them, perhaps because their mimeographed letters, unprofessional appearance, and crude writing didn't seem too serious a threat. I had, however, always wondered why they were sent to that address on Oxford Street.

Some might have found this all rather eerie, but to me it seemed almost a comfort. Here was a dossier that proclaimed to be a secret file of intelligence on my activities, and it listed an address—perhaps the simplest detail of my life to investigate—where I had not lived for the last eight years.

Not only that, but I realized many years later that, if the prosecutors had asked me somewhat different questions, there might indeed have been a case for my detention, however unjust. During all this time, I had been holding clandestine meetings with the far left, hoping to integrate them into our non-violent campaign. By association alone, I had known the communists, who were banned under Pinochet's constitution. And even if I had disagreed with them, this association alone may have constituted a "crime."

But Pinochet's police never asked those questions; they were too fixated on linking me to the attempted assassination. They had decided upon a narrative before I was ever brought for questioning and were determined not to change it, however poor the fit. There are bureaucracies even in intelligence, I thought to myself. And Pinochet's police work on me hadn't been the system's finest moment.

I forced myself to stop peering into the upside-down file as I saw the prosecutor return, and I prepared myself for another round of our grueling dialogue.

At the end of it all, the prosecutor seemed to have melted ever so slightly, showing a bit of empathy even as his face remained cool. "I am going to declare you *arraigo*," he told me, a designation used by judges to prevent those who had committed crimes from leaving the country.

"Sir, you know that nothing that I have done warrants this," I protested.

The prosecutor didn't look me in the eye, but simply pulled a pen from his shirt pocket and began saying. "Sir, this is the only option I have. On the phone just now, I have received countless calls instructing me to keep you in prison, detained as the intellectual author of all that has happened. I have refused to do so, but the *arraigo* is the least that I can do without having problems of my own."

Then, he added, "I only have this," showing me his pen. "They have guns. That is the reason I have to order you to stay in the country. I am alone."

I couldn't say much to that, and I left his office feeling sad about what he had said, not just because things looked rather hopeless for me, but because I was thinking about all the institutions of Chile that had been corrupted, that were ghosts of their former selves. Pinochet would go to any lengths, and use any means, to maintain his power—no matter the price.

"Mr. Lagos, Mr. Lagos. Are you awake?" One of my fellow prisoners tapped my side to grab my attention. It was 3 A.M., but he couldn't wait. "Mr. Lagos, I have a radio with batteries—we can hear the news."

I rolled toward my companion and we leaned into the small radio, desperate to hear the news—any news. And what we heard was well worth the lost sleep: Argentinean President Raúl Alfonsín was speaking out against my detention, together with Jimmy Carter and the European Union.

It was becoming clear, even from the isolation of those quarters, that the chorus calling for my release was growing louder and louder. Of those toiling behind the scenes to make it happen, perhaps none worked harder than the Spanish ambassador, Miguel Solano, who had been on vacation when I had been taken into custody. I had seen his wife Alicia in Los Dominicos on that famous Sunday, and the moment that he learned of my arrest, Spanish President Felipe González had ordered him back to Chile to work for my freedom.

Solano recounted all this to Luisa as soon as he was back in Chile, and he promised to do all he could to help. But the one thing he could not do, he told Luisa, was to visit me. "Explain to Lagos that if I come to visit him, it will mean that I have failed. Because it will mean there is nothing more I can do."

The ambassador worked tirelessly and met with Luisa almost daily, updating her on his inching progress. One Saturday, he learned that the undersecretary of the interior, Alberto Cardemil, would be attending a rodeo more than 100 miles south of Santiago in the city of Curicó. So Solano went. He tracked down the official, trying to catch him at a moment of leisure—and also make it known how far he had come (and would go) to get me out. But the ambassador hit a wall at every turn, and he was coming to believe that it would be impossible to secure my release.

Then one afternoon, the ambassador came to visit me—a signal that he knew he could not succeed. Embarrassed and overwhelmed with defeat, Solano came that day with a huge cake—big enough for all my fellow inmates to share—as some consolation for the freedom that I wouldn't yet taste.

Things got worse before they got better. Just days after the Spanish ambassador visited with his bad news, the guards came across some scribbling on the bathroom wall, derogatory phrases condemning Pinochet. It was a grave offense for political prisoners, and the punishment was the suspension of our visiting hours. When my wife came to visit that week, she was turned away.

Luisa immediately found a pay phone and called Radio Cooperativa to inform them that they had suspended my visitation rights. Within minutes, the news had spread throughout the entire country; Radio Cooperativa was the single best way that the opposition had to communicate. And since it was a channel controlled by the Christian Democrats (rather than, say, the socialists), shutting it down permanently would have been tricky even for Pinochet.

Luisa is a clever and brave woman, and she soon returned to the commissariat to try and speak with the captain. This time, she was of course allowed. Luisa had made life very difficult for the police, the captain explained to her, a complaint for which she had not an ounce of sympathy. "I'm sorry," Luisa told him, "but every time that our freedoms and our rights are impeded upon, I will denounce it. And that's just what I have done this time."

A world away from where I was being held, Pinochet's regime was under heavy pressure at the U.N. General Assembly in New York. As tales of human rights abuses mounted in the international media, and our movement gained momentum domestically, Chile had become increasingly isolated. Of course, Pinochet didn't portray it that way. Chile's diplomatic relations were excellent, or so he told the country. One of the best examples of his spin machine in action came during that year's U.N. session, when, for the first time, Chile's foreign minister was scheduled to sit down with his European counterparts en masse. To the Europeans, it was a moment to engage—to get more concessions from a dictator than isolation could provide. But to Pinochet, it was a sign that the ice was melting.

How wrong he was. In the days before that meeting with the Europeans— the one Pinochet's PR machine desperately needed—the Spanish delegation, led by Francisco Fernández Ordóñez, refused to take part until I was freed. His European colleagues quickly signed on to the boycott.

Pinochet couldn't afford to let that meeting go, so he had to release me— and immediately so that his foreign minister could still meet with the European delegation before the General Assembly session ended. On Friday, September 26 at 7 P.M., Captain Acuña came to inform me of the news: I was going home.

The door to my quarters flew open, and the captain walked hurriedly in. "Quickly take your things and let's go," he told me, an instruction I met with a rather dumbfounded stare. We all just sat there for a moment. I remember looking at my cellmates, frustrated that I could do nothing to secure their own releases. I understood that I must be getting out due to diplomatic pressure, and that many would not be so lucky. Now I had to bid my fellow prisoners goodbye in a huge rush, ill befitting the time we had spent together. Within seconds I was gone.

"I have instructions from the director general of the Carabineros to take you home and ensure that you don't run into any trouble," the captain told me as we were walking away from my cell. He ordered a car to take me back home. "And if it's all right, I would like to accompany you to your house." How odd it all was: After weeks of being his prisoner, now I was suddenly almost a dignitary, requiring his protection.

We took the police vehicle and drove to my house. There were no officers packing me into my seat this time; no guns pointing out the windows or toward me. There were no sirens; we stopped at all the traffic lights. As we pulled up toward my condo, I saw all of our neighbors, who had heard of my imminent release on the radio, waiting outside. The crowd was huge. My mother had come from her house to wait.

"I wanted to be the one to free Mr. Lagos," Acuña said, looking forward in the car, perhaps so his eyes would not betray his otherwise professional air. "I was fulfilling my duty when we took you into custody, but I also wanted to be sure that you arrived safe and sound at your house. I leave you now in peace."

I was free. And there was only one logical way to spend the next day: We decided to take those famous bedside tables to my in-laws' beach house in El Quisco and pick up our dog, Teodoro, from the vet. And before doing both those things, we went to visit those who were still in prison.

In the brief time I was detained, the world had changed. Our long hours of negotiation and debate could never have produced so clear a political outcome as the failed assassination attempt on Pinochet: Now, violence was completely discredited as a tactic. Every political sector, from the Christian Democrats to the further-left socialists, was beginning to see things our way.

I had changed as well. As those dark days in prison came to an end, I began to realize what a public figure I had become. To learn that Jimmy Carter and Argentina's Raúl Alfonsín had spoken out about my arrest—to realize that European diplomats had canceled meetings in my name—was empowering. It was also a challenge: The world was throwing its weight behind the idea that we could bring about nonviolent change. Now we had to deliver.

Our first opening came, ironically enough, from Pinochet's constitution itself. One of the institutions created in that 1980 document was a constitutional tribunal that would validate the laws passed by the national Congress and the junta government. Its first ruling in September 1985 ordered the creation of an electoral tribunal for the upcoming 1988 plebiscite. That vote couldn't take place, the tribunal said, without electoral registers. So the registers were re-opened on February 25, 1987, after having been closed and unchanged since the beginning of Pinochet's regime a decade and a half ago. Of course, the first person to register was Augusto Pinochet.

The tribunal's decision began an intense debate among the opposition about whether to register ourselves for the vote. In the end, we decided we had to do it. To succeed nonviolently, we had to take democratic openings whenever they arose. Besides, we would have to register scores of opposition supporters if we ever hoped to beat Pinochet in the plebiscite. The general by then was actually on more fragile ground than he appeared. Winning the 1988 plebiscite was the only way he could stay in power. He had never had the support of the masses, but he had their fear. Now even that was disappearing as the opposition grew.

Still, we also knew that the plebiscite was unfair and far from an ideal opening. In essence, Pinochet was running against nobody; one could only vote Yes or No to his rule, not choose between competing candidates. So before moving straight to the Yes or No vote, we decided that we must first demand truly free elections—a change in the constitution that would allow other candidates to run against Pinochet in 1988. If Pinochet wanted to be a candidate, fine. But there should also be other options on the ballot. If Chile could open its electoral registers, why couldn't we have a truly free vote?

In March 1987, we created a "Committee for Free Elections" to push forward our cause. The committee was organized under Sergio Molina, a distinguished economist who had served in the Ministry of Finance under President Eduardo Frei Montalva from 1964 to 1966. Joining him were many political figures from the middle, the left, and the far left, some famous from their political lives and some made famous by the tragedies they had suffered under the dictatorship. The Democratic Alliance joined the drive, establishing our own committee, and I suggested that the Socialist Party do the same. I became the head of this latter group, created to complement the Christian Democrats' and the Radical Party's participation under the AD umbrella.

The next people we had to bring on board were our allies abroad. The campaign against Pinochet was by then 15 years old. As thousands of exiles had left the country, they had taken with them the stories, the evidence, and the momentum necessary to stoke outrage around the world—on subway walls in Paris, telephone poles in London, and concrete partitions in Spain. The workers' union in Sweden raised collections. Labor leaders in Germany organized events. Students in the United States protested against human rights violations. Candlelight vigils were held for the disappeared. Chile was an international cause célèbre, and the more the world cried out, the more its leaders took note.

This was international solidarity, one of the most important components of our democratic defense. It began as a spontaneous outpouring of sympathy but grew more organized over time.

We tried to take advantage of the support to ratchet up the pressure on Pinochet. In October 1987, all of us who were involved in committees for free elections of various political stripes traveled to Germany, Italy, and Spain. We could tell that our cause had inspired the European public. But what we had to do was to reassure the politicians and make the case that our opposition alliance was capable of more than just fighting. If Pinochet had one thing going for him, it was the veneer of stability he provided for Chile. We had to prove that after he was gone, we too would be able to govern.

P inochet didn't agree to free elections—not that we had expected him to—so it was time for Plan B. In the months before Pinochet called the plebiscite, there were three things we would have to do: create a new party, register voters, and recruit an army of election monitors who could be in every corner of Chile where votes would be cast. There were 35,000 electoral tables in the country, so that's how many sets of eyes we needed to watch the vote—at a minimum.

The first order of business was creating a new political party, since voters would have to register under some political umbrella to get their names on the electoral register. The trouble was, under Pinochet's constitution, both the Socialist Party and the Communist Party were banned. We'd have to create a new entity that could serve as a "big tent" for the various factions on the left, what we would come to call the Party for Democracy, the PPD. Working backward from the plebiscite, which would certainly be in the second half of 1988, we figured we would need several months to train monitors and another several to register voters and make our case. So at the latest, we would have to register our party with the Electoral Service by the middle of March 1988. And to do so, we would need 35,000 signatures, distributed in 8 or 10 regions across the country. It was November 1987, and we had four months.

The first step was easy: We needed just 180 registered signatures to officially declare our intention to create the PPD. Around 6 P.M. on November 20, I left my office and invited Angélica Alzamora, my secretary, to join me in this new, democratic party. Together we descended down the building's steps, walked to the metro, and took it straight to La Moneda station, from where we walked together to the Círculo Español for the small festivities to celebrate the party's creation.

The ceremony was modest, but emotions ran high. "Today, we are here because we love Chile," I told the small crowd. "We are here because we want to see Chile return to her republican, democratic tradition. We are here to create a party that will, together with the other democratic elements in Chile, be an instrument to unseat Pinochet. We are here to say to the Chilean people that we are standing on our feet without fear but with conviction, without hate but with the force of our ideas, to fight against the dictator."

Our drive to create the PPD cemented, we took one more logistical step: On February 2, 1988, the "Concertación"—a collection of all the parties who favored a No vote on the plebiscite—was formally born. We were 17 parties with one aim: democracy.

There was one key holdout. The previous March, Clodomiro Almeyda had flown to Santiago, stepped off the plane, and returned to Chile for the first time since the coup. He didn't come back in secret; he didn't try to hide who he was when he filed in line at the immigration queue to check his identity. Instead, he went directly from that plane to the government tribunal that had declared his exile and announced that he was back. He was finished with exile. The running was over.

Almeyda came back because he felt he had to—in part as a statement of his own determination to bring Pinochet down, but also because we had reached a new moment in Chilean politics in which it was no longer possible to fight from outside the country. Politics was going to have to be done locally. We would have to roll up our sleeves and get our hands dirty, building up our parties, challenging the dictator, and rallying the hope that was suddenly becoming infectious. Almeyda was back because Chile had changed.

But Pinochet was not about to make Almeyda's return easy. The socialist leader was sent down all the way to Chile Chico, a far-flung corner of the country more than some 850 miles south of Santiago. Almeyda was in Chile, but he was going to be damn near impossible to access.

I, however, didn't have a choice. I had to bring Almeyda's militant faction over to our side. So, along with my brother-in-law, Pedro Durán, I made the arduous journey down to see him. It was my first time in Chile Chico, a city not quite four miles from the Argentine border, near the large Lake General Carrera, which sits on the Chilean side. The roads were all unpaved, but the path they cut through central Chile Chico was a beautiful one. The city was flat, almost a desert, with the soil sweeping up from the ground at each pass of the wind.

Almeyda was staying in a home kept by Arab-Chileans, so our meals were spiced with a hint of flavors—saffron and olive—that evoked the Middle East. There we were, eating grape leaves and phyllo-dough pastries at the end of the world.

For all our disagreements, Almeyda was my friend, and I was pleased to have him back in Chile. But what it meant more than anything was that the hard work was about to begin. The Socialist Party was still split, and we would have to work hard to win over his faction. I was in Chile Chico as much to greet him as to begin that conversation: I was urging Almeyda to start electoral registration.

"Give me a bit of time to move in this direction," he said. I'd made my case; now it was up to him to bring the radicals around.

The campaign to register voters for the plebiscite was the kind of affair for which the term "grassroots" was created. We traveled across Chile on a whirlwind tour, going from town to town seeking support and educating potential voters. Sometimes our meetings were in high school stadiums, sometimes they were in backyards. Sometimes there were hundreds of people, sometimes just 10 or 12. One February afternoon in a town close to La Serena, Las Compañías, we were met by no more than 11 women, waiting in the hot sun. In Collipulli, we held a meeting of about 15 people in a dirt-floor garage full of cars. In Puerto Natales, a torrential downpour made our meeting of just 60 people an uncomfortable affair. We traveled with little more than the clothes on our backs, and we couldn't afford fancy paraphernalia or flyers. All we could do was hope for ears to listen, and usually we found at least a few. Our goal in all this was not just to obtain the 35,000 signatures that we needed to register; it was also to reach out to people in every region of the country and begin to build a party structure that could organize our efforts.

Nowhere was all this more difficult than in the neighborhoods of Santiago, where people—living in such close proximity to the dictator—were terribly afraid. They were also simply busy in a way that rural people were not. Our winning strategy was to go directly to the people as they went about their lives. We set up a petition booth at the Paseo Peatonal, a pedestrian hot spot in the heart of the city. We went to the people in the *ferias* and the supermarkets. We caught them mid-routine, and they signed up in droves.

The mayor of Santiago tried to stop us. We would need permission to set up tables on the street, he insisted, and it was certain that we wouldn't be granted it if we asked. So I thought of another solution: We would create walking tables, similar to those used by young cigarette sellers hawking their products on the streets. Slowly but surely, we gathered the mass of signatures that we needed to create our party and, more importantly, sparked a true debate by our mere presence. That alone was a sort of victory.

No matter how much the streets buzzed, to the mainstream media, our campaign did not exist. A few magazines dared mention the PPD by name, but in the newspapers that everyone read, our name was as foreign as another language. Radio steered clear, with the exception of the Catholic station and Radio Cooperativa. We were going to have to bring our message to the masses by ourselves.

By the middle of March, however, we reached the crucial numbers of support. So we gathered all our signatures in a box in our office in Domínica, 10 blocks from the office of the Electoral Service, and walked them straight to be registered. There were a couple hundred of us carrying signs, raising our voices to celebrate as we headed toward the office, stopping traffic and attracting looks of surprise, encouragement, and sometimes fear along the way. Then suddenly there we were, standing before the director of the Electoral Register. I remember it being a very strange act, proudly handing our box of signatures to a man appointed by a dictator we were hoping to overthrow. Yet when we entered his office, the man played out his role in the most professional of ways, as if there were not a celebration awaiting us outside, as if thousands were not awaiting that moment, that day.

O n July 7, 1987, one of the Chicago Boys' own came back to La Moneda. Sergio Fernández was a lawyer, not an economist; he had never gone to Illinois. But at the same time that the Chicago Boys had rolled the dice on the Chilean economy, Fernández had completely reorganized the state. The former minister of the interior was credited with leading Pinochet's government to success in the previous plebiscite, in 1980. Pinochet wanted him back by his side for another go at the ballot box. He called the new arrangement his "cabinet of projection." Fernández's job would be not only to ensure that Pinochet would be the junta's chosen candidate, but also to win the 1988 plebiscite and end the growing questions about the regime's legitimacy.

The first task was not as easy as it might appear. By the second half of the decade, even some members of the junta, particularly José Toribio Merino of the Army and Fernando Matthei of the Air Force, were growing weary of Pinochet; they thought it would be easier to get electoral approval for a civilian than for a dictator who had already been in power for 15 years. They could acutely sense that the country was tired—tired of the protests, tired of Pinochet, tired of things not quite working right. And the pressure was only growing. Almeyda was back in the country, as were the prominent communists Luis Guastavino, Julieta Campusano, and Mirella Baltra. A socialist senator, Erich Schnake, had resolved to come back, ending his exile. Even the institutions that Pinochet himself created were now throwing up obstacles in his path. The constitutional tribunal ruled that the election had to take place within 30 days of the announcement of the junta's candidate.

It was also around that time that Pope John Paul II arrived in Chile. By now well known for the subtle political messages he had sent throughout the communist world, in Chile, the pope pushed hard on human rights. He met with the opposition and traveled throughout the country. He preached to the bishops of Chile, urging them not to be afraid "to pass moral judgment even in political matters." But then, in a move that would forever create doubts about the true impact of his visit, he met with Pinochet at the presidential palace. During their meeting, Pinochet placed the pope right in front of the window overlooking a small crowd gathered in the plaza below—and then opened the shutters, allowing everyone to see the two men together. When the crowd applauded, it must have seemed to Pinochet as if the pope was proclaiming his solidarity with the junta.

So perhaps that day in August 1988 was inevitable, when the ruling generals walked solemnly one by one down the red carpet that led from the ministry of defense to the press podium and informed the country who would be the candidate for the plebiscite. The ballot was called for October 5. Pinochet's arrogance was in many ways his undoing; he believed that the referendum would be a mere formality, and that nothing could overtake his 15 years of momentum.

Or perhaps he just hadn't done the math. We had—and had figured out how to beat an electoral system rigged in the regime's favor. Pinochet had mandated that once you were 18, you were allowed—but not required—to register to vote. Once you did, however, you were obligated to cast a ballot in every election for the rest of your life.

With the opposition deterred from registering and fear casting a shadow over any past polls, Pinochet was all but assured rousing victories in previous votes. But the crucial element for us was that every single person we registered would *have* to vote. We knew by then that some 8.2 million Chileans were old enough to register. Assuming that Pinochet had the support of 40 percent of those 8 million, he would secure about 3.2 million Yes votes. To beat them, we needed to ensure that as many people as possible registered—and if they registered for us, at least we could be nearly certain of a No vote. Having just 7 million would be enough to win, but it was not a slam dunk; we really needed 8 million names on the list—in other words, nearly the entire country.

Everywhere we went, we explained the numbers to the people, driving home the message of the importance of every last vote. On the day when we hit that magic number, 7 million, I remember saying among ourselves, almost afraid to jinx it but still too excited to keep it inside, that Pinochet had already been defeated.

I t was only when we went on television, many now believe, that the No campaign truly took off. After we had registered our party, Channel 13, the station of Catholic University, decided to invite us to its program *Face of the Nation,* where I would eventually wag my finger at Pinochet. We knew up to that point that we had taken big steps toward democracy, but it wasn't until our television debut, and after having men and women approach me in the streets, that I realized the quantitative leap we had taken in just a few short months. Suddenly, Chileans had seen for themselves that they had a real choice of parties, of leaders, and of futures for the country. We had stood up to Pinochet on television, and the sun still rose the next day. I hadn't been re-arrested.

It didn't end there. A few days earlier, the constitutional tribunal had granted 15 minutes of daily air time to each side of the referendum vote. And every day, more of the country began to tune in. The arguments for Yes were not new; Chileans had been hearing them for the last 15 years. But the arguments for the No campaign were the first breath of fresh air in over a decade. We were subtle and strategic with our time, focusing on positive messages. We had to persuade people that we could govern the country, not just oppose Pinochet. We had a song and a symbol, the rainbow, all the brainchild of Patricio Bañados, a famous opposition television presenter. He had been silenced during the dictatorship, and his reappearance alone was a sign of how the times had changed. There he was, speaking with a smile, campaigning against Chile's most brutal period at last, without fear.

Of course, there were serious topics to tackle, not least the human rights violations that a Yes vote would prolong. But if we wanted to win, the last thing to do was frighten or polarize people. In many parts of Chile, voters believed that Pinochet had the power to see and know who had voted Yes and who had voted No. We had to tread lightly, navigating the nuances without neglecting the details. We didn't want to talk about the deaths, the disappearances, and the violence. Our message was about moving forward. But, in a quiet acknowledgment of the disappeared, we settled at last on a simple scene in our television commercial: a widow, dancing *la cueca*—alone because her husband had disappeared.

It was only when Chileans saw and heard all this on television that they began to believe victory was possible. The optimism was infectious. On one of my trips to the far south, I was joined by a friend who was a supporter, but skeptical that we could actually win. So I invited him to accompany me to fly more than 900 miles south to Balmaceda and take the bus to Coyhaique from there for a rally. About 40 miles past Coyhaique was Puerto Aysén, a port city where old sailboats are more common than shipping containers. The town's name means "where the ice ends," and some of the ice there dates back longer than even the port.

We arrived late and found not a soul awaiting us. The only thing that weighed harder on us than the silence was the premonitions of failure. But one man finally arrived to greet us, and he assured us things were better than they seemed. "Yes, things are difficult here," he said, "but I have faith in your supporters." His voice had the tone of a man who has secret good news about which he can say nothing.

I pressed for details. "So where is the meeting?" I asked.

"It's at the gymnasium," he replied. Perhaps, we thought, that's why there was no one in the city.

From the cool night, we stepped into a gymnasium full of people. And the silence shattered. They were *loud*—enthusiastically shouting and singing. We made our way dumbfounded with delight to center stage. There was no equipment to speak of, but the locals had taken several benches from the closest classroom and set them up, along with a hand microphone.

I began my speech with a slogan that we had by then adopted on television: "Chile, la alegría ya viene (Chile, joy is coming)." It was the campaign's song as well as its unofficial motto. And the moment I said those words, the crowd burst into the melody without prompting. I stepped back for moment, trying to realize what had happened. Just two days after our television campaign had begun, Puerto Aysén—at the southern tip of the world—knew our song.

"That's it, Lagos," my skeptical friend told me later. "I'm convinced."

Of course, in many cities and towns, fear still lingered. You could feel the goose bumps on your skin in Pedro de Valdivia, a small nitrate-mining area in the Atacama desert in Chile's far north. I arrived there one afternoon to a humble lunch with our local supporters, who sheepishly told me that the people of the town had not believed that I, Ricardo Lagos, was actually coming.

"After lunch, no one is going to come and join you," they said, their eyes toward the floor as they stirred their food. "Those who are here now are the only ones who dared to come and meet you."

"But we have an idea," one man continued. "We wanted to ask you to walk through the village." The people, they reasoned, would see me through their windows, looking through the peepholes of the doors they dared not open.

We set out from the lunch walking slowly, deliberately, through the town toward the central plaza. The streets were as sparsely populated as my reception—just two people sweeping the worn cobblestones of the city square. They kept sweeping, as if we didn't exist.

But little by little as we continued on, people began to come out. First, there were eyes peering over the windowsills and pointing fingers. Several said hello, but from inside their houses; no one came out to speak to me.

The people of Pedro de Valdivia were scared because they thought they'd be dismissed from the company, but they were not alone in their trepidation.

I next went to María Elena, another nitrate town owned by the same company. It had a larger population and a sizeable labor office that had invited me to a meeting with the workers. The day after our meeting, all of the workers were fired.

We had come to expect such reprisals, and I promised the workers that I would come back, even if it was in the middle of the plebiscite. And I kept that promise, taking the long trip, first by plane, then bus, then bus again, and arriving a few hours later. I knew it would help if I were not there alone; with me that day was an Italian television crew and several others from European countries. There were 30 of us set up in the plaza, right in front of the central market. And from there, we began to call people into the streets to join us.

The people streamed toward us, even as the mayor's office tried to stop them. First, his office began to play very loud music, the volume all the way up so that no one could hear what I was saying. But I spoke very loud—I screamed—so that people could hear me.

In effect, that's exactly what we were doing in every village in Chile: shouting for freedom so loudly that everyone—even those who tried their best not to listen—couldn't help but hear us. We had to show the world that there were voices for freedom in the poorest Santiago suburbs and the fear-stricken heartlands. Even in María Elena.

A journalist approached me at a rally that spring and whispered in my ear: The plebiscite had been called for Wednesday, October 5. "Ah, Pinochet has already lost," I told him. And how funny fate is. He had called the referendum vote on the feast day of my patron saint, San Froilán. "Surely the best gift that I could have is that we win the No," I said. It would be like calling an election on your opponent's birthday and expecting to win.

By then, however, I was confident for far less superstitious reasons. As we worked tirelessly to build Chile's hopes, we worked even harder to ensure that they were not disappointed. In Chile's classrooms, parishes, backyards, and gardens, we were training thousands and thousands of monitors to verify a free vote. We taught them how the tables should look, how the process would work, and what to watch for if there was any rigging. Those first classes lasted six hours without any break because we couldn't afford to hand out sandwiches or snacks. Slowly, we whittled down the curriculum to four hours, beginning at 6 or 7 in the evening and lasting into the night. We trained 35,000 monitors, each awarded a certificate from the PPD saying that we had trained them to be our representative in counting the votes. The Christian Democrats, the Radical Party, and other opposition groups did the same. And as a result, there were monitors from the No campaign at every single table across the length of Chile. And on top of our own monitors, foreign observers from all over the world started pouring in.

With the manpower in place to do our own parallel count, what we needed now were the structures—an executive committee of command for the No—that would coordinate each No party's tallies. We set up a data center in a hotel in Santiago, led by the future secretary-general to the presidency, Genaro Arriagada, and armed with hundreds of people and every piece of equipment we could find: phones, faxes, typewriters, and a lot of paper and pens.

But as the days inched closer, we realized how much was still out of our hands. On the Saturday evening before the plebiscite, my home phone rang frantically. It was my brother-in-law, Pedro, who had been asked to pass on a message: Lionel Acuña, the same officer who had held me in prison, urgently wanted to speak to me alone.

I hadn't seen Acuña, who was by then a colonel, since he had driven me home from prison two years earlier. Like that odd day, he greeted me warmly. But his voice quickly turned more serious. Seven buses had been stolen in Santiago, he said, recounting what he believed had happened. These were normal buses, traveling the normal city routes. But they were also of the same model and make used by the Carabineros. "We think they were stolen in an operation," he said gravely, "by the intelligence service"—in other words, Pinochet's secret police.

What did Pinochet want with the buses? We could pretty easily imagine his devious plan: the buses would be painted to match the Carabineros' buses and deployed throughout the city. But if needed, those "Carabineros" would stir up trouble, arresting, inciting violence, and producing disturbances in Chile's most vulnerable (and most traumatized) neighborhoods. "We, the true Carabineros, can do nothing," Acuña continued. "I am afraid that they will use them the day of the plebiscite to make it appear as if what they are doing is being done by the civilian police."

Perhaps it seems like a silly thing to worry about now, but such an incident on the day of the vote would have devastated Chile. Violence and unrest would destroy the opposition's credibility; Pinochet could easily claim that his rule was the only way to ensure stability. It was an argument that many foreign governments (and even many Chileans) were still willing to buy.

We were determined that it wouldn't reach that point, and the moment I left that meeting, I started making phone calls. I called Alejandro Hales, a human rights lawyer who had contacts in the Carabineros and was close to the Christian Democrats. "Patricio Aylwin told me the same thing this morning," he replied. "I am going to go see him immediately." Aylwin, it turned out, had gotten similar information from sources I did not know and still do not know to this day.

For the first time, I suggested that we each try to speak with a member of the junta—Aylwin with the director of the Carabineros and myself with the commander of the Air Force, Fernando Matthei.

I called the cousin of my ex-wife, a general in the Air Force, to see if he could help pass the word to General Matthei. We could stay in contact, he assured me, but he thought it unwise for me to meet with Matthei—even if Aylwin was there as well. Instead, General Matthei suggested that if I had something to tell him, I should simply pass the world along through the same general I had already approached. As I recall it, we met to "play tennis," the Air Force general and I, and between games, I told him what we knew about the buses. Meanwhile, Hales was able to track down General Rodolfo Stange, the head of the Carabineros, who received us the following day, October 2.

It was 5 P.M. when Aylwin, Hales, and I arrived at Stange's official residence, a beautiful home in Ñuñoa. We told the general what we knew. To our surprise, he was unfazed by the announcement. "The information you have is wrong. There weren't seven buses that were stolen, there were 14, and all of them are the same make and model as those that are used by the Carabineros to transport personnel. We believe that it is part of an operation, and certainly now those buses have been painted as those of the Carabineros."

He continued, all of us listening. "But don't worry. We have a plan too. In these last days, we have been painting the logo of the Carabineros on the tops of all of our buses with florescent paint. If our helicopters see that there is a bus that does not have this logo, we can order its destruction. I assure you, we are taking care of the matter."

The butterflies in our stomachs were far from quelled. After we left, I asked Heraldo Muñoz to warn the American embassy, and he spoke personally with Ambassador Barnes. In Washington, the Chilean ambassador was summoned to the State Department at midnight and warned in strong terms that any interference in the election would have grave consequences for bilateral relations. Meanwhile, I spoke with Volodia Telteilboin, the well-known Chilean communist writer, to be sure that the Communist Party acted with maturity on the day of the plebiscite, so as not to produce (or respond to) any provocations or disruptions. And that is exactly what they did.

By that time, spring was beginning in Chile. It was not unusual for me to sleep away from home, as I had done for much of the last year in Chile's villages and towns. But this time, as a security measure, I had begun sleeping next door to my house, which made me feel farther from home than I'd been even in the most distant towns. I woke in the mornings wondering if I would be able go home after the vote. There I was, the man who had spent his last decade convincing Chile that an end to Pinochet was possible, and I was still afraid.

Six students volunteered to watch over my house one day before the plebiscite. Our children were all in other houses, too, most with my in-laws, who lived in the same community (by then, the exile imposed upon them had finally been lifted). I was a bit farther away, in another house.

October 5 came at last. I rose and met journalists who accompanied me to the part of the city where we had set up to monitor the voting. Our headquarters was a hotel in central Santiago, Hotel Galerías, close to the Central Command for the No, which was in a house about eight blocks away. The rooms were packed with people bustling from phone to fax and back to the press room. It would have been uncomfortably cozy had we been in a mood to notice. And talk about strategically placed—it was right in front of where Pinochet's camp was counting the votes and right across from the Ministry of Defense, where the official results would be announced.

I went to the voting booth around 10 in the morning, a time I have stuck to in all the elections I have voted in since. My table was located in an old, regal schoolhouse arranged around a central plaza. The booths were all around—in the classrooms, on the second floor, and finally in a semi-enclosed gymnasium.

As I walked through the front gates that led into the patio, I felt a silence come over my fellow voters. I made my way through the crowds toward my designated voting table in the back, immediately on the right when you enter the outdoor gymnasium. But as I started walking, the silence changed to cheers. The people were applauding, first on the ground level and then into the rafters of the second floor.

I remember knowing at that moment that we had already achieved the most important thing that I could imagine: Chile had shed its fear.

Indeed, it took courage even to go to the polls that day. All of Chile had risen from bed, eaten their breakfast, and made their way to the voting tables—all without so much as looking at each other. No one's eyes were lifted above ground level. It was as if your eyes—should someone see them—would betray your vote. They were tense elections precisely because everyone knew just how profound an impact the result would have on the future of the country. If they were successful, it would be a new page in Chilean history.

The day went on, and we prepared ourselves for a long night. I tried to nap to prepare, but was awakened at 3:30 P.M. by the visit of one Pierre Mauroy, the former prime minister of France, whom I had met five years before at the re-inauguration of Argentina's Alfonsín. "Since I am no longer the prime minister and I'm free from political duties, today I am here as a comrade," he told me. "I've come to share the victory of the plebiscite with you." He spoke in French, of course, but translation was not necessary. The passion of his speech was so strong that I knew what he was talking about.

The monitors started reporting around 4 P.M., and the vote count was lightning quick; there were only two ballot options.

Unfortunately, the first count from the Interior Ministry at about 7 P.M. put the Yes vote at 54 percent and the No at 43. Then there was a second count around 9 P.M. The Yes was still winning, but the margin had narrowed considerably. We were silent as we heard the figures read aloud.

Inside, however, my thoughts were racing. We needed to have our own count, tallied by the thousands of monitors we had watching in polling stations around the country, and we needed it now. "I will announce the result when we have 10 percent" of the results, Genaro Arriagada told me when I inquired, "but so far we have not reached that percentage."

"That's impossible. We have results with more than 10 percent and it looks certain that we have at least 54 percent or 55 percent!" I protested. "I beg you; let's release something quickly. Otherwise people will surely become very nervous, and the government's numbers will be the only ones." Aylwin must have agreed, because after speaking with Genaro, the two decided that they would release a preliminary result at 9:45 P.M. By our count, we were ahead by 10 points.

In fact by then, I was already certain that we had won. The PPD's own vote center had tallied a first count that put us firmly ahead. But since all the parties—ours, the Christian Democrats, and the radicals—were united under the Central No command, to announce our own figures would have betrayed the unity that sustained the Concertación for the No. So I could say nothing concrete. I told the international journalists watching that we were calmly awaiting the results with great conviction in the fact that we would win.

Around 10:30 that night, the regime made its first concession. Sergio Onofre Jarpa, the former minister of the interior, acknowledged that the No vote had won in a television interview. We were immediately joyful, but it was still far from any official confirmation of the tally.

The official silence, meanwhile, continued. And continued. So long was the delay that the national television station began showing old movies to fill the space. On the most important night in Chile's recent history—the night that could end 17 years of dictatorship—the people of Chile were watching the cinema. Finally, we began to protest. Our data center had some 80 percent of the tables reporting, and we would soon release our own results. In the end, that's what happened—at 1 A.M. on October 6.

Long after the night had fallen, but with all of Chile still wide awake, Aylwin walked up to a podium set up at our data center, right across from the Ministry of Defense. There was a crowd gathered. Television cameras from all over the world were watching, broadcasting the result from north to south. Aylwin's voice pierced the silence with force, penetrating all of our ears, reaching through our veins, and going straight to our pumping hearts. Speaking on behalf of the No command, he read the results: a resounding victory for No, at 54 percent.

The applause that followed was incredible, and if I listen hard enough, it is still ringing in my ears. I rushed from my perch on the stage to embrace Aylwin as photographers snapped our picture. It was an image that would travel the world in minutes—a visual expression of what the triumph of the No vote had meant.

Meanwhile, Pinochet was frantic. Shocked and betrayed by his own ignorance, he tried to proclaim a state of emergency so that he wouldn't have to step down. He had even drafted the declaration; he was ready to stay.

But the promise of true democracy had touched even the other members of the junta that night. Matthei knew that the result would be difficult for Pinochet to accept, so he pre-empted the general. Before entering the room to discuss the results with Pinochet, Matthei told the journalists outside that the No vote had triumphed. Thus, it was ultimately the junta itself—Matthei and Merino—that finally told Pinochet no. He had to recognize his own constitution and live up to the result.

"Do what they want," he finally told the other generals, despondent. He felt he was surrounded by traitors.

Matthei left the meeting with Pinochet and told the press that the government had "accepted" the victory of the No vote. Sergio Fernández, the minister who was supposed to clench victory for Pinochet, still found some comfort; the Yes campaign had won a large number of votes, nearly 44 percent. "So where's the champagne?" Matthei quipped.

At 3 A.M., the undersecretary of the interior, Alberto Cardemil, recognized the victory of the No vote. In total, 7,236,241 voters had cast their ballots, and 3,111,875 voted Yes. A total of 3,969,495 voted No—putting Yes at 43 percent and No at 54.7 percent. Empty ballots accounted for 0.9 percent and invalid ones for 1.3 percent.

After confirming the results at the PPD headquarters, at 2 A.M. I went to Hotel Galerías, where hundreds of foreign friends were waiting, together with all our PPD volunteers, to celebrate. I entered the room to a captive audience, their eyes glued to the large screens set up, with Cardemil reading the results. Applause broke out; shouts of joy filled the room.

I stood in front of the few tables that made up our make-shift podium space, thanking everyone who had made the day possible—which was in fact all of Chile. I saw European parliamentarians with tears falling down their

cheeks. They had not cried since General De Gaulle came to Paris as a libera-
tor in World War II, but that night there were tears. That's how much had been
done by the Chilean people.

The following day, a humor magazine published the headline: "The general runs alone and finishes second." Another summed up the previous decade:
"With a pen and paper, we have defeated Pinochet and his dictatorship."

FIVE

INTERREGNUM

The people exploded onto the streets. Without permission or premeditation, without organization or prompting, they flung open their doors, lifted their eyes after 15 years of looking downward, and celebrated in a way that they hadn't been able to since anyone could remember. To wake up that morning was to realize that you had been carrying a heavy burden for the last decade and a half. And it was gone. You couldn't help but run into the streets and join the celebrations. When the Carabineros came to disperse the crowds, they weren't met with jeers; they were met with the same contagious joy with which people greeted their neighbors. The crowds hugged the policemen they once feared. It seemed as if the very soul of a people had been transformed.

We still hadn't slept when morning came to the Hotel Galerías, where we had been savoring the moment for hours. There wasn't a sleepy soul to be found.

I stayed in the hotel throughout the following day, until around 6 o'clock, when I made my way through the crowds and out in front. My plan had been to walk to the television interview I had scheduled with CNN, about seven blocks away at the Hotel Carrera, a place that today acts as the Ministry of Foreign Affairs. But I could barely move, let alone make my way across downtown on foot. Throngs of people swarmed me, greeting and hugging me as I passed. They shouted my name. They sang, they cried, they reached to touch my hands and face. Whichever way I turned, the crowd quickly followed.

There was simply no denying it; we were in a new Chile. The next day, October 7, we held an official victory rally in Parque O'Higgins, the same place where Pinochet had once sent us because he was sure our small ranks would be dwarfed by the vast expanse of space. The park overflowed with humanity as people came from all over Santiago and the outlying regions. They gathered standing, bunched together but never noticing how they must have been squeezed side by side. All eyes were fixed on the stage where we would begin the rally.

But what would we say? The plan was to give no speeches, only greet the crowd to kick off the joyous occasion. Yet as I stood there on stage, I felt the heavy responsibility of governing that had passed to us. Standing there before us were the hopes and fears of an entire nation. These were the people who had fought with us—and even many of those who had fought against us. It was our task not just to prove ourselves worthy to those who were already on our side, but to all of Chile—even those Pinochet supporters who were suddenly afraid for their futures.

Eighteen months later, I took a job as the minister of education, and when I showed up to take my new post, I found that the offices were covered floor to ceiling with paintings of nautical escapades. What any of it had to do with education, I wasn't sure. But in the early days of the junta, the Navy had controlled the Education Ministry and seen fit to adorn the walls with portraits of Chile's naval heroes and their deeds. To me, it only made sense that a painting of October 7, 1988, decorate my office instead. The famous Chilean artist Gracia Barrios donated several pieces, including one called simply, *La Celebración del Triunfo del No* (The Celebration of the Triumph of the No). I had it hung directly behind my desk. And each time I felt lost or felt the urge to think of quitting, I would see that painting and remember: I'll have to answer to all of Chile if I forget what that day stood for. That painting has followed me everywhere since—through my presidential campaigns, to La Moneda, and to my office today.

A week after our victory rally, on October 14, our coalition, Concertación, declared itself as a coalition of post-plebiscite political parties. Our work was far from over; we'd still need to ensure that the next president would be one of our own. It was an awkward intermission. Until March 11, 1990, Pinochet was still in charge of Chile. And we were still technically in the opposition.

In the coming year and a half, what was officially the Concertación of Political Parties for Democracy would have to codify our political platform, agree upon a single candidate to win the election, and negotiate with Pinochet to reform his undemocratic constitution. On top of all this was the fact that, for the 43 percent of the country that had just voted Yes, this new Chile was terrifying. We would have to reassure them that there was nothing to fear from a Concertación government.

Not long after the election, I went to visit Genaro Arriagada, who had been the executive secretary of the No command, at his house in a wealthy neighborhood of Santiago, to plan how we could offer a conciliatory gesture toward Pinochet's supporters. As my car pulled up to Arriagada's home, however, I found it surrounded with reams of angry protestors, all supporters of the junta. This was Las Condes, a neighborhood where many of Pinochet's elite constituency lived. They were shouting as loudly and angrily as our own supporters had been joyous—only they were calling for Pinochet to stay. And the last person they wanted to see was surely me, the man who had helped bring down their leader. We pulled around the side, entering in the back to avoid the commotion.

Arriagada was the kind of man who likes to get straight to the point. And in that meeting, we were both very clear about what we needed to do: We would issue a magnanimous statement indicating that we were gracious winners, ready to hold talks with the Pinochet government and ready to govern for all of Chile.

When we concluded our meeting, Arriagada realized that it would be quite difficult for me to leave unnoticed amid the angry protestors. The crowds were growing larger, and we feared being swarmed if either of us were seen. "The biggest problem is that you are bald, and people will see and recognize you," he told me. (For the record, Arriagada was also bald, and he had been for far longer than me!) So before I left, he gave me a hat, a black one of the sort that European sailors wear. With that cap, I slipped outside through the multitudes who were shouting outside.

I'd come to talk with Arriagada about reconciliation, and what I'd seen was a reminder of just how badly it was needed. Those crowds plainly demonstrated how deeply polarized the country still was. Undoing the years of division would take more than a few mere statements. Our government would have to transform the way Chileans thought about politics. No longer could one's political opponent be seen as a bitter enemy. If we weren't careful at that moment, Luisa often reminded me, Chile could easily go back to the bad old days. "With all that we have suffered and all that has happened, never think for a moment that we are somehow now on the other side of that hurdle," she would say.

Today, more than two decades later, many don't remember or understand what it meant to live for those 17 years under Pinochet. They don't understand how people used to walk through the streets, eyes averted, their mouths closed, all the time afraid of the torture, the exile, the loss of their dignity. There has never before been a generation in Chile as marked by history as mine, those who lived through the coup and the dictatorship. We share a common, overwhelming desire to ensure that such a dark period never happens again. We never harbored a desire for vengeance, as many assumed. Truth and justice were about keeping the past out of our future.

We were also too busy making plans to spend much time looking backward. While the outside world looked on our campaign with admiration, they were also anxious about the unknown prospects of Chile without Pinochet. What would happen next? Would Concertación be able not just to protest and campaign, but also to govern? Could the opposition become the rulers?

It is a sign of just how backward Chile's constitution was that even the parties that had supported Pinochet agreed it was in need of serious fixing. Within weeks of the plebiscite vote, we began negotiating with the National Renewal (RN) Party, which had supported the junta. (The more conservative Independent Democratic Union Party [UDI] never did want to change the constitution.) There was much that needed changing: Article 8, which prohibited leftist parties, had to be eliminated altogether; the parliamentary seats designated for the junta's appointed senators would have to go; and the electoral system—which gave an unfair advantage to Pinochet—had to be amended.

As clear as we were on our own side of what needed to be done, Pinochet was even clearer: The margin for changes was miniscule. At first, he refused any reforms at all. It was only because national sentiment had so fully turned against him that he eventually had to join in the negotiations. On October 21, Pinochet sacked his interior minister, Sergio Fernández, the man who had failed to bring him victory, and brought in his former minister of finance, Carlos Cáceres, to fill the spot. It would be Cáceres with whom we would hold all of our negotiations.

We gathered among ourselves first, negotiating with the RN, to set the parties' proposals in order. Everyone agreed that Article 8 should go. Civil authority would have to be re-established over the armed services, in part by eliminating the National Security Council, an executive committee stacked with military officers. Getting rid of that odd body would curb Pinochet's influence over the subsequent president, the Senate, and the Supreme Court. Finally, there was agreement that the electoral system would have to be reformed. With our camp in order, Aylwin and Jarpa, on behalf of the Concertación and RN, respectively, had begun serious discussions with Cáceres by the time the Chilean summer was in full season the following March.

From day one, Cáceres had very little room to maneuver, and each time he reported back to Pinochet with even the most modest advances, the dictator would berate him as if his work were an absolute betrayal. Pinochet was not as strong as he had once been, and slowly but surely, the junta leader would have to make at least a few concessions to the now much stronger opposition. But he never did compromise on the most important matters.

In the end, 54 constitutional reforms emerged from our discussions. To our disappointment, however, only a few of these truly represented significant change. Article 8 was dropped; the number of senators rose from 26 to 38, diluting ever so slightly the influence of the 9 senators still to be named by the military (although any president who had served for more than six years was also guaranteed a Senate seat—meaning Pinochet would become senator for life and have immunity from prosecution). The presidential term for the transitional government that would be elected in 1990 was cut down from Pinochet's eight years to just four. After that, all subsequent holders of the office would again serve for eight years. The president lost his ability to dissolve parliament.

Where our negotiations reached an impasse was in modifying the electoral system. As it stood, two senators would be elected in each district—the first from the party that garnered the most votes, and the second from the party that took runner up. If one party took two thirds of the vote, the party that took the other third would still see one of its members enter the Senate. It was a system that we found absurdly favorable toward the minority coalition—which of course was no accident. Pinochet was about to become the opposition, and no matter how unpopular he became, he would retain seats through this perverse electoral calculus.

We argued tirelessly to fix it, but I was pessimistic about our chances. We failed even after trying what should have been a very clever gambit. Pinochet's constitution, it turned out, had a serious strategic loophole. As it was written, certain clauses could be amended only with a two-thirds majority vote, while others could be changed with a simple majority. But included in the section for a simple majority was the clause stipulating a two-thirds vote for the other, more sensitive parts. If we could muster a majority to alter that clause, we could, in effect, do away with the two-thirds requirement for real change. In short, we could amend the entire constitution with a simple majority—and that's what Pinochet feared most. He had lost his majority, meaning his entire constitution was in peril.

But even with that two-thirds clause as a bargaining chip, we never got any further. We knew that taking advantage of the constitution's flaws would draw anger and further polarize an already divided country. If we wanted to undo the constitution with a simple majority, we would have to call a plebiscite. The country might not take kindly to such a move—some would see it as a victor trying to consolidate his gains. So we proceeded with negotiations. And each time, we were told that making fundamental changes to the electoral system was a red line for Pinochet. No one could change that.

For perhaps the first time since I began fighting against the dictatorship, I felt distraught. We were fast reaching the point after which electoral reform would no longer be possible. If it didn't happen now—before the elections—it might not happen at all. And it could take years or even decades to reverse the flawed system. On top of that, opening up a fight over the issue within Concertación could pull apart our coalition. There was a clear split already between those who favored taking what reforms we could and those who wanted to walk away if we couldn't also change the electoral system. There was too much at stake, and we were still too new of a political bloc to stand up to such a divisive challenge.

Besides, what was implicit in all this, although of course we never said it, was our certainty that after those four years with a transitional government, each of the parties in Concertación—the socialists, Christian Democrats, radicals, and so on—would regain its unique political identity. Concertación would no longer be necessary because democracy would have been re-established. We wouldn't need four more years of being crowded under the same political tent. Or so we thought. Perhaps there would come a time when one party or another from our pro-democracy camp would benefit from the system's bias toward the minority.

Reality was looming over us as we gathered all the party chiefs together one night to sort out what we hoped to do about the stalled constitutional reforms. We were running out of time to negotiate with the RN and with Pinochet, and soon we would have to simply say yes or no to the entire package of changes. We couldn't cherry-pick the issues where we had been successful and simply say "no" where we had failed; this was all or nothing. Either we kept the electoral system with all its flaws, knowing that we would receive in exchange other reforms that had been hard negotiated, or we could walk away in protest. With nothing.

I was torn. As soon as I had finished reading our party's report on the negotiations, written by José Antonio Viera-Gallo, Patricio Aylwin stood up. The weight of what we were discussing was clearly bearing down on him. We had made great progress, he told the group, and we had to go forward with what we had. If politics were the art of the possible, we had apparently reached that point, and it would be silly for us to walk away now. My eyes wandered around the room as he spoke, trying to read the faces of the other party leaders. They nodded their heads, mumbling among themselves. They all seemed in favor of doing what Aylwin had suggested.

I couldn't stop myself from rebutting. I looked across the table from where I was seated, exactly across from Aylwin, and I began to lay out my reservations. But as soon as I finished, Aylwin, who has always been a tranquil and pensive character, unleashed all the force of rhetoric he could muster. He spoke with conviction and even frustration, looking me directly in the face, asking me if I wanted to go to Chile for a referendum on constitutional reform—one that would be as hard and as polarizing as the one we had just held—all so that we could change the electoral system.

He was right. I realized that saying no to the little progress that had been made in the negotiations would mean asking Chile to go to another plebiscite to approve our broader, more sweeping measures. And that, I also realized, would be the end of Concertación. Such an endeavor would surely tear us apart.

"Patricio, I don't know why you are becoming so angry when I am just asking, no more!" I said. Laughter erupted, the tense moment shattered. "The only thing I am worried about is that, if we cannot fix the electoral system, it will render it nearly impossible for us to govern."

Aylwin replied, "Ricardo, we have been discussing this same question with Sergio Jarpa and RN. They are of the same mind as Concertación, and so we are certain that once a new national Congress has been elected, our first project can be electoral reform."

"And what guarantee do we have? Do we have something written?"

"Tomorrow, we have been invited to dinner at the home of Rivadeneira, one of the jurists who was working on the negotiations with RN, and there, we will propose this compromise to reform the electoral system later, given that Pinochet has given us no further room to negotiate now."

I conceded and left the debate there, planning to go the next day to Ignacio Rivadeneira's house as a leader of Concertación. I felt much better after that meeting, having heard his reassurances and having understood that we were not the only political party concerned. We left the meeting agreeing to work toward electoral reform beginning in 1990, from the moment that Pinochet was gone. It was already May 1989. So in less than a year, we could pick up the thread again.

The next night, however, the only person not attending the dinner was Jarpa—the leader of the RN. It was a grim omen, and I left with a pit in my stomach, knowing that the electoral system might not change. With Concertación now claiming the electoral lead, RN was about to become one of the biggest beneficiaries of the flawed system. I don't need to say that, to this day, the electoral system in Chile has not been amended.

In the 18 months leading up to that summer, Concertación had been preoccupied by one question: Who would stand as our presidential candidate in the upcoming election? It wasn't easy—not only because there were so many parties but because, as a nascent coalition, there were no rules or procedures in place through which to decide. The long period of dictatorship had made even the most democratic among us forget how to be democratic among ourselves.

For me, the first priority was to get my name out of the running. I knew that I could not stand for the presidency—at least not yet. Chile was still too polarized, and I was still too far to the left (too against Pinochet, to be precise) to risk setting Chile's reconciliation back further. This decision came as a huge surprise to everyone. Many PPD supporters had assumed that my name would be on the list. Their clamoring for my nomination began less than a week after the plebiscite. At a meeting in Los Condes, one of the nicest neighborhoods in Santiago, I was greeted by handfuls of demonstrators shouting what has become Chile's universal presidential cheer. Their voices rose up forcibly: "Se siente, se siente, Lagos presidente!"

Not realizing there were reporters in the crowd, I got out of my car and thanked the crowd. We took the responsibility that the plebiscite had bestowed upon us so seriously, I told them. But I could not be a candidate. I understood that having my name—after all the strident statements I had made in the campaign against Pinochet—could be seen to half of Chile as a provocation. And the interests of Chilean unity had to come first. My announcement threw a bucket of cold water on the meeting, where my disappointed PPD peers were as shocked as the demonstrators outside. The next day, a daily newspaper published the news.

Later that day, Raquel Correa, the same journalist who had spoken with me on the night of the finger, came to my house for an interview that would run in that Sunday's *El Mercurio.* "Is it true," she asked me incredulously, "that you will not stand as a candidate, Mr. Lagos?" No, I told her firmly, I wouldn't. "Are you sure?" she prodded on.

We finished the interview, and as she gathered her things, Correa stopped me, the doubting look still on her face. "Ricardo, I want to ask you one favor," she said. "I know that you are going to be a presidential candidate. So I just want to ask: Since you denied it, and since I know that I'm right and you'll eventually be a candidate, can I have the first interview with you as a candidate?"

I laughed and replied, "I'm afraid, Raquel, that I am going to keep you waiting."

Correa would wait almost a decade for me to run. This time around, the field was for others. The Christian Democrats eventually chose their candidate to be Aylwin, the radicals named Enrique Silva Cimma, and our colleagues in Almeyda's wing of the Socialist Party named Alejandro Hales, the well-known lawyer. The PPD and the socialists of Ricardo Núñez fell in line behind Silva Cimma.

Slowly and surely, one by one, those candidates began to drop out, as it became clear that Concertación would pick Aylwin. Having a Christian Democrat would be the least polarizing choice, and among that party, Aylwin was the clear leader. If Aylwin was Concertación's candidate, that was good enough for most of our supporters, and there was no need for a formal vote.

Indeed, we were lucky we had Aylwin as an uncontested leader when the time came for drafting parliamentary lists. In each of Chile's 60 electoral districts, Concertación could field just two candidates. But of course also in each district, every party under our coalition umbrella had a candidate anxious to compete. Whittling down one solid list was painstakingly hard and may have been impossible had Aylwin not been able to moderate among all the competing sides.

But we at last finalized our list, so all that remained was creating a common political platform around which Concertación's many parts could rally. In many ways, this was the easiest part, since it had begun not months but years upon years earlier, in all of our parties' think tanks and academic circles. Constitutional reform, removing the elements of dictatorship, was our very raison d'être. Economic policies had been imagined and detailed in dozens of papers and conferences; social plans had been agreed upon as we watched the country's poverty grow worse and worse. Even our international program had, in a way, been in the works for years thanks to the international solidarity campaign and the many friendly governments abroad who had worked for a democratic Chile.

On March 12, 1989, the U.S. Food and Drug Administration (FDA) made a devastating announcement. Two grapes from Chile, they said, had been found to contain cyanide. Earlier that month, an anonymous caller to the U.S. Embassy in Santiago had threatened to put the same deadly chemical into the country's exported grapes. The FDA would be investigating further. But in the meantime, fear gripped consumers across the United States, who shunned Chilean grapes—then responsible for about 70 percent of our country's fruit exports. On the docks of Philadelphia, where Chilean products usually land, dozens of shipments of grapes were allowed to go bad. Over the course of that growing season, some six million crates of grapes were dumped, and the industry lost about $240 million.

Pinochet blamed the opposition for the fiasco. Concertación, he argued, had turned the United States against Chilean products. Of course, we denied this adamantly. What interests of ours would it serve to alienate one of Chile's biggest export markets? But our denials couldn't do much to calm the storm. The grape crisis shook a country already on edge and made many wonder what would really happen after Pinochet. Would Chile's export partners suddenly cease to take our products? Would Concertación know how to manage Chile's economy?

There were certainly some who blamed us for the troubles. One day when I arrived home, there at the gate of our condominium complex were piles and piles of grapes—perhaps three truckloads—left to rot, as if I were the responsible party. The United States never did find more grapes with cyanide, but in Chile, the damage was done.

But the elections still came that December, right when the new growing season for grapes had begun and memories in the United States were fading. More importantly, Concertación looked strong. We had succeeded in staying together through political negotiations that could easily have torn us apart. There was one presidential candidate, one parliamentarian list, and one common program. Now we just had to sell it—to help voters understand what we could offer them in the next election.

That next phase of campaigning was, for me, quite personal. I was running for a Senate seat in Santiago, a position that would represent about three million Chileans—half of the city's six million—if I won. But what my candidacy actually meant in practice was that I had to campaign twice: first in the neighborhoods of Santiago on my own behalf and then throughout the country in support of Aylwin. I had become the de facto face of Chile's left, and so my solidarity with Aylwin was paramount if he was to win the votes of PPD supporters.

It was terribly difficult, not least because the financial resources at our disposal were laughably few. Luckily what we did have was support, both at home and abroad, that helped us push through. The most unusual form of help that came to us was the gift sent to us from the labor unions of Sweden: a used bus. This was no ordinary bus, however. This was a bus built for campaigning. The front contained the usual rows of seats for a dozen or so passengers to squeeze in. The back, however, could fold out into a mobile stage for skits or presentations. It came equipped with sound equipment, including microphones and speakers. Back in Sweden, it had been a post office van, the front used for shuttling people and the back for packages and parcels. In Chile, it was perfect for retail politics.

That bus became our mobile home as we traveled the length of Chile, arriving one day in the fast-growing port city of Puerto Montt, more than 600 miles south of Santiago. The climate there is rainy, and since it was by now winter, the air almost hovered on our bodies, especially moist. We decided to organize a rally in the city's covered stadium, which had room for about 8,000 people. Pulling up to the stadium at around 7 o'clock for a 7:30 P.M. event, we saw that it was already packed; the seats were filled, and hundreds were standing outside, hoping to get in.

We began our program right away, welcoming the crowd and building up the spirit of those attending. The local Senate candidate, Aniceto Rodríguez, had just begun to speak when we saw a cloud of smoke descend over the indoor stadium. It was tear gas.

The fumes filled the stadium faster than we could understand what was happening. Utter pandemonium broke out. Half-blinded and screaming, covering their eyes, the people ran for the doors. We tried to calm them, but who knows if they even heard what we said. Behind us at the microphones, the crew was also running—but this time to keep the equipment from becoming tainted with the stuff. Had they not done so, a terrible fire could easily have broken out—with everyone still trapped inside. Looking back, I have no doubt that members of Pinochet's secret police must have been in that theater, and it was they who had unleashed the tear gas.

Within minutes that seemed like hours, the crowd was outside. We left, too, and were surprised to find that the people hadn't dispersed, as we had expected them to. Instead, they suggested, why not continue the rally outside, under the light rain that fell from the sky. We had the bus, we realized. The crowd followed us about 10 blocks, right to the shore, where our bus had already been set up for an outdoor performance the next day. As quickly as we could, we moved our equipment from there back to the city plaza, where we unfolded the stage and set up for the rally, part two.

The day afterward, we went back to see the stadium. Strewn across the grounds were some thousand spare shoes—just one of each type—that had been left behind in the hurry to get out. We called up the local radio station and had them announce that the people of Puerto Montt could come and fetch their lost shoes.

When all this had finished, I wrote to our Swedish donors to tell them all that had taken place. I thought this bizarre incident would aptly describe not just how we used that bus that they'd given, but how close we were to democracy—yet with so far still to travel.

Practically every day on the campaign, we saw reminders that democracy was still far from taking hold in Chile. Another came not too long after, at a conference on press freedom held at the Hotel Crown Plaza in Santiago. Most of the country's magazines, newspapers, and television stations leaned quite obviously toward Pinochet's camp, a legacy of years of press intimidation.

Among the invitees to speak that night were me and my opponent for the Senate seat in Santiago, Jaime Guzmán, who happened also to be the mind behind the Pinochet constitution of 1980. Guzmán was scheduled to speak first, followed by me, in a debate of sorts meant to be carried on television. The cameras were set up on the sidelines and ready to roll; the reporters all clutched their notepads to scribble notes as Guzmán began to speak to great applause. But as I walked to the podium for my own turn, I noticed that the cameramen were taking apart their tripods and putting their equipment away. By the time my first words were spoken, there was not a soul left to film them.

"Well, it seems that you have all just had the opportunity to see what press freedom is in Chile," I told the crowd. "When my opponent in this debate, Jaime Guzmán, spoke, the cameras were looking on. Now, they've gone. They have made certain that whatever I say here will stay in this room." Laughter filled the room, and I began the real speech that I had planned on giving. But for all those watching on television that night, it was a one-sided debate.

By far the hardest part of the campaign was raising money. Luckily, to this day in Chile, campaigns are not terribly costly, since advertising on television is prohibited. Still, radio and newspaper advertisements are not free. I've always avoided this part of politics, and in the Senate race, I also put money second, despite the many warnings that this would imperil my chances of being elected. I preferred to get out there and simply meet people.

As we reached the end of the campaign, however, I learned the truth of what I had feared all along: that despite rallies that attracted thousands, tireless campaigning, and even great support, Concertación could lose elections because of the peculiar electoral system. By the time election night came, I knew that I had lost my Senate race. I received 399,720 votes, and my fellow candidate from Concertación, Andrés Zaldivar, received 408,227. Together, more than 800,000 people backed us. But since the parties of the right received the next-most votes after our party, Guzmán would claim the second seat with a mere 224,396 votes. As a result of our electoral system, even though I had taken second place, I wouldn't be getting a seat. It was a great blow to our party, but luckily, there was other news to celebrate. Aylwin won the presidency with 55 percent of the vote. The PPD won 4 Senate seats and more than 15 deputy seats. The Socialist Party and the PPD combined received almost as many votes as the Christian Democrats. In the end, Concertación won 72 of the lower house's 120 slots despite the odd electoral math. In some districts, our candidates won so many votes that we had captured two deputy seats.

In the Senate, we also won the election, but Pinochet's camp would still have more representatives, since added to the right's victories were those senators appointed by Pinochet himself. Aylwin would have to govern in consultation with the right on many occasions, as would also be the case for his successor, Eduardo Frei, and later my government as well. It was only after the designated Senate seats for presidential appointees and ex-presidents were finally done away with in 2005 that Concertación could finally win a small majority.

For me, the end of the election was both exhausting and sad. Sensing my disappointment, a friend lent me his place outside Santiago, where I stayed for several days away from the bustle of the city. I left from there directly to pick up my daughter, Ximena, from the airport; she had just finished doing her post-graduate degree with her husband Gonzalo in Belgium. Even more importantly, they were arriving with my first granddaughter, Emilia, who was just three months old. Luisa had gone to stay with them at the University of Brussels in August, when Emilia was born. But this was my first chance to see my granddaughter. As we left the airport so happily, I with Emilia in my arms, a small crowd broke into applause. My granddaughter had lifted my spirits.

S ometimes luck comes from the most unexpected places—like the loss of my Senate race. Aylwin was intent on naming his cabinet, something that we all agreed he must do quickly. So I returned to Santiago, refreshed from my few days of rest, and called together the PPD, explaining to them that I would go and speak with Aylwin about the matter.

Aylwin began as everyone did in those few days: with his condolences for my losing the Senate race. But he quickly transitioned. "Lagos, I want you to join the cabinet," he told me directly. The post he had in mind was the minister of justice.

I was surprised and asked him who else he was considering for the cabinet more broadly. He imagined Enrique Silva Cimma as foreign minister and Alejandro Foxley as minister of finance and chief of staff. Enrique Krauss, a Christian Democrat who had worked with former president Eduardo Frei Montalva, would be minister of interior.

"Mr. President, I think you are making an error," I finally replied. "If I am the minister of justice, and we are hoping to take some measures to advance human rights, we will surely run into difficulty." As with my presidential candidacy, I realized that I was still too controversial a figure—too opposed to Pinochet—for sensitive posts. "I think it's better that the Justice Ministry go to another person." Aylwin reluctantly agreed, and we closed the meeting, each going our ways and promising to keep talking in coming days.

A few days later, I ran into a friend, and we began speaking casually about the cabinet. As we discussed, I began to realize the importance of one particular post, the minister of public works, and I told my friend as much. During the military regime, nearly every aspect of Chile's infrastructure had been neglected, growing more and more dilapidated over time. The Ministry of Public Works would have to start rebuilding the country one road and bridge at a time. This friend, I later learned, passed along my musings to Aylwin, planting the idea that perhaps I should be nominated as minister of public works.

I laughed when Aylwin asked, until I realized that he was serious. I protested again. This would be such an important ministry; were there not others more qualified? I knew next to nothing about engineering. So I quickly offered him other suggestions of who might do a better job.

"Look, Ricardo," he told me, silencing my protests. "This country will not understand if you are not a part of my cabinet. Public opinion will not understand if someone of your stature and your reputation is not in the cabinet." His words struck me. "You have played such an important role to this point, and you will have to work with this government now. These are the compromises that we must make. So tell me what portfolio you will accept within my cabinet. Aside from the Ministry of Interior, Foreign Affairs, and Finance, all other posts are open," he laughed. "And I assumed you wouldn't like Defense."

I sat there, thinking. He was right, of course. What else could I say? After so many years as an academic, all I could think to say was "education—minister of education."

"Really?" he asked me. It wasn't considered an especially powerful post.

I replied yes.

"Fine, minister of education then. If that is what you would like, you will be the minister of education." He continued, "There will no doubt be many problems with education. The teachers are demanding quite a bit."

Nineteen eighty-nine was ending, and summer was on its way. The change of government was as impending as the season, still now in that awkward springtime interlude before the onset of summer.

It was also in this strange interregnum between the election and Aylwin's presidency that the two factions of the Socialist Party at last decided to reunite. The "renewed" Socialist Party first led by Ricardo Núñez, now by Jorge Arrate, joined with the socialists from Clodomiro Almeyda's camp. It was an exciting moment after so many years of trying to reconcile. We celebrated our success at the Hotel Tupahue, knowing now that the Socialist Party—united after nearly two decades apart—could at last play a serious role in the government.

In mid-February, I went to La Moneda, along with other Aylwin ministers, for the first time since Allende's death. We had come to make the most of what was supposed to be a civilized transition. All our ministers would meet Pinochet's, and we would be briefed on where programs had begun and finished. I spoke with the outgoing minister of education in a cordial chat. But he left off one rather important detail: The day before he left office on March 11, 1990,

Pinochet would pass an education law that transformed Chile's education system. The ministry was essentially privatized: Schools would receive a certain amount of government spending per student, whether they were public or private institutions. What that meant in practice was that the ministry was rendered powerless overnight, incapable of regulating the new system. Pinochet had taken that one last chance to infuse his neoliberal ideology into Chile. Worst of all, since this was a "constitutional law," it would require a two-thirds majority in Congress to repeal it.

Yet on that day in La Moneda, our minds were elsewhere as we re-entered the palace. After two decades spent fearing it, we were back. Memories of Allende came flooding in, even as my thoughts were preoccupied with all the work we would have to do next. It was overwhelming, and as I left the building that day, and journalists crowded around me, my eyes welled with tears.

SIX

THE MORNING AFTER

I n 1911, Pablo Neruda, Chile's national poet, fell in love with literature. He was just a young boy when he moved to Carahue, a small town in the country's south, so that his father could work with the railroad. Each day, Neruda's father rode the train from Carahue down to Puerto Saavedra, a small port on the Pacific Ocean. It was a modest job in a modest town, but it was where the future poet would discover his most profound love.

Not long after they had arrived, Neruda's father began taking his young son to join him on the daily journey. Neruda was entranced by that first train ride. He saw how the locomotive worked; he saw the moving scenery as they whizzed down the tracks. He watched the steam blow from the engine with a whistle as the cars hit the rail with a click-clack, click-clack. It was, for him, incredible.

But like anything that becomes routine, the romance began to wear thin for both father and son. Neruda grew tired of taking the same route, day after day, and his father began looking for other ways to leave the boy in safe hands while he was working on the railroad.

One day, Neruda's father thought he would try the local library. Its collection was modest—just a few hundred books, really—but from that moment, the young boy fell in love with what would soon be his craft. As the poet recounts in his memoirs, an older librarian, a poet named Augusto Winter, guided him through his first literary journeys, ever in awe of how voraciously the young boy absorbed book upon book.

Neruda's story was often on my mind as minister of education. What power there was in the simple collection of books and the guidance of a librarian! I wondered on countless occasions if there was another library and another librarian out there—in some far-flung village or town—that was at that very moment cultivating our next Nobel Prize winner, and if not a library, then perhaps a school or teacher or program? I knew that our goal should be to reach the point where every piece of the education system would be as conducive to learning as Neruda's public reading room had been. To get there would take a near complete overhaul of our education system, which I found in dire shape when I assumed my duties.

From the beginning, I wanted to send a message to Chile's people: This is going to be hard, but we're going to do everything we can to ensure that the system serves every student equally well. The country's educational infrastructure was broken, and the challenges were enormous. But my goal, aided by countless plans and memos cooked up over the previous two decades in the opposition by Concertación-friendly think tanks, was to transform our classrooms into laboratories of innovation. We didn't know what was going to work. But we were going to find out.

What we did know was how bad it had gotten under the dictatorship. As they did in nearly ever other sector of the Chilean economy, the Chicago Boys took to experimenting with the market in education. When Pinochet took over in 1973, all teachers had been part of the Education Ministry, paid from the top and regulated from there as well. The Chicago Boys radically decentralized: Teachers would answer to the municipal councils, and anyone who had the desire could set up a school. As the power spread out, so did the funding. Each student was granted a voucher, to be received by whatever school he or she attended—be it public or private. Catholic schools that recruited students took their public funding with them, so long as they remained tuition-free.

The problem with all this was not enrollment. Unlike our peer countries around that time, for example, those in Africa or Asia, Chile had enough schools to go around. Over the course of the twentieth century, enrollment had jumped from 30 percent to 94 percent in primary school.

The real problem was quality. There were many places that were so far flung that the market simply didn't reach them. After all, you would have to be crazy to start a private school in the rural areas at that time. There was no profit to be made from teaching a handful of poor students in the middle of nowhere. So the public schools that took on that role were as poor as their students. Nationwide, only about a third of students tested at their grade level. Just one teacher often stood before dozens of students, all in different grades, each with their own level and lack of materials. So common was this predicament that for the 1,200 schools in the rural areas, there were a mere 1,500 teachers. That mattered not just because it rendered classroom management impossible. It mattered because those lone teachers were isolated, as cut off as their respective villages, and they were completely unable to learn from or interact with their colleagues.

Inner-city schools lacked resources as well, since impoverished neighborhoods were just as unattractive from the market's point of view. Teachers were overwhelmed with the task before them. Underequipped and badly paid, many struggled—particularly in the rougher areas—just to keep up with their students. Pupils didn't have it easy, either. Forced to learn in abysmal conditions at school, they often had to work after class, either in petty jobs or at home. It was no wonder that social mobility was a fiction in Chile.

In short, the education system represented Chile's inequality at its worst, replicated over and over by the Chicago Boys' system. Rural schools had fallen behind for their inferior resources and neglect. Even the textbooks had, up to that point, been an afterthought. One language book used in those rural schools, for example, used example sentences such as "Pedro takes the metro to go to class." But most rural students had probably neither seen nor used a metro. And they had certainly never taken one to get to class.

The trouble was, we couldn't fix the system without a two-thirds majority vote. Decades later, that's a majority in Chile that—thanks to the flawed electoral system—we've still never had.

Inequality in Chile—particularly in education—had to be fought with a simple equation: Give more to those who have less. Our government funds needed to "discriminate" in favor of the poor. Impoverished schools needed funding far more than the elite academies along Santiago's main boulevards.

Fixing the education system meant starting from the bottom, rather than perfecting or tinkering with the top. Prove that a child of any age or economic class could outperform the fate of his background, and we would produce a social revolution just as profound as our political one.

The first step was to figure out who was falling behind. Chile has just over 9,000 primary schools, and for many years, the country had used a standardized test to measure how well or poorly they were doing in mathematics and language. Using the test results, we could easily pinpoint the neediest subset of schools—the lowest 10 percent.

Those lowest 10 percent became the backbone of Chile's education overhaul through a program named for them—the Program of the 900. We would give students the resources they needed and turn teachers into innovators, able to make the most of their newly resourced circumstances. The program would have to be paid for with outside help, since Foxley, through no fault of his own, couldn't get me the funds; Pinochet had already fixed a budget for 1990 that we couldn't amend. The Swedish government stepped up, and a year later, seeing how effective the program had been, the World Bank took over as our benefactor, even replicating the program elsewhere.

We began, in the spirit of Neruda, with libraries—small collections of books in every classroom. In the rural areas, we also brought in new textbooks more appropriate to the circumstances. Classroom libraries began with 30 or 40 titles, each on a different subject and at a variety of reading levels. It wasn't much, but it was enough to turn the students into voracious consumers of knowledge—so much so that word spread up a generation; parents started asking if they could also come to the facilities to read. Of course, the answer was yes.

The teachers were our second entry point, and here the goal was transformative. Our hands were tied by the education law in many respects; we couldn't bring the teachers under ministry oversight, nor could we take away the role of the municipal councils. So we had to be creative within the existing system.

There was no more powerful incentive we could use than pay. When I entered office, teaching was a terribly underappreciated profession. It wasn't uncommon for me to find teachers who were paid no more than the minimum wage—the same salary paid to manual laborers. The toughest posts in the most difficult neighborhoods and furthest-flung towns paid the least. The best teachers were all competing to teach at the Instituto Nacional (National Academy) or another of Santiago's finest, well-resourced schools.

Our equation—giving the most to those with the least—required a complete change of direction. We wanted to raise all salaries to a humane level, but the pay structure also had to depend on how qualified and motivated the teachers were. A small percentage of the increase would be based on how long the teacher had been in the system. But two other factors would decide the bulk of the salary rise: how difficult the neighborhood was that you were teaching in and how much additional training you undertook.

First, we needed to recruit a lot more teachers to the poorest schools and reward them for working under trying circumstances. To encourage young graduates to enter the profession in the first place—and to work in the harder spots—we needed scholarships and promises that their pay would be worth the effort.

We also wanted to inject more incentives into the classroom. Doctors, lawyers, and businessmen were always looking for a competitive edge—a new innovation that could take their work to the next level. We wanted teachers to look for the same thing. To institutionalize that culture, we introduced a scheme through which each school and each teacher could draft proposals for new projects or plans to improve their schools. The Ministry of Education would approve the best through a competitive process.

Within months, the requests started coming in. Some schools sent plans to improve their course materials in math, science, language, and social studies. Another group of teachers wanted to broadcast programming on a new radio station, Radio Escolar, a sort of elementary learning channel. We read proposals to start scholarship programs for the poorer students, to publish teachers' work in scholarly journals, to build scientific laboratories, and much more.

In rural areas, we tried to bring teachers together to discuss their experiences and collaborate, ending their geographic isolation. I remember organizing one class of instructors about 125 miles south of Santiago and realizing that, for the many teachers who attended, it was the first time they had been given the opportunity to interact with and learn from their peers. They didn't waste a moment in exchanging stories, sharing experiences, and passing along their own personal tips.

Finally, we knew that teachers couldn't do their work alone. Sometimes, the right person to coach a struggling student wasn't another adult or superior, but a peer—an older student mentor who could relate to the pupil's struggles and fears. For a very small stipend, we invited university students into lower-level schools, where they would work with individual students and sometimes larger classrooms as well. The younger students won an invaluable advocate for their work, and the mentors won often much-needed financial help to finance their studies. Many of those mentors would go on to become Chile's new generation of teachers.

Despite the boost we hoped to give the teaching profession, however, it was the teachers' union that was, at first, the hardest sell. Inherent in all of our programs was the intention to end tenure for school principals, who were to be our engines of change in the educational system. The problem was that once educators reached these top administrative posts, all their incentives to keep improving effectively disappeared. To be sure, many of them worked tirelessly to do the best they could. But many others didn't, and it was slowly debilitating the future of our country's children.

I met with tens of thousands of teachers across the country, trying to persuade them that the changes underway were to their overwhelming advantage. At a time when the economy was growing (although not yet booming), we were promising increases in salary that exceeded inflation by 36 percent over the coming several years.

Persuasion was even more difficult than it should have been, however, because the country's teachers were now under the control of Chile's municipalities, and when I took office, all the mayors had been appointed by Pinochet. We had held democratic national elections, but it wasn't until 1992 that the country would choose their own local leaders.

These Pinochet holdouts were not fond at all of our education reforms, not least because they managed to find similarities to what Allende had once attempted to do. Our mentor program in particular drew great criticism. The right argued that it would serve as a sort of indoctrination into leftist ideology—that these young university students who received money from the state were teaching politics, not just reading or math. They disapproved also of some of our new contributions to the curriculum, such as a new mandate to teach students about human rights. To the political right, the term itself had always been a tool for attacking Pinochet, and again, they cast our plans as such.

So my meetings with teachers inevitably involved talking with mayors as well. One in particular, in the far south of Chile on the archipelago of Chiloé, stands out. I had met an especially stubborn crowd of local politicians as I made my plea for change, and I quickly realized what was going on.

"I know that as mayors, you never thought that you would see me—Ricardo Lagos—as education minister. And certainly, I know you never imagined having to negotiate with me," I told them. Silence. "But I never thought I would have to negotiate with Pinochet's mayors, either!" I continued. "And yet here we are, and we have to work together." It had been the elephant in the room, and acknowledging it helped us move beyond it. At last, some discussions began.

Everywhere we visited, we made slow progress, bringing teachers and administrators on board with our new programs. We realized, however, that we weren't going to win when it came to the tenure system. School principals, like the mayors, were appointed by Pinochet. Whenever discussions turned to limiting their tenure, everything ground to a halt. Meanwhile, in Congress, we lacked the votes to change the tenure system.

Yet even with the most contentious issue off the table, the union remained resistant. They decided to go on strike to protest all these reforms, which I was promoting through a new "Teachers Statute." I warned Aylwin what was coming, and I asked him for permission to address the nation, explaining how our measures would dramatically improve Chile's education system. Aylwin, however, was behind me in the project, and told me that, this being his government, it was he who should address the people.

"But Mr. President, that's precisely the point," I told him. "You are the president. If I address the people, and this takes a turn for the worse, you can just fire me. I can take the blame, and you can walk away unscathed."

In an incredible moment of either naiveté or selfishness on both our parts, Aylwin decided to address the nation himself. I had offered to take the fall, and Aylwin mustered the political courage to ensure it didn't come to that. It worked. The teachers' union stepped down, and our education statute was passed in 1991. Tenure didn't disappear, but the incentives for a more dynamic profession were now in place. Two decades later, the teachers' union would surely go to the streets if anyone tried to roll back our reforms.

The average Chilean child in those days began his or her studies with elementary school, attending faithfully for the eight years that were at the time required by law. Once the children hit high school—when they were old enough to work and mature enough to know that their families needed them too—the enrollment numbers began to fall. Particularly in the neighborhoods where so many were already poor, this was the fastest route to future impoverishment.

Both the beginning and end of that system needed rethinking. Going to preschool was a luxury that about half the country didn't enjoy. All children, you could say, were born equal, but by the time they reached first grade, Chile's inequalities were already entrenched. So we spent the next two decades building preschool capacity for everyone.

High school was a more complex problem. We had to make staying in school more attractive than working. We had to make going to school, in effect, a paying job, offering students a small retainer, a "retention stipend," for staying enrolled. If your family needed you to contribute economically from such a young age, you could do it simply by remaining in class. The amount wasn't much, but it was enough to convince students to stick around—and to set an example for their brothers and sisters to do the same.

Hoping to do more, I solicited the help of the World Bank, by then a donor for the Program of the 900. I hoped it would also help fund our middle-level education plans. I was surprised by the reply that I received: Donors would be angry if the World Bank shifted in any way from its mandated focus on primary education. Not for the merit of our programs, but the myopia of a donor's priorities, I didn't win any grants. Only after several years and a change of government did the World Bank finally realize the chance it had missed and offer to help. It was just one example of the troubles so many developing countries face when their needs simply don't match up to what the donors want.

The other tool we had to discourage dropouts was the legal mandate, which was finally raised from 8 to 12 required years of schooling in 2003. It was an honor to finally sign that into law as president of Chile.

Lower dropout rates have had a monumental impact on university access. In 1990, only 200,000 students were enrolled in higher education. Today, that number has quadrupled, and 7 out of every 10 new students are the first generation in their family to attend college. Which is not to say that the work is finished; inequality is still pronounced. Just 14 percent of the poorest Chileans make it to university, while two out of every three of the richest do.

Just like their younger peers, Chile's adult workers needed to keep boosting their skills if we were to keep on growing the economy. One answer came through libraries, an impressive number of which now span the length of the country. We received funding for a project from the Bill and Melinda Gates Foundation in the late 2000s to boost that number, spending $10 million in foundation money and $10 million in government funds to equip the country's 300 public libraries with computers and Internet access. Today, those libraries offer Internet-literacy classes such that every community—particularly in the poorest areas—can get online.

And use it they have. In the small town of Putre in the extreme north of Chile, between Arica and Bolivia, the Internet has helped draw tourists to the lofty mountain peaks, as every visitor sends his pictures and stories of his experience circling the globe. In the other extreme end of the country, the Guaitecas Islands in the southern archipelago of Chiloé, fishermen of Chilean sea bass are now proud users of twenty-first-century tools. I traveled to this far-flung place, isolated even from airports anytime bad weather rumbles in the skies, on February 20, 2004, to grant certificates in Internet proficiency to 18 newly minted trainees. Their tales were gripping: "This has changed our lives," they told me. "We catch a large number of Chilean sea bass, which sell at a high price on the international market. We had no idea the price that we could get for exporting our fish to Europe!" Their prices, and lives, have taken a turn for the better as their catch is served on tables in Madrid and Barcelona.

In all this, perhaps the most difficult bit was the seemingly simple chore of keeping progress moving, year after year. When one goal was met, it was replaced with another. Not just in Chile, but everywhere, elites tend to reproduce themselves, as do the poor; too often the children of the privileged and the impoverished remain like their parents. Breaking that pattern is the greatest question facing our time—and the answer may someday yield a true social democracy. We're closer, but still far from that moment.

Not long after I finished my term as president in 2006, student strikes broke out across Santiago and several other parts of Chile. The students' main grievance? Their education system was still vastly unequal. Quality still varied widely from place to place.

They were right, of course, despite all the progress that had been made. But what struck me most when those young men and women came to the streets was that this was the first generation of Chilean democracy. Born in

1990 or 1991, these young Chileans had organized themselves not to protest against a dictatorship or an unjust government system. They were there to announce that they wanted a better way to learn. They were a sign of how far Chile had come—and how our work is never done.

I went to meet the cardinal for tea at his modest middle-class home in Santiago. The reception was cordial, but the topic was sensitive. It was some time into my tenure at the ministry, and I had stumbled upon a problem so socially complex that I knew I couldn't tackle it without first consulting the Catholic Church. What was to be done about the 10,000 teenage girls who became pregnant each year and were forced to drop out of school?

Chile's rules at the time were strict: A pregnant student had to go to night school. She should be removed from the classroom so as not to prove a poor example to her peers, the reasoning went. They shouldn't see her pregnant. Maybe the policy had originally been devised with good intentions, but the result it produced was jarring. A massive number of young women were swept away into evening or night school even as the men who impregnated them could remain and study as if nothing had happened. More, the women who chose to abort their children could also continue with class, since the visual signs of pregnancy would never appear. It all amounted not just to injustice but even a perverse incentive to abort—to avoid being socially punished for bearing a child.

As far as I was concerned, the remedy was painfully obvious: We had to allow pregnant students to continue with their regular studies. If anything, seeing their young, pregnant peers would dissuade other students from becoming pregnant, I thought. Still, I knew that changing the rules would spark a conflict—not least with the Church.

By this time, everyone in Chile knew that I was not a practicing Catholic. That was precisely why I had to take so much extra care not to offend the Church—or the majority of Chileans who belonged to it. Before doing anything, I had to have that audience with Carlos Oviedo, the bishop of Santiago and a cardinal within the Church.

I met him at his tidy quarters in Ñuñoa, in the same house where all of the men holding his clerical rank had lived. He was a gentle-looking man, with square glasses and an equally rectangular jaw line. Leading me inside for tea, he sat me down at a table adorned with a few dessert pastries. Oviedo had just moved to the capital, having previously been the bishop of the north of Chile, so I started off with some light conversation, asking him how he was, how he found the new congregation, and how he was settling into the city. But I was there to make a point, and I quickly segued into the topic of what was to be done for the pregnant students.

I explained to him why I believed that the current system was unjust— putting my arguments in terms that I hoped would appeal to Catholic doctrine. Those who chose life over abortion, for example, were relegated to night school, while those who aborted could continue as if nothing were wrong. I explained also that I found it terribly unjust to punish the girls and not the men who had impregnated them.

From there, I transitioned softly into what I hoped could be the solution to all this: letting the young women remain in school to continue studying with their peers. During an adolescence that would certainly prove complicated in so many other matters, I explained, surely their education was one anchor that the girls would be able to depend upon.

The cardinal's face all this time grew soft, filled with empathy and even a bit of surprise about learning such details about the matter. But I didn't expect his support immediately; no matter how powerful my case, there were social forces that made this a delicate matter. After I finished my points, but before I let him answer, I told the cardinal that I didn't need his response right away. I only wanted him to think about the issue, and that we could be in touch. He graciously thanked me and inquired about a few other details, and then we turned to other matters within the government, and how to improve the transition from a long dictatorship to democracy. It was an interesting talk.

Before going, I told him that I wanted to make a decision about what to do soon, and I would be grateful for his opinion before doing so. And then I got up to leave. He smiled at me and said, "Go ahead with what you have suggested; I believe that what you're doing is the correct course." I stopped halfway to standing, my knees almost locked in position.

We changed the policy immediately, with the cardinal's tacit support. He gave his nod of approval by not saying anything at all—by not denouncing what many other priests in the Church certainly would. But aside from brief discussions in the press, there was little uproar. It was as if we had fixed something that most everyone had known was broken, but no one wanted to admit.

Indeed, never have I been so certain that a small change has made such a difference. Years after leaving my post as the minister, I remember visiting countless schools where—of all the reforms we made—it was that single decision that received the greatest applause from the students. An afternoon tea with the monsignor and one change to the rulebooks had recast the fates of tens of thousands of young people.

One family arrived at my office a few months later—on Christmas Eve of 1991—to show me, in person, exactly what an impact the decision had made. A grandmother, her daughter, and her granddaughter entered my office that day, lining up in front of me humbly. "It's because of you," the grandmother began to speak, "that we decided to have this child. Because before that, my daughter would have had to stop going to school." On very few occasions have I received such a moving Christmas gift.

M y eyes were fixed on Augusto Pinochet on March 11, 1990, as he seemed to lord over the Parliament, in Valparaíso. It was the day that he was to leave office—when Aylwin would be transformed from my Christian Democratic colleague into my president. Yet dressed in his finest coattails, military medals adorning his chest, Pinochet looked as if it were his strongest hour. He and his ministers looked proud and obstinate as they gazed upon the ornate room, organized around a long table that stretched from one side to another. Aylwin's new ministers, by contrast, myself included, dressed only in dark business suits. Seated in the front row, we greeted the incoming president as he entered to applause. Pinochet, still commander in chief, stood at the front of the room, where the head of Congress was calling the session to order. He invited Aylwin, as the new president, to join him and Pinochet.

The general coldly, painstakingly began to remove his sash and place it firmly in the hands of the speaker, who then bestowed it upon Aylwin. Then, with as much haste as he could muster, the dictator moved from the ceremony's center, past the row where I was seated, and made straight for the side exit.

As he did, I realized that I wasn't the only one looking at Pinochet. For the first time in my life, the man I had spent decades fighting against—but never met—was looking me straight in the eye. It was a fleeting moment, but he must have seen me and realized that it was I, Ricardo Lagos, the man who had worked so hard to bring about his fall. It was so curious, I remember thinking.

It was the first time I had ever seen Pinochet in person. And now, there before me, was the dictator who had been defeated at a game governed by his own rules, all because his people finally said no.

From the moment we took office, Aylwin and all of us in the government were working to undo Pinochet's dark legacy. Aylwin held his inauguration ceremony in the national stadium where so many thousands had been tortured 17 years ago. As if to signal that we had finally entered a new era, the venue was transformed into a festival, a Chilean flag stretched across the entire length of the stadium's soccer pitch. It was attended by international delegations and, more importantly, some 70,000 Chileans. Hundreds of thousands more would have come but just couldn't fit. Local bands sang Chilean melodies, and cheers celebrated Aylwin's first speech as president.

There we were in a new Chile, but of course the hard work of making it a real change began every morning and never concluded by the time we left work each night. When we met as a cabinet, we would painstakingly discuss each new program, every trial and challenge, our conversations ranging from the celebrations of success to debates over what to do next. We needed to decide, for example, how to handle the former state firms that Pinochet had privatized. Aylwin's view was that it was better to simply turn the page. We all understood that it was better not to go down the road of state expropriation—at least not while Chile was still so divided.

Through all of this, it certainly helped that Aylwin had one of the most adept men possible in the minister of finance position. Foxley had taken it upon himself to control inflation and keep the books in order—and on top of it, to begin a long process of opening up Chile to the rest of the world. Foxley was essential to countering the notion that only Pinochet could run Chile's economy. As Aylwin brought a democratic Chile back to the world stage politically, Foxley did the same economically. The growth that his smart policies produced helped to keep Chile growing and people's lives improving.

What we were doing resonated throughout the world—the way we were tackling the haunting memories of those 17 years and the terrible consequences they had wrought in every conceivable corner of the country. A year into my term as education minister, in 1991, I traveled to a UNESCO conference in Paris, where we held a lunch for all the ministers of Latin America, as well as the French education minister, Lionel Jospin, at the Chilean Embassy, a fashionable building on the Avenue de la Motte Picquet neighborhood. During our lunch, I noticed that Jospin kept peering out the windows of the embassy, down at the square of Santiago de Chile that is in front of the embassy.

I approached him and without my even asking, he said, "That's what I'm looking at, minister," pointing out the window. "You see that tree there? I slept many nights there, between the 10th and 11th of September, every year after 1974, when we came to protest against Pinochet. We were calling for the preservation of democracy and the end of human rights abuses."

He continued, his gaze fixed out the window. "As the dawn came on one occasion, I awoke and realized that, from this very window, someone had been watching us. I never thought that I would be here, as a minister, on the other side, together with you, as a host."

Jospin wasn't the only one my peers and I encountered abroad who had been a part of—in one way or another—Chile's democratic restoration. Tony Blair was another whose political career was nudged along by Chile. He once told me, as well as Isabelle Allende, the former president's daughter, that his outrage over the coup and his interest in human rights in Chile played a large role in his foray into politics.

Two years after Augusto Pinochet had looked me in the eye, I finally had to meet him. That first, short moment of shared glances had been enough for me, but just days before Aylwin shuffled his cabinet so that I could prepare to run for the presidency, I shook hands with the general.

The event began with the annual military parade, which takes place the day after Chile's independence day. After the procession, we returned to La Moneda for tea. It was September 19 by then, and I knew that my campaign would soon take me out of the cabinet. Aylwin knew too and was eager to use that fact to win him some company at the rather dreaded event to follow, a party to celebrate the "glory of the Chilean army," held each year at the military officers' club. I never volunteered to go. Aylwin twisted our arms: I understand that some would prefer to step aside, he told the cabinet, so I would like those who are leaving to go with me. It would be our last chance as members of his government.

I entered the ceremony ahead of Aylwin, alone as protocol stipulated, and mingled with a group of cabinet and other officials. Then the host of the evening, Pinochet, appeared with his entourage, all moving in my and Aylwin's direction.

Aylwin was the perfect gentleman, but he was also quite obviously stressed to have to act cordially to such a man. He turned to Pinochet, introducing each of us. And as he reached me, his voice laced with irony, Aylwin said: "And this is my minister of education, who I suppose needs no introduction. You must know him." Of course, we had never met.

Pinochet held out his hand and mine rose to meet it. Our greeting was cold, neither of us smiling. I'm sure that somewhere there must be a photo of that moment. (In fact, one surfaced during my campaign in the form of a poster asking voters if they would elect this man who shook hands with Pinochet.)

The reception looked set to continue for hours longer, toasts raising over *pisco* sours and old military friends recounting their trials and travails. But after just 40 minutes, I saw Aylwin retire from the festivities, and I took his cue to follow.

I began to walk toward the stairs, heading down for the first floor to exit. But at that moment, Pinochet appeared to see me off.

I'll never know if it was me he wanted to see, or he truly just had a message that he wanted to give me: that the Military Academy was waiting to obtain its official credentials as an institution of higher education. Pinochet's representative there, General Jorge Ballerino, had told him about the progress and asked the former dictator to follow up.

We were making progress in that direction—toward recognition—I told him flatly. And that was that.

The first time I ran for the presidency, I knew that I would lose the primary in Concertación to the Christian Democrat, Eduardo Frei. Much of it came down to his name; his father had been a well-respected president just before Allende's government. I had no illusions, nor did anyone on my team—Frei was ahead of me by a huge 20 percent. Still, it seemed important for me to contest—both to involve the public in the political process and so that Concertación's candidate would have the legitimacy he or she would need to win the broader election.

My campaign was as much about strengthening Chilean democracy—proving that even Concertación was open to internal competition—as it was about actually reaching La Moneda. Anyone registered for Concertación could vote in the primaries, which we had to organize by ourselves, without state help. From the polling stations to the ballots to the monitors, we held Chile's first primary election. Hundreds of thousands of Chileans came out to vote.

My predictions were right, and Frei beat me by a large margin of 63 percent to 37 percent. That same day at 8 P.M., we held a press conference together, and I indicated my intention of working for the new presidential candidate, who would be the flag-bearer for Concertación. He went on to win the national contest with a solid 58 percent of the votes cast. Chileans clearly liked what was happening under Concertación, and they were willing to give us a bit more time to go further.

I was only tangentially involved in the formation of Frei's cabinet, but he asked me to take on the post of minister of public works. I knew it would be an important role in his administration; Frei is a hydrological engineer, and his promises to introduce Chile into the modern global economy implied a massive investment in public infrastructure. So when Aylwin passed the presidential sash to Frei on March 11, 1994, I was suddenly in charge of Chile's infrastructure.

If there was any winner from the High Middle Ages, it was an unlikely city-state on the coast of Italy, built and lined with canals. Venice was perfectly positioned to define the era, not just because of its convenient geography on the shipping routes between Europe and the Middle East. The real reason was because Venice was ready for that moment in history, and those decades and centuries became the city's own.

Years before its monumental rise, Venice began investing. It ships were among the best in the Mediterranean and its ports the best equipped to carry and welcome trade. The city's canals made it a major transportation hub. And when Venice became the transit point for the crusaders, carrying them and then equipping them, again and again throughout the centuries, its place in history was secured.

Chile could be the next Venice—it was the vision that I had always imagined. After centuries of being condemned to isolation by the Andes to Chile's east, the Pacific Ocean to our west, the Atacama desert in the north, and the Antarctic glaciers in the south, suddenly now, our geography was perfectly aligned for the coming Pacific century. Using that luck properly, we could transform Chile into a regional and world giant. Our products could set sail to the world's most dynamic economic hubs. If Chile wanted to become a tiger of its own, we would have to be a bridge between the growing tigers of Asia and South America.

We had to upgrade our infrastructure to accommodate the scale of this opportunity: that meant our ports, our airports, our roads, and our systems of communication. To be a Venice, we would need to link Asian trade and commerce with the markets of Latin and North America. Goods could come in through our largest ports near Valparaíso, San Antonio, and Quintero, plus others in the north. From the docks, products could travel by road, by rail, and by plane to the rest of the continent. The Chicago Boys always believed that this would happen automatically; but there was nothing automatic about the roads we needed to build from Chile's north into Brazil, the 13 links we established between Argentina and Chile, and the airport runway extension that finally allowed the biggest jets to land in our capital. We needed a public policy—guided by the vision of Venice.

First, however, we had to defeat a terrible conundrum. There wasn't enough money in the government's budget to fix up our infrastructure. In fact, it wasn't even close. We would never have enough until Chile's economy grew—and it never would with such dilapidated internal networks.

To find a way out of the vicious cycle, we had to be creative. Poor infrastructure was keeping Chile's productivity down, which in turn lowered government revenues and our ministry's ability to fix up the country. The gap between where we found ourselves and what was needed had three components: internal infrastructure to connect Chile's cities, villages, and towns; human and social infrastructure to improve our quality of life; and export infrastructure to open Chile up to the world. To conquer all three, the government could invest no more than $700 million each year in infrastructure—a massive increase from the $300 million that my predecessor had had in office in 1990, surely, but still far too little. I estimated that we would need four times this much over the next 15 years to achieve our goals.

The answer to our financial woes came with the first project: an expansion of the highway that served as Chile's spinal column—the route that tracked from Arica in the north, south to Santiago, and all the way down to Puerto Montt at the tip of the continent. At least half of the road's 1,800 miles desperately needed enlarging to hold its current traffic. Building a road up to the high standards we sought would be pricey, costing between $2 and $4 million per mile and between $2 to $3 billion in total for a multi-lane highway. It was a monumental investment given our budget. And if we built roads at the speed at which Aylwin's administration had, it would have been 2020 or 2030 before the entire new highway was built.

There were no two ways about it, I realized: We would have to raise private money to pay for our plan. The answer was to enlist private companies and allow them to charge a modest toll.

It may sound strange to hear a socialist such as myself suggest the privatization of Chile's roads' construction and operation. My workers at the ministry certainly thought so, and they lashed out at the idea. The engineers, architects, and other professionals in the ministry were used to their public projects having public funding; many feared that a private scheme would usurp their role as the builders of Chilean infrastructure. Those fears—and the larger debate— spread to the Chilean public as a whole. We were talking about transforming the country's main highway into a toll road. The amount wasn't substantial, but the change of mindset it required certainly was. My main argument to convince the skeptics was a simple cost-benefit analysis: The time saved on a new road would surely outweigh the small toll you'd pay for its use.

The plan worked; we were able to build the road, which was finished by 2004. I finished most of the inter-city roads during my presidential term, at a cost of another $4 billion. Over the next 10 years, $10 billion of investment was recruited to rebuild our network of highways.

All of this boosted our commerce, lowering travel times and making shipping more secure and precise. The time it took to go from Santiago to Concepción, for example, dropped from eight hours to six by bus. Whereas one vehicle used to be able to make the one-way trip three times in every 24 hours, now they could take four trips, using the extra revenue to pay the tolls (and there would still be added profit left over). Travel time to the airport in Santiago went from 80 minutes to just 20. Bus drivers, chauffeurs, and truck drivers all told us how the new roads had improved their working lives.

This had a second, residual effect that we could never have fully antici-pated: Our connecting Chile with better roads had rendered construction much easier for the ministries of education and health, who seized the chance to boost their own social infrastructure. Elementary schools, high schools, hospitals, and health centers sprung up all over the country.

We used the public-private system to improve our ports and airports as well, eventually building eight of the latter. Later in Santiago, we doubled the size of the metro from 25 miles in 2000 to 55 miles by the end of my presiden-tial term.

We also realized, during my presidency, that we could use this same sys-tem of concessions to double our prison capacity. Food and linen services would be contracted out even as state-funded guards kept the order. We could do the same for hospitals, where we easily attracted outside firms to provide the hotel-like services taking care of the residents' rooms and food.

C hilean wine was born of high pedigree into the 1870s aristocracy. It wasn't uncommon for the richest landowners at that time to travel to France, and on one fateful trip, they brought grapes back with them. Cabernet Sauvignon sailed across the Atlantic, across the equator, and down to the other side of the world where it was planted. Chile's wine industry was born.

The first Chilean wines probably weren't very refined, and they certainly wouldn't have been especially tasty to the cultivated French palate. Yet in one of history's great ironies, just decades after Chileans took the grape from France, the French came to Chile to get it back. A terrible blight had wiped out vineyards across the continent's wine-producing regions. So the French traveled to Chile and took the Cabernet Sauvignon on a return trip. Mean-while, Chile kept producing, in slowly improving mediocrity, for years. Using just a few varieties—cabernet, merlot, pinot noir, and sauvignon blanc—the winemakers harvested the grapes and aged them in wooden barrels. Their best blends were sold at home in Chile, and a less tasty wine called Vinex—*vino de exporter*—was made for international sale through the 1930s and 1940s.

One hundred years after it began, however, Chile's wine industry had its second revolution, this one led by Miguel Torres, a Spanish winemaker. Torres realized that Chile's climate could easily produce wine for European tastes—if the product was massaged and refined. The first thing to change would be the barrels; no more wood, since metal was what the Europeans used. Exported wines would be shipped out in bottles, rather than the bulk containers that Vinex had come in for so many years.

With a few tweaks and a lot of care, the modern Chilean wine industry took off. Torres proved that Chilean soils and growers could produce fine wines. As our economy opened up to the world, sales grew as well. Today, some of the best bottles are shipped abroad. Most are best when consumed after 6 to 10 years—perfect for the tastes of an emerging global middle class.

I watched with humble delight as I saw the industry profit from the better roads that we were building and the more efficient ports that sprang up to ship the fruit of the vine. I am a bit of a wine aficionado, so my delight was selfish as well. My home in Santiago, my office, and my house in Caleu all have well-stocked wine cellars full of excellent Chilean blends. And my favorite? I will leave that to your imagination, so that you, readers, might try our Chilean grapes.

When I was just 22 years old, I traveled to the far north of Chile, more than 400 miles from Santiago, to a small mining enclave called Domeyko. We stayed at a guest house run by the mining company operating there. The rooms were modest, and a set of towels was laid out on every one of the beds. But we soon realized that they were never used; there was no running water in the town. Thirty-five years later, when I arrived in Domeyko, imagine my surprise to realize that the towels were still unused. In those 35 years, during which the world had seen so much modernization, Domeyko remained the same.

By the time I came back to this desolate northern town, I was minister of works, which meant that the responsibility for water now lay partly with me. Before I left, I promised that I would return—and bring with me running water. The community was thrilled, if skeptical that we could really deliver. They handed me a small statue of a man in a truck whose bed carried a small barrel of water. It was the symbol of this village, which drew all its water by hand from a well. The guard watching over the city's font would allow residents to draw water for drinking and nothing more.

The water we needed to turn on the tap lay almost two miles outside the village, along the main road that passed by the town. The trouble was, this water belonged to the mining company operating there—or so the firm believed—and they wouldn't hear of our diverting it.

That argument wasn't going to work on me. The water belonged to the community, I told the company officials. When they remained unyielding, I threatened to expropriate the land, placing the territory (and hence the water) under the control of the Ministry of Works. It never reached that point, luckily; my brinkmanship worked. About six months later, Frei and I were back to celebrate Domeyko's first running water.

Domeyko was certainly an exception in those days; the majority of Chileans had access to sewer systems and taps. What was far less secure, however, was the cleanliness of that water. Our treatment facilities lagged behind the standard, even in Latin America.

The sector's organization was a big part of the problem. Under Pinochet, the water industry remained in the hands of the state, but it was massively decentralized and placed under the purview of an autonomous board. The effect was similar to what had happened with schools; the richest pockets of Chile had the best water systems, and the poorest areas of our country went without.

But as with so many priorities in those days, our government budget simply wouldn't cover the investment needed to bring our water system up to speed. As with the highways, we once again turned to the private sector. President Frei had already made some reforms; during his government, the state water company was privatized into three large firms, one in each of Chile's major cities. I modified the system so that these new private investors would act as operators rather than owners, while the water itself—the actual H_2O—remained in the hands of the state. Our rationale was precisely to avoid situations like what happened in Domeyko, where something as vital as water was "owned" by a private entity that didn't necessarily have the people's best interest in mind. And it has worked. In the decade since it was privatized, the system has improved dramatically. Close to 100 percent of the water that circulates through Chilean pipes is treated; nearly every person in Chile has access to this crucial lifeblood.

China is rising, and Chile is today positioned for a monumental historic opportunity: to partake and participate in the new Asian economy. As the center of gravity in world affairs moves toward the Pacific, Chile will finally have a front row seat to history. We have to be ready, and that was always my vision—one that helped make Chile's infrastructure among the most robust in Latin America,

It is only fitting that I made my first trip to China as minister of public works in April 1998. It was a 15-day trip, and I traveled with my sales pitch in my pocket: Chile is your portal to Latin America, I told Beijing. China's leaders also clearly had expectations of me; days before I left on the trip, the ambassador approached me in thanks for accepting the offer to visit. "Here in Chile, you are a minister. But in China, you will be welcomed as a leader," he said. "There are many ministers but few leaders." Perhaps they had done their research and were betting high on my political future. Or perhaps it was because Chile had been the first country to recognize Beijing's China at the U.N. General Assembly in 1971, when I was a delegate.

Toward the end of my trip, I was received by the president of the Chinese Assembly, Li Peng. During an amicable conversation, I made my pitch about trade between our two countries to his welcoming nods. Then he changed the tone a bit. I would be pleased to hear, he said, that Chile would not have to abstain at the United Nations when the Human Rights Commission issued its annual condemnation of China's respect for human rights. The United States had agreed not to bring it up during the commission's next meeting.

Li's words caught me off guard. I had come to China with no intention of broaching such sensitive topics, but now that the issue was there before me, I could hardly keep from replying.

"Mr. President, we learned our own lessons the hard way about human rights during our years under Augusto Pinochet," I told him. "But in all those years, we were always very disappointed that China never voted for the restoration of human rights in our country, in Chile."

My delegation was horrified, and my host may have been as well. What I had just said to this high-level Chinese official could easily get me into trouble and set back our efforts to elevate Chile's economic relations with China. After the meeting, our ambassador warned me we might be sent home. I was sure that the next meeting I had scheduled, with President Jiang Zemin, would be canceled.

To everyone's surprise, however, the visit continued as planned. The next day, when we arrived for tea with Jiang, my staff was dreading what might occur. Instead, the Chinese leader opened the meeting with a remarkable invitation: "I have been told that you are a very important person in Chile," he said to me unexpectedly. "And I think, since you are coming from such a distant country, from Chile, you should have something important to tell me. I will stop here and listen to you, Mr. Lagos."

The message I had intended to deliver was in fact one about economics and trade, and so I began my usual speech—how Chile's ports were an access point to the continent and our country was ready to be Asia's bridge.

"I looked at the program for your visit," Jiang stopped me and said. "And I see that you have visited all of the beautiful places in China. You have not gone yet to where the poor people live.

"I will see to it that next time you come, you see that too—the many difficulties we face with our poor. That's why so many of them move to the cities, to find work. It's not an easy thing for people to move," he continued. "That's also why we only allow our peasants to stay in the cities for a few months before they go home.

"I just returned home from the United States—what a beautiful country! And there, I met an old classmate of mine from here in China now working at IBM. I was so happy to meet my old friend in America. But as I walked around campus, I noticed many signs and posters claiming that I am a dictator. If only they saw all our poor people and all the problems that I have!

"And so I asked Bill Clinton: Why don't you take 10 percent of China's population into America? It would be no more than 120 or 130 million people. And it would be in the name of freedom. 'Impossible!' he told me.

"I replied to him, 'So you are also a dictator, because you have put limits on where people can go. How can I run China if I let everyone that wants to move to Shanghai do so?'"

I understood his point. Without ever saying the word human rights, or even acknowledging my comments to Li Peng, he had explained his philosophy—interests first and human rights later. It is one I still puzzle over and cannot myself condone.

But today China is part of Chile's reality, and for the better. We have a free-trade agreement with Beijing, and China has invested in our mining and other industries. There are even Chinese wineries that have learned from our example.

Looking back at that trip, and all I saw in rising China, I realize how lucky I am to have been minister of education and of public works before I became president—to have seen the worst of Chile's troubles but also the breadth of opportunity unfolding before us.

And indeed, after those two ministerial posts, I was finally ready. In August 1998, a little over a year before the next election, I resigned as Frei shuffled his cabinet, and my second presidential campaign began. This time, I won the primary with 70 percent of the Concertación vote against my Christian Democratic opponent, Andrés Zaldivar. It was the largest voluntary voter turnout that Chile had ever seen.

So my sights were set on La Moneda, facing the candidate of the right, Joaquín Lavin. He had mellowed since the end of dictatorship, from an adamant defender of Pinochet's "revolution"—while a fiery journalist for *El Mercurio*—to a pragmatic, fix-it mayor of the wealthy neighborhood of Los Condes. He won a reputation for making things work and reaching compromise, always trying new things. Some of his projects bordered on the ludicrous (for example, a much-trumpeted attempt to seed clouds so that it would rain in a time of drought—which it never did). But at least he tried to do something, which no one could criticize. His privileged background would prove to be his Achilles heel.

Ten years in power had been a long time for Concertación, and we had surely taken advantage. Chile was a different place than we had found it in 1990—so much so that by the time I would come to office, our difficulties would look as much like those of Europe and the United States as any country in the developing world.

SEVEN

PINOCHET'S GHOST

O n October 17, 1998, Tony Blair was playing Saturday morning tennis Chequers, when an aide approached him with the news: The London Metropolitan Police had taken Pinochet into custody on a Spanish arrest warrant. The issuing judge, an ambitious human rights legalist named Baltazar Garzón, wanted to put Pinochet on trial in Madrid for abuses committed against Spanish citizens under his regime and for Operation Condor—the cynical regional security alliance that targeted political exiles across Latin America, including former Chilean officials like Carlos Prats and Orlando Letelier. The police found the 82-year-old Pinochet at a London clinic, where he was recovering from back surgery, and it was there that they took him into custody. Within minutes, the wires were exploding with the news. Blair was as shocked as anyone, he later told me, not realizing that the Metropolitan Police had been tracking down our former dictator.

My phone rang as soon as word reached Chile. It was late evening by then, and I was preparing to go to dinner at the house of a friend, when the minister of foreign affairs, José Miguel Insulza, rang.

"Ricardo, do you know what has just happened?" he began urgently. "Twenty minutes ago, Scotland Yard has taken Augusto Pinochet under arrest in London under a warrant from Baltazar Garzón." My heart dropped; I didn't know what to say. This would change everything—just days after I had left the cabinet and was preparing my presidential campaign.

Chileans were shocked. Over the coming days, as a long battle began over whether to extradite Pinochet to Spain for trial, tensions grew. Many in the Socialist Party wanted Pinochet to stay put, perpetually in limbo there in London, never to return to Chile again. The parties of the right, however, were outraged. It was a grave offense, they thought, to see their leader humiliated. On November 3, the Senate approved a resolution, by a narrow one-vote margin, condemning the arrest. The measure passed only after a shouting match broke out in the Senate's public gallery, the dictator's family and friends making their case audibly heard. Pinochet's arrest had polarized the country. There were bomb threats, rallies, and nascent outbursts of rage on the streets to the point that President Eduardo Frei addressed the nation, warning against those who would wish "to introduce the germ of violence" back into Chile.

All the meanwhile, Pinochet was passing his house arrest in a comfortable neighborhood in London. He could have been "under arrest" anywhere; being over the age of 75, it was quite normal to be kept at home while awaiting extradition or trial. And a long wait it was; the legal battle over his extradition to Spain dragged on for almost two years. His supporters on the Chilean right began a broad campaign to demand his release and return him to Chile, raising money to help finance his legal and living expenses. In Britain, Pinochet won the support of former Prime Minister Margaret Thatcher, whose free-market philosophy jived nicely with the Chicago Boys' own. It helped, too, that Pinochet had apparently backed Thatcher in the conflict over the Falkland Islands (also called the Malvinas) with Argentina in 1982, and whenever he visited London, he could be spotted heading for tea with the Iron Lady. Only a week after Pinochet was arrested, Thatcher fiercely lobbied the government for his release, arguing that "many British lives were saved" by Pinochet's actions over the Falklands. (Blair reminded Thatcher that he had to abide by the separation of powers and let the courts decide.)

Pinochet had immunity back in Chile, but surely if he was to be put on trial, I thought, it would have to take place in the country where the bulk of his crimes were committed—not in Spain. To watch our former leader prosecuted overseas would be a travesty for Chilean democracy, not because the trial was happening in the first place but because a foreign power had to do it for us. It would signal that we couldn't find the political will and judicial courage to do it ourselves.

I said as much the day after Pinochet's arrest. (In an odd twist of fate, I had already planned to give a press conference that day—although on an incredibly different subject. Yoko Ono had come to open an exhibition, and we were set to talk about her work, my campaign, and my plans for new cultural policies.) I understood the progress that that warrant represented, I said—we now lived in a world in which no one could run from the offenses of their past. The whole world, not just any one country or people, would hold autocrats to account.

Yet while human rights campaigners the world over rejoiced at the "Pinochet precedent"—this idea that malicious heads of state could no longer hide behind their own rigged legal systems—I was troubled by the thought of what might happen. Pinochet could very well see justice, but his victims—in Chile, not Spain—never would. I reached out to the British government to gather a sense of what it might be thinking about the arrest. Allende's daughter, Isabel, and others traveled to London to make their case for trying Pinochet right then and there. I didn't agree, but at the moment, it wasn't my role to interfere.

In part, that was because I was running for the presidency when all this took place. After Pinochet's arrest, I suddenly found myself in a country that was once again polarized by ideology and the power of one man. The mood at home was inflamed by the intense passion abroad. There was a powerful constituency of Chileans from the left in Britain who had fled Pinochet's regime and who now attended every trial proceeding. And there were many Chilean elites in London who backed Pinochet. The court gallery in London, like our Senate box back at home, would often deteriorate into shouting matches.

My presidential rival from the right, Joaquín Lavin, made a pilgrimage to visit the old general at one point, under incredible pressure to do so from Pinochet's rank and file. Lavin himself was rather more cautious about the whole thing; he preferred to focus on "the future" rather than let his campaign get weighed down in a battle over the past. Still, it was perhaps the only thing the two of us agreed on: Pinochet had to come back home.

Pinochet finally came back to Chile on March 4, 2000, just days before I was inaugurated as the next president. Jack Straw, the British home secretary, announced the decision to send him back, primarily on the grounds that he was in no health to stand trial.

The general's plane landed to great fanfare. There was a massive military deployment awaiting his return, the band breaking into music the moment he came into view. They played his favorite song, and television crews gathered around—we all watched it unfold on television. Pinochet was in a wheelchair when he descended from the plane, a crane literally lifting him out of the carrier. Then, the moment he touched the ground, in what his supporters would hail as a "miracle," Pinochet stood up and walked. He took his cane, lifting it from his side, and waved it into the air as if a rallying cry. But instead of placing it back down to assist his walk, he began stumbling forward without it. He was back in Chile.

It wasn't nearly as triumphant as it seemed, however. Scarcely a single member of Congress was there to welcome him, although many from the right would later greet him at his home that evening. Pinochet's legacy was starting to weigh them down. The tension that marked those days was a reminder of what a great hold the dictator's legacy still had over the country. Here was a man whose arrest had repolarized a nation that was slowly becoming whole again. What became more and more apparent was that if we wanted to truly heal, Chileans would have to come to terms with Pinochet's crimes.

Pinochet must surely have thought that his troubles were over when his plane touched down in Santiago, but in fact they had just begun. Five months later, in August, the Supreme Court lifted Pinochet's immunity from prosecution, opening the door to the hundreds of cases that were waiting to be brought against him. Countless individuals and families had filed charges long before Pinochet was even out of office, but until then they had been blocked by his immunity and by the fact that the victims in question had simply disappeared (until there was a body, the cases were still "open"). After the Supreme Court's ruling, the charges only multiplied. And this time, no one seemed to question whether there was reason to bring him to trial.

But the courts had less than two years to move on those prosecutions before Pinochet got lucky again. On July 9, 2002, the Supreme Court ruled on Pinochet's fitness for trial—this time noting that his vascular dementia, a condition he'd exhibited for several years by then, disqualified him from attending the proceedings. He was not well enough to stand trial, the judges ruled; continuing the prosecutions would amount to a form of cruelty.

There was just one problem with that determination, however, from Pinochet's perspective: If he was too sick to be on trial, surely he was also not well enough to continue in his post as senator. Public opinion began to coalesce against him remaining in office. If he cannot attend to his trials, why should he be involved in crafting the policy of the state? He couldn't have it both ways, and that same month, Pinochet finally resigned as senator for life.

The news for Pinochet kept getting worse, and in a few short years, much of the positive legacy he had worked so hard to maintain essentially evaporated, exposed as nothing more than an authoritarian façade. The image that the Chicago Boys cultivated for their president was that of a purist—a disciplined leader who was willing to tighten not only Chile's belt but his own. Nothing did more to shatter that illusion than the revelation that this supposed moral pillar of the state was, in fact, grossly corrupt.

In July 2004, a U.S. Senate investigation revealed that Pinochet had stashed between $4 and $8 million in as many as 125 personal accounts at Riggs Bank in Washington and eight other U.S. financial institutions. Among several aliases he used were Daniel Lopez and Augusto "Ugarte," the latter being his mother's surname. Six months after the initial investigation, Riggs Bank clarified that Pinochet's accounts in fact amounted to $10 million. The dictator had funneled money abroad to other offshore banks as well, under pseudonyms. In total, his stash amounted to some $30 million—a few million here, another million there. His corruption probably began in the 1980s and extended to the upper ranks of the junta. Many had suspected that the fine cars and nice houses that the military top brass had supposedly purchased with their modest salaries were in fact ill-gotten gains. But it wasn't until the U.S. Senate started digging that the extent of the corruption became clear.

As a result of these revelations, Chile's Estate Defense Council, a body of lawyers whose mandate is to guard the security of the national Chilean finances, began another set of legal proceedings against Pinochet, eventually leading to his placement under house arrest in November 2005. The following year, in April 2006, the Supreme Court acknowledged Pinochet's responsibility for the atrocities committed in "Operation Colombo," in which Pinochet's secret police planted false stories abroad to propagate the myth that the dissidents he had disappeared were in fact hiding overseas, preparing a guerrilla attack on Chile. By the time he died in December 2006, Pinochet faced a multitude of charges for human rights abuses and corruption. He was also prosecuted for tax evasion—and several of these cases remain open to this day as

Chile tries to repatriate Pinochet's stolen loot, much of which is tied up in his widow's estate.

Pinochet's own actions did better than any opposition ever could have at shattering his spotless record. In the end, it was the corruption, more than anything else, that laid waste to the dictator's legacy. To many, the disappearances and all the other abuses were something of an abstraction; here was tangible evidence that the "captain general" was actually stealing from the Chilean state. He had no excuse for it either; he had no pressing financial needs. No, he was exactly like the dictators all around the world who rule, in the end, for themselves. It was a devastating revelation for a man who was touted as, yes, a strongman, but at the same time a good and honest economic broker. Making matters worse were the numbers of his supporters who had raised money to support his living expenses during his house arrest in London. The donors were outraged, and the entire right wing was taken aback at having been tricked. They never said it in public, but private conversation was rife with disillusionment. Many of his deepest supporters were shaken in a way that they had never been by all the evidence of state-sanctioned torture and murder.

Of course, to many Chileans, Pinochet's financial crimes were nothing compared with the terrible suffering that his dictatorship had wrought. But those abuses were committed by more than just one man. Pinochet wasn't just a bad seed; something about Chile at that time had allowed him to flourish. We needed to find out what—and make sure that it was purged from Chile's character for good. Because to understand the awful nature of what our society had inflicted upon other human beings was to understand ourselves.

It is a fair question to ask whether any of this would have been possible if Garzón had never filed his warrant and the British police had never arrested Pinochet. It might have taken longer; it might have been even more politically divisive. But Pinochet couldn't hide in Chile any more than he could anywhere else. And bringing him to justice at home was, in fact, the true Pinochet precedent.

Two thousand Chileans disappeared between 1973 and 1988—gone, without a trace or any hint of what became of their fate. They were taken from their homes, off the street, from their places of work. They were sent to Dawson Island prison, to the hundreds of torture centers set up throughout the country, to a network of black prisons hidden in old army facilities, schools, gyms, farmhouses, and factories. For two decades, no one knew where they went. Two thousand families were still desperately trying to find out the truth. Ambiguity was one of Pinochet's most potent weapons of politics: As long as the disappeareds' stories remained secret, an entire group of Chileans—indeed, an entire generation—would remain trapped in the past.

Aylwin knew this when he entered office, and he understood that tracing the roots of the disappeared would be the best place to start in broaching the most difficult topics of the past 17 years. So he set up a commission to examine who had gone missing, when, and why. He chose Raúl Rettig, a former senator of the Radical Party and a vice president of the Bar Association, as the head of inquiry, leading a commission staffed with members of all political persuasions. The goal, as the commission's report later summarized, was "to draw up as complete a picture as possible of the most serious human rights violations that resulted in death and disappearances which were committed by government agents or by private citizens for political purposes; to gather evidence that would make it possible to identify individual victims and determine their fate or whereabouts; to recommend such measures of reparation and restoration of people's good name as it regarded as just, and also to recommend measures that should be adopted to hinder or prevent new violations from being committed."

The Rettig Commission was fundamentally based on the records of the Vicariate, as well as the thousands of habeas corpus cases that were filed by the families of the disappeared when their loved ones went missing. They drew on public records and gathered testimonies from witnesses and family members who volunteered their stories. A few members of the parties of the right participated. The military did not.

It was an important step forward, but the commission had one fundamental disadvantage: The Chilean judicial system didn't have a mechanism to process disappearances. Until the bodies were discovered, any cases opened were merely unsolved kidnappings. And since the Rettig Commission lacked subpoena power, it was toothless in trying to force the military to explain where the bodies had actually gone.

After nine months of work, questions were left unanswered, cases left unsolved. What limited progress was made stirred up controversy all the same.

Many of those who had suffered under Pinochet were relieved and heartened when the commission's report was released, on February 9, 1991. Not everyone was so touched, however. Many on the right called the report biased, since it had not included the military's perspective. Some argued that there had been no "Caravan of Death" assassinating opposition members and dumping their bodies to sea. They believed that most arrests had been undertaken lawfully, and that executions were in accordance with the military's Judicial Code. This was exactly the sort of report that would divide Chile, they claimed—a classic example of history being written by the victors. Certainly, these wounds were still raw: At that time Pinochet was still commander in chief of the armed forces, the right wing still held a legislative majority in the upper chamber, and it had been mere months since Concertación had taken over.

Military leaders were also outspoken about the report. They denounced its findings, arguing that the commission's work was an inaccurate depiction of events, and that they rejected the conclusions outright. The Navy, long the most radical branch of the military, issued the most firmly worded statement; the Air Force, a more moderate force, was slightly less combative.

I was at the Ministry of Education at the time, where I argued that Chile's young people should have access to the report—that it, together with the ideas of human rights, gender, and environmental protection—should be added to their curriculum. These topics were added in the end, but not without a heated political battle.

For all the controversy, the details in the report were difficult to rebut, and for the great majority of the population, its release had a great impact. For the first time, the families of those who had disappeared received symbolic compensation for their loss—one that was now recognized by the state. The families of those disappeared also won a small amount of money and were guaranteed certain social opportunities that they might otherwise have had to sacrifice. For those who lost a father or a brother, the family had lost a salary and the resources to send children to school and take care of aging parents' health. The Rettig Report restored opportunity to those from whom it had been unlawfully taken away.

News of the Rettig Report spread across the world as one of the first examples of a transitioning society making a concerted effort to understand the past. It marked a clear before and after in Chilean history. And three years later, when another famously divided society transitioned to democracy, experts from the Rettig Commission made their way to Pretoria, South Africa, to help Nelson Mandela set up his own truth and reconciliation process.

The report also gave Aylwin the chance to give Chileans something that they had deserved for two decades: an apology. On March 4, Aylwin stood before the Chilean people on national television, and after presenting the commission's findings, he took responsibility on behalf of the state. As president, he was in a position to make amends for the historical mistakes of his predecessors, even though he obviously had nothing to do with the abuses himself and had spent much of his life trying to oust Pinochet. It was an act so magnanimous and profound that it forever sealed the relationship between Aylwin and the people of Chile. Needless to say, until the moment of his death, Pinochet never had the courage to do as much.

B y 1999, as Eduardo Frei was preparing to leave office, the need for further investigation was clear. The Rettig Report had gone far toward uncovering facts, but it still left gaping holes. It failed to uncover where so many disappeared bodies had been laid. Nor had it reconciled any of the players—it had not forced the two Chiles to sit down and work together.

So Frei set up a new process, calling it aptly the Mesa de Diálogo, or Table for Dialogue. If the Rettig Report was about establishing who had gone missing, the Mesa was about finding the bodies—about discovering their fates. "[Finding] a solution to the problem of the disappeared requires knowing the final resting place of their remains, when it is possible, or the establishment, in any case, of their fate," the commission's report states. "If we succeed in this objective, we will have succeeded in providing a sense of peace to the families of those disappeared. But the necessity of understanding their fates goes beyond simply this; it is also about ensuring that our society has a concrete understanding of what took place and what must never happen again."

Doing all that required that the military be involved. It would mark the first time that the armed forces agreed to look into their past.

By the time that Frei became president, most of the officers involved in the 1973 coup had retired. Most of the men from Pinochet's closest rank and file were also gone. But the military was, if anything, even more heavily influenced by the Pinochet years because its leadership had come of age under the general's rule. They had known no other Chile. Many in the military had passed through the intelligence system and had participated in Pinochet's peculiar interpretation of the rule of law.

The Mesa de Diálogo was meant to find out just how much damage had been done. But it was also a means to change the very culture within the military, confronting its leaders with their victims. The setup was literally that of a table, with four sides occupied by the four pillars of the commission. On one side sat the armed forces, represented by its highest echelons of authority. Across from them were human rights activists. The third side was reserved for the Catholic Church and other religious denominations. Rounding out the dialogue were lawyers and politicians from all sides of the political spectrum.

The first days of the Mesa were like ice. The minister of defense, Edmundo Perez Yoma, who mediated the discussions, didn't know where to begin. There were to be 22 public hearings, but in those first days, it was hard to get anyone to speak. Distrust permeated the proceedings as Perez asked each group to begin telling its side of the story. But slowly, painfully, and emotionally, the Mesa started to work. For the first time, the opposing sides of our history were sitting together, discussing and trying to agree upon a definition of the past.

No matter how far the dialogue moved on most issues, however, one topic always froze that slowly thawing table back to ice. It was proving impossible to resolve what was to be done with the countless disappeared cases that were still pending as kidnappings on the legal books. I came to office not long after the Mesa's work began, and one of my first acts as president was to confront the military leadership about the missing remains of the disappeared.

But first, the generals wanted to send me a very public message. During the first week of May, less than two months after I was inaugurated, the commanders of our military branches—Army, Navy, Air Force, and Carabineros— met for a public lunch in a show of support for Pinochet, who was by then facing trial. The press was in attendance, following the meeting closely. Their interpretation? This was a *coup de serviette,* a napkin revolt. The generals were openly defying the president.

More than being angry, I was embarrassed—shamed for our country. Here we were, a fledgling democracy trying to make its way, and our military was trying to assert that it still had a voice in running the show. It was an outrage—an obvious display of support for Pinochet—and I was determined to tell the generals as much. I knew that they were testing the waters, trying to discern just how much power they still had.

I called each general to meet me separately, explaining that the next time they did such a thing, I would denounce them in public. Imagine the generals of France or the United States pulling such a stunt in front of their president, I challenged them. Never would such a thing happen. And next time it did in Chile, I would call upon the people to keep the military in its place. For the first time in recent history, Chile's people were the more powerful force.

It took two more meetings, neither of them comfortable but both terribly necessary, for the military to start to open up. This time, I invited the generals to lunch—the heads of the Army, Navy, Air Force, and Carabineros—and I confronted them about the need to open up their archives to the Mesa. I put the weight of history on their shoulders: Chile's future depended on their actions. They needed to tell me, and the rest of Chile, where we could find the bodies of those who were lost.

Not long after that meeting, Army General Ricardo Izurieta paid me a visit at home. He was dressed in his freshly pressed uniform, a clear signal to me—and perhaps to himself—that this meant business. Military men had always felt uncomfortable coming to my home in uniform, knowing that I had no attendants to care for them, as they had come to expect. I had no servant to hang their coats and hats neatly on the coat rack while we spoke; it was just me who would drape them around the back of a chair. So I knew that if a man came to see me in uniform, he meant business.

He began our conversation in a soft tone. "Mr. President," he said, "it is not so easy for us to tell you where the remains are of those who were disappeared." His voice was sullen as he continued. "You see, many of the bodies were disposed of in the sea. They were carried there in helicopters and dropped."

My pulse stopped. Many years earlier, we had heard the stories about the men who were taken on helicopters and killed, the hundreds who perished this way. I never knew if the rumors were true. I had been among the first to speak publicly about what was going on, spelling out what we had heard in a magazine interview; before then, no one had dared to say these words above a whisper. Now, years later, the head of the armed forces was standing before me, explaining the intimate details.

I could hardly utter a reply. "But did they carry corpses to the sea—or living people?" I swallowed hard. "Were they already dead when they were taken to the sea?"

"They carried corpses, Mr. President."

"How many?"

"At least 200."

Within days, the Mesa had the same information that had shaken me to the core. Two hundred men and women's corpses had been thrown to the bottom of the ocean, weighted down in bags filled with rocks to compensate for the floating effect of their empty lungs.

And this was a mere tenth of the 2,000 disappeared.

Slowly and carefully, the military began to tell us more about where the rest of the remains were. They told the Mesa about one site in an old abandoned mine on the road between Santiago and Valparaíso. Immediately, an evacuation team was dispatched. But after weeks of digging, expecting to find dozens of remains, the team found something even more eerie: no full corpses, but only a few small bones. These men and women's corpses had been disappeared a second time. Their bodies were buried, and then moved. And again, it was Pinochet who had stolen the souls.

It was as if the dictator knew—anticipated—that someone would come back to dig up his crimes. In the last years of his presidency, the military had gone back to its grave sites and exhumed the bodies. It took the corpses elsewhere, relocating them to new sites that even fewer men knew of and that Chile's judicial system was unlikely to ever uncover. Their work was fast and messy; clothes, shoes, buttons, and small bone fragments were left in the cavities where the corpses previously lay. It gave the Mesa just enough information to know what had taken place. But it also prolonged the suffering of so many whose loved ones' bodies were still missing. To this day, many remains have never been found.

The uncertainty of it all tore us apart. These families had already waited so long for news. In 1990, while I was minister of education, I received a letter from a group of families in the town of Valdivia—the relatives of more than a dozen people who had disappeared right after the coup. They had somehow learned where the bodies were supposed to have been buried. But all those years they were afraid to dig them up or even to mark the graves as being their loved ones' own. Now that Aylwin was in office, they thought perhaps they could go ahead. Still, they were nervous that perhaps their doing so would trigger outrage and somehow harm the new government. The solution they settled upon was to write to me for counsel. Should they dig up the bodies? Or should they wait for a more propitious moment?

I read the letter and was profoundly moved. Here was a group of people who had literally been waiting for dozens of years to uncover their relatives' fate, and now they were as concerned about the fate of our larger Chilean democracy as they were about their personal torment. How mature the people of Chile were! I took the case to Aylwin, and we decided to tell them to go ahead, taking their case before a tribunal that could then order an excavation of the site.

But the wait didn't end. The bodies were among the many corpses that Pinochet dug up and moved. When the families exhumed the site, they found only a few small bones, some buttons, some pieces of clothing. The bodies had been there, but Pinochet had covered his tracks, denying those families the closure they needed.

It was a story repeated over and over across Chile. In Paine, a small village about 15 miles south of Santiago, a group of families wanted to dig for their loved ones, whom they believed were buried in a nearby mine. When they finally did, they found only calcified bones, an effect of the minerals in the mine that Pinochet's people may well have anticipated. Now not even the bodies would be found.

Pinochet had covered his tracks in other ways too. When the Mesa released its report on January 5, 2001, its many revelations were clouded by what wasn't included: the entire period from 1974 to 1976, at the height of the operations of Pinochet's secret police. The records for that period were simply gone. Many believe that the head of the organization, Manuel Contreras, took the files with him when he was ousted from the military in 1979. The Mesa couldn't fill the gap with interviews or testimonies; how would they know whom to even ask? The secret police could have detained anyone during that time, and their secrets would remain secret.

The unsolved mysteries still tear at my heart—and countless hearts across Chile. Yet there were openings, and what the Mesa did more than anything was prove to Chile that its people were not permanently, irreconcilably divided. As the hearings went forward, the four sides—military, church, human rights, and civil society—began to see one another as partners in a project of truth-seeking. When they first met, it would have been impossible to imagine what happened toward the end, when General Manuel Salgado, then one of the highest-ranking members of the armed forces, extended a handshake to Pamela Pereira, a lawyer who had represented many victims of human rights abuses and whose own father had disappeared. "Give me your hand at the end of these discussions if we have succeeded in understanding what happened to our loved ones," she told the general.

I read the report through in its entirety on a warm January day, and a profound sadness descended on my being. So long after we started, there were still 600 disappeared persons about whom we knew nothing. A decade since democracy was restored to Chile, we were all still grappling with the most difficult question of the past: How was it possible that our society had let this happen? How could human beings in my country commit such crimes against their own people?

I finished reading late into the evening, and I looked around my dark office with distress. I was 50 blocks from home, but I wanted to walk. My feet moved fast, crossing the sidewalk without realizing how many steps I had taken or how many streets I had passed. Half the reason I moved so fast was simply so as not to be recognized—or to seem hurried enough that I wouldn't be stopped on the street. But it was also out of focus. I couldn't tear my mind away from the images of the people whose paths I crossed. Men, women, young, and old. These were Chileans. I peered deeply into their faces as they passed, searching for some explanation of the kind of humanity that had inflicted such pain upon itself. I did not have, and still do not have, an answer.

In an odd way, Chile's disappeared were the most visible tragedy of the dictatorship. When they were taken, court cases, advocacy groups, and the Vicariate arose in support. Their absence created a gap in society and instilled a perpetual fear among those who were left behind. Maybe they would be next?

But there was another kind of disappearance in Chile during those times: exile. Pinochet robbed some 30,000 Chileans of their country, forcing them to transplant their lives abroad. I had been through the experience myself, although voluntarily, to avoid the worst of the purges. My family had felt the impact too; my brother-in-law Pedro fled to Honduras and then Peru, only to end up in Paris for years, where he became a skilled photographer and learned to speak French. Like so many other Chileans, he made a life abroad. But it was never a home.

We wanted those Chileans back. Many of our most talented thinkers, writers, engineers, and politicians had fled, to the loss of all of Chile. So throughout the 1990s, we tried our best to facilitate their return. We allowed them to bring back their possessions tax-free and helped integrate them back into Chilean life. Modest reparations followed—a symbolic recognition of the pain the Chilean state had caused.

But exile is not an easy thing to end. I was fortunate to be able to return after a relatively short time. For those who had spent the longest time away, some as many as 30 years, returning home was a kind of second exile; returnees no longer knew the country, and their friends and even family often remained abroad. Children born or raised overseas spoke beautiful Swedish or French or English and were in no hurry to return to a country they had only seen in pictures. Many of the Chileans whom I visited in Sweden, for example, were accomplished in their new setting, whether as members of parliament, university professors, or television journalists. How could we ask them to come to a place they hardly knew anymore? Many never did, and others who tried to come back found themselves eager to go abroad again.

Like those exiled, the many thousands of workers who had lost their jobs under Pinochet were hard to help. The dictatorship had forced thousands to leave their posts within the civil service and other parts of the state. These weren't the unfortunate victims of government downsizing; they were fired for their political leanings or suspected sympathies with the left. It was by then impossible to reintegrate most of the workers into the bureaucracy, some 15 or 20 years after they left. So we sought financial damages on their behalves. Special commissions examined each case to determine whether the worker was fired for political reasons or simply for poor performance. Our reparations surely didn't fix the past, but they at least dignified the victims.

I n the dark, furious days after the coup, they came for Gustavo Molina, a soft-spoken doctor and academic. He had roomed with Allende once upon a time, and that was enough. On January 8, 1974, the junta's men took him and two other doctors, Giorgio Solimano and Reynaldo Martinez, threw them into a station wagon, and shipped them to Tejas Verdes, known as Prison Camp No. 2. The military had transformed the facility near Valparaíso, previously an army engineering school, into a torture factory equipped to hold several hundred prisoners at once.

Ostensibly, the point of all this torment was to uncover a "plot" against the military regime. After taking power, Pinochet's junta invented an operation, said to be in the planning stages among the political left, to undertake a counter-coup. They called it Plan Z. It was a complete concoction, but many in the military believed it was a real threat—and thought they were doing their country a service by torturing out the details from the leftist insurrectionists.

In that fight to find coup plotters, Tejas Verdes grew into the epitome of institutionalized abuse. The torture was bureaucratic and mundane, beginning at exactly 9 A.M. and pausing for lunch at noon, only to resume from 3 P.M. until the end of the day. The bureaucrats got to know those they tortured, establishing odd relationships with their daily subjects, in a twisted coworker-like way. One day at the end of a torture session, the man interrogating one of Molina's companions, Solimano, turned to his victim as if in ordinary conversation. The military man began to drink a glass of mineral water and asked, "Doctor, will it make me fat?" Ever the professional—Solimano was a nutrition expert—he replied that, no, it would not.

"If you ever find me outside, Giorgio," the torturer continued, "what will you do to me?"

Nothing, said Solimano. He was a doctor to help people.

"Don't you see?" the bureaucrat intoned. "This is a profession, just like yours."

The doctor's experience was typical of what torture became in Pinochet's Chile—constant, bureaucratic, systematic. Chileans had carried out terrible crimes against fellow human beings. And doing so became simply a habit, a chore—work.

For the exiled, we could offer help with return. For those who lost their jobs, we could pay them compensation. But what could we do for those whose very humanity had been compromised day after day while unjustly in prison? It was the toughest issue left to solve.

It was also the most politically explosive. The right was adamant that a full-fledged investigation would tear Chile apart. But by the end of the Frei administration, the victims were demanding that something be done. I realized that a decision of such historical magnitude had to fall to the president. What was needed was a presidential commission with the independence and authority to establish a record of the truth, led by someone whose integrity was beyond reproach.

It had to be Monsignor Valech, the man who had run the Vicariate de la Solidaridad during the 1980s and who knew better than anyone what had taken place in Chile's past. Tall and strong, with a deep baritone voice, he had become a beacon of moral authority during the years when Chile's government had none. He was born into great wealth, but I only discovered this much later; he had traded his riches for the priesthood and never looked back. It was largely thanks to Valech that the Vicariate stayed out of Pinochet's reach. When the dictator sought to open up the church records, exposing the victims who had come there for protection, Valech stood firm, drawing support from the Vatican. Pope John Paul II sent a personal representative to help firm up the monsignor's position.

Valech's main partner on the commission would be María Luisa Sepúlveda, a woman whom he surely knew well, since she had spent the years of Pinochet's dictatorship working as a lay worker in the Vicariate. She was there at all hours—day or night—always ready to open her arms to anyone who arrived in need of help.

The commission's mandate was "to identify those who lost their freedom and were tortured for political reasons . . . and to propose measures of reparation." Its work would be based on testimony—declarations that we would call upon all affected Chileans to make. We gathered and trained dozens of psychologists, social workers, lawyers, doctors, and judges to work across the length of the country, hearing the stories of what had taken place. In towns, villages, and big cities, we would establish branches of the commission. Embassies and consulates abroad would welcome the testimonies of refugees and exiles who wanted to come forward. Anyone could make an appointment; they could spend as long as was needed telling their stories. If we did it right, we hoped to establish a concrete record for every one of the tens of thousands of Chileans who had been imprisoned. Truth would be the objective; this was no tribunal. Victims could press charges through a special court system if they later chose to do so.

The statements made before the commission were private—and they had to remain that way. What had taken place during those 17 years was the most personal denigration of human character that one can imagine. Women were raped; men were tortured, electricity applied to their genitals. They were screamed at, beaten, starved, and manipulated psychologically in ways that defied recovery. Those Chileans who came forward had to take a leap of trust, placing their experience into a historical record that was incomplete without it.

And so the work began. In all, 35,868 people came forward, 37 percent from the Santiago area and another tenth from abroad, in over 40 countries. Every day, an average of 114 people testified, and at high points, that number reached 240. Everyone's information was recorded, verified, and catalogued. In many cases, the stories could be checked against the habeas corpus records filed by families at the time that they were taken into custody. Torture was verifiable through the patterns that we saw emerge; certain facilities preferred electric shock, others surrounded naked women with rats, offering the creatures the chance to gnaw at their genitalia. Other facilities used waterboarding. The more we learned, the more of a record we produced—which we could use to check new testimony against. Every instance of abuse was documented with the person's age, profession, and gender and where the torture had taken place. Still, we were reluctant, in a way, to summarize the violations into mere numbers and statistics. Doing so would apply the same cold logic the Pinochet regime applied when it committed the crimes. Instead, all of it now represents a dark chapter in Chile's official history books.

For many, it was incredibly difficult to relive the details of all they had suffered. But for others, it provided a sense of peace that the passage of time could not. The same state that had caused them so much pain was finally willing to listen and seek justice. The commission was in and of itself a gesture of pardon and change—a means by which the state could beg forgiveness for what had taken place.

Thirty-five thousand testimonies later, Chile finally had a historical record of torture in the Valech Report. To read it is to take a walk to the depths of the human spirit, what Dante Alighieri must have imagined when he thought of hell. Some 29,000 Chileans were imprisoned during the dictatorship, and the majority—an astounding 94 percent—were tortured. (The other 6,000 testimonies couldn't be verified; or the tribunals established that they had, in fact, committed crimes—stealing, assault, murder—to justify their sentences.) It was all systematic, calculated, and part of a real pathology of violence that dominated Pinochet's state. Ostensibly, Pinochet was quashing leftist plots. In reality, he was only ruining innocent lives.

If the report was a glimpse of hell, it also offered a road to Chile's redemption. It finally brought together our two Chiles—left and right—each seeing the other completely and neither denying the others' pain or perspective any longer. We were looking, finally, in the mirror, faced with the sheer magnitude of the atrocities that had taken place. When we asked how it had been possible—how Chile had let it happen—we finally all knew how to reply. There was no explanation, nor justification, nor possibility to deny.

"How could we live for 30 years in silence?" I asked the country when I released the report publically. "Surely, it was for fear. The report says that 'Lifting the veil of torture, of humiliation, of physical and psychological violence, is very difficult to do. Even between husbands and wives. And that same silence deepened the pain and suffering that the victims shared—giving the impression that it was erased, its pages were ripped out and removed from the record of our history.' Silence could not overcome hatred."

Now, three decades later, we had finally restored a measure of dignity to Chile and its victims. We knew at last what we had lived through and knew that we must never let it happen again. Those years were like a madness that overcomes the soul, purging Chile of its norms and traditions. In the Valech Commission, those values were finally restored. As I told Chile, never again would we live through this hell, nor would we deny that we had.

The air was windy as I walked the streets of Valdivia in late 2009, going door to door to campaign for Concertación's next presidential candidate. I had left the presidency three years earlier but I remained, and still remain, politically active. One of the things that will always invigorate my soul is traveling from town to town and city to city, meeting ordinary Chileans. Local election campaigning was a nice excuse.

At one particular house during that trip, the family invited me inside. The grandfather was sick and in his last days, so the family asked me to see him in his bedroom. The man was frail, laid immobile in his bed.

He knew me instantly and his eyes lit up. "President, I am in the Valech Report," he told me proudly. I asked if he might have a copy of the report somewhere so that he could show me which entry corresponded with his name. The man beckoned to a family member, who pulled the book from a shelf nearby, and the man continued. He flipped through the pages, knowing exactly what number he was headed toward. He stopped and pointed to his testimony. "This is me," he said. "Could I ask you to sign my report?"

As my pen scratched the opening pages, writing even as I was moved by what the report had meant to this man, he turned again to me. "After this report, I can die in peace," his voice was filled with a sort of tranquil joy, "because I have been able to see you and thank you for what you have done."

The Valech Report didn't divide Chile; it gave us all a record of the yesterday that made our today—and still makes our tomorrow. Each of the Chileans who testified before the commission received a copy of the report by mail, together with a note thanking them for their contribution to uncovering the truth. And no matter where I visited in the country, I always encountered Chileans who thanked me for the report.

Like the old man in Valdivia, many of them were proud to say: I was No. 14,506. It was a number that acknowledged the weight of their suffering and made it possible to move on. The report restored public confidence in the country's institutional ability as a consolidated democracy—so strong that it could stare such a dark past in the face and emerge more unified, more sensitive, as a result.

But the most important thing about the Valech Commission was where it finally took Chile. Some people were surely puzzled by the report, but there was not a soul who denied it—or what had occurred in Chile anymore. The armed forces had collaborated so fully and completely with the process that ignoring what took place was untenable. They opened up old facilities, pointed out black prisons on the map, and let the democratic institutions of Chile override the bureaucratic military processes that they had hidden behind for years.

In fact, the army itself was changed by the report. Reformists in the military had been carving away at Pinochet's legacy for several years by then, and the report proved a chance to make a truly clean break.

"Our institution has committed to the end of human rights violations," Army Commander Juan Emilio Cheyre declared just before the report's publication. When the findings were released, the military closed its intelligence service, long the notorious vehicle for Pinochet's abuses. Then, that same general offered what historians already call a mea culpa on behalf of his institution, much as Aylwin had done years earlier on behalf of the Chilean state.

"The violations of human rights can never ever have ethical justification," Cheyre proclaimed, adding, "The Chilean Army took the hard but irreversible decision to assume the responsibilities that, as an institution, fall on it for all the punishable and morally unacceptable events of the past. Moreover it has repeatedly recognized the misdeeds and crimes committed by personnel directly under its command. It has censured them, criticized them publicly and permanently cooperated with the courts, so as to contribute, wherever possible, to truth and reconciliation."

All this is still an ongoing process. It was only in 2010 that the Supreme Court finally established that Carlos Prats had in fact been murdered by the military. And it was just months before this book was written that Prats's daughters were received by the military in a show of respect for their father. How things had changed—when the young girls were growing up, they had called Pinochet "uncle" and thought of him as a close friend of their father's. Prats had been certain when the coup took place that Pinochet was not a part of it—that he would have reasoned against it. That same man—the friend turned junta leader—would murder him.

"Truth and reconciliation" and "post-conflict justice" are buzzwords today. They crop up in every recent post-conflict history, from Sierra Leone to Rwanda to Cambodia. A formula derived from Chile, South Africa, and others has been applied across the world. What I took away from our experience is that the act of seeking reconciliation is a self-fulfilling mechanism: When you ask the questions, truth becomes an inevitable end. Chileans *wanted* to talk about the truth, something that the media was quick to pick up on. They noticed how popular their programs were on the topic, and they began competing for who could produce the best coverage.

Was it the passage of time, the prequel proceedings, or the tribunals that finally brought our country closer together? The answer is surely everything—it took all of this to reunite our two Chiles into one. Time was necessary so that everyone could have the distance needed to examine the past. But so too were the repeated investigations, the consistency of approach, and the determination of the individuals involved at each step of the process. In the end, what was produced was a record so complete, so comprehensive, and so powerful that it was no longer possible to be in denial.

Equally important, we now had the political power to stand strong in the face of difficult findings. There was a time in Chile's history when, if we had asked the generals to stand down or change, they simply wouldn't have complied. Fears that we could regress, even see another military revolt, were not entirely unfounded. As the leaders honored with the people's mandate during those years after Pinochet, Concertación had to prove that we were capable of governing, of being different, of moving forward—even while we dug up the past. The two had to progress in tandem.

To this day, I know of no other country in the world that has tackled the issue of political prisoners in the way that Chile did. Unlike deaths or disappearances, political prisoners are still active members of society; so are the torturers. That requires agility, respect, and an unwavering standard of justice that is both fair and compassionate.

When U.S. President Bill Clinton visited Chile in 2005, I relayed our experience, telling him about the details of the report. I should send him a copy, he suggested. Regrettably, it was only in Spanish, I replied. "It wouldn't be a bad idea to translate it," Clinton told me. He had a point; we translated the executive summary into English, and I sent him a copy right away. Ours became perhaps the most exhaustive investigation into political abuses that the world has ever known. That's how we exorcized Pinochet's ghost.

As I traveled throughout the beginning of my presidency, one question seemed to always awkwardly come up. Every foreign leader wanted to know: Does Pinochet's legacy still weigh upon Chile?

In many ways, it was harder to convince the world that Chile had moved on than it was to convince ourselves. Despite the reparations, the ongoing commissions, the Mesa, and the Rettig Report, Pinochet still haunted us on the world stage. Surely such a man must have cast such a dark cloud over the country that it would take years to lift, they seemed to think. What finally convinced the world that Chile had moved on was, of all things, a cabinet reshuffle—a move that, in my mind, was entirely about governance. In the summer of 2002, I needed to make some concessions to the Christian Democrats in hopes of improving my relations with them in Congress. My minister of defense at the time, Mario Fernández, was a Christian Democrat and a well-respected member of the party. I asked him to take over as secretary-general of the presidency, Chile's equivalent of a chief of staff. (The post had previously been filled by a member of my own PPD.) And to the position of minister of defense, I transferred Michelle Bachelet.

Bachelet began her political career quietly, and she had gone unnoticed for years. She ran and was defeated for a seat on the city council of Los Condes, a wealthy neighborhood in Santiago, back in 1992. A doctor by training, she later joined the Ministry of Health as an advisor.

Around that time, the military was trying to demonstrate its increased openness to civilian control, and one of their first measures was to open up courses at the military academies for civil servants within the government. Bachelet's father had been in the military—among those who opposed the coup—and she had grown up immersed in Chile's armed services. So she decided to enroll in the classes, where she surprised everyone by finishing first. The reward for such an outstanding placement was to travel to Washington to attend the Inter-American College of Defense. When Bachelet returned from Washington, she took up a post working with Perez Yoma in the Defense Ministry.

Bachelet was surprised when I offered her the minister of health post at the beginning of my administration. I called her to my apartment for the news, and I remember her response. She was of course excited, but mostly taken aback. "Mr. President, I am so surprised. Of course, if you think I can do a good job, I will take the post," she said. But her face looked as if she wanted to say something more. "It's just that I thought you were calling me here to place me somewhere within the Ministry of Defense, not to name me a minister."

When the post did open up, Bachelet seemed the perfect candidate for the next minister of defense. She had a deep understanding of military strategy, and she had proven too that she was an effective administrator.

But of course, to the public eye, this was a very different kind of choice. Bachelet was the first woman ever to be appointed to the office and, even more, the first socialist to occupy it since Salvador Allende's time. Bachelet also had another history with the military in Chile: she had been tortured and imprisoned by soldiers at Villa Grimaldi, an extensive prison complex just outside Santiago. Her father, a general in the Air Force, had also been arrested during the coup and later died in detention. Needless to say, her appointment sent an indisputable signal that the military was now completely subordinate to civilian control. And to the world, it was also a signal that we no longer lived under Pinochet's shadow.

Now there was just one thing left to do. Sixteen years after the referendum that ousted Pinochet, his 1980 constitution was still officially in effect. It was a deeply authoritarian document. As they had said of Franco's regime in Spain, *Todo quede atado y bien atado:* Pinochet had left everything closely wrapped up. The constitution, the entire system—everything was nearly impossible to unravel. The military still had an incredible amount of power over the president. It took a huge majority to amend the constitution, and, on top of it all, the flawed electoral system ensured that we would never dramatically overpower the right.

At first, knowing that it would be difficult to change the laws on the books, we simply changed our behavior. A meeting of the National Security Council, for example, could technically be called by either the president or two generals. But I made it clear to the generals that they must never do so—or I would denounce them before all of Chile. "If you call a meeting," I told them, "you had better find somewhere to host it. Because it won't be in La Moneda if I do not agree to have the meeting." The longer we behaved like a democracy, the more popular it became for us to do so, ridding ourselves of the last vestiges of the Pinochet constitution.

Then finally in 2005, we were able to amend it. We got rid of the National Security Council and gave presidents the power to dismiss commanders in chief. In all, the reform introduced 51 significant changes, including provisions for the independence of the Constitutional Tribunal, the Supreme Court, and the Electoral Commission. The presidential term was reduced from six to four years after my own—fully half of the length that Pinochet had given himself during his last "term" in office.

What a day it was when I finally signed those documents and saw a new Chile reborn. It was my name that lined the bottom of the constitution as president of the republic—instead of Augusto Pinochet's.

Now, several years later, a debate is opening about whether and how to draft a new constitution altogether. It is a project many Chileans have long supported, and one that only became possible once the air was cleared and the authoritarian remnants of our past were finally vanquished.

When I was a young boy in school in Santiago, my friends and I often wandered toward La Moneda, approaching its front gate and embarking on an awe-inspiring journey from one end of the presidential palace to another. The colonial building, built in majestic white with beautiful wood columns, was open for all Chileans; after all, it was our republic. The two main courtyards saw hundreds of passersby each day, walking through the seat of power and remarking at what must have been going on behind those doors. I loved that walk through Chile's center, feeling as if I was somehow touching part of the history.

Those gates were closed late in the 1960s, and when Pinochet decided to occupy the restored La Moneda, the gates remained closed, just like so many aspects of Chilean society. On my very first day in office, I re-opened them. The palace belonged to everyone. Hundreds and thousands of Chileans came to pass through, remembering their own walks in childhood or seeing La Moneda for the first time. Tourists were amazed to discover they could simply walk through the presidential gates—no metal detectors, no long wait. Those open doors were what we meant by democracy: Everyone was allowed.

Three years later, I decided to open another gate. The thirtieth anniversary of the military coup was approaching—September 11, 2003—and something was needed to commemorate the date. I remembered a question that I often received from passersby as they walked through La Moneda's courtyards. Where, they wondered, had Salvador Allende died?

On that anniversary, we would finally commemorate that place where Chile's democracy died. It happened on the side of the palace, where for 70 years a small door had opened directly onto the street. One particular president at the beginning of the twentieth century, Federico Errázuriz, had opened the passageway for his mother, who lived close by and was accustomed to frequent visits. From there forward, the door became a private entryway for Chilean presidents. It was the first door they walked through when they were transformed from civilian to president and the last door they left, leaving the head-of-state office and rejoining the civilians on the street.

Allende's body left through that door—as did the last defenders of La Moneda who escaped the bombardment during the coup. Allende had hurried those who were remaining down the stairs and out into the streets, insisting that he would be last. Then he never followed. He closed the door and ascended up the stairs, telling them he had forgotten something. He sat down on a red sofa with a gun pointed into his mouth and killed himself.

Pinochet bricked up the door. He was never a civilian; he had never planned to give up his role as head of state. To him, the door was illogical and of no symbolic importance. So when he reconstructed the palace after the bombardment, he simply didn't build that doorway back. For 17 years, it didn't exist.

In March, I ordered the passageway to be reconstructed and ready by September 11, 2003. The door was opened on that solemn day, with Tencha Allende, the ex-president's wife, nobly at my side.

It was a symbol of how Chile had regained its respect, pluralism, tolerance, and unity of national spirit. There and only there did the sacrifice of the last 30 years really make sense—amid the spirit of those who died there, and those who fought with everything they had to restore Chile to its former civilized self.

Today as I think back, it has not been easy to declare that the ghost of Pinochet no longer haunts Chile. But in the 20 years that we fought to exhume and understand our history, we came out stronger from our digging. Chile looked into its past, saw the pain and horror, and emerged whole. We saw the errors committed and vowed not to repeat them—nor deny that they took place. And it was through that very act of truth-seeking that we discovered something we didn't even expect: the most profound qualities of the Chilean spirit—to forgive and never forget.

EIGHT

THE CHILEAN WAY

I f there is one overarching lesson of the six years that I served as president of Chile, and the many years I worked in Concertación, it might be this: A good government stands on three legs. In order to prosper, any modern country needs democracy, economic growth, and social equality. Lose any one component, and the whole apparatus could easily come crashing down. Work hard on all three, and you'll find the sum is greater than its parts.

By the time I became president in 2000, Chile had made monumental progress toward re-establishing democracy. My predecessors also earned high marks on economic growth; under Concertación in the 1990s, the economy grew at an average rate of 6.3 percent a year. But if our first 10 years were about reclaiming our liberty and prosperity, my term as president would have to be about making sure that victory was shared by all. We needed to couple our economic progress with social justice.

My tripod theory of government was quite a change for Chile. For nearly all of the country's history, our leaders had focused on one pillar or another, always neglecting the other two. Pinochet, for example, built his regime on the idea that economic growth alone—spread unequally and unfettered by democracy—could ensure stability. Even Allende had a preference, focusing on redistribution over a strong overall economy and polity. But it was Pinochet's vision that triumphed, and at the turn of the century, the richest 10 percent of Chileans held almost half of our country's wealth.

We now know just how wrong both sides of that debate were. We failed to understand then that a country cannot be strong when it stands on just one leg, be it economic or political. We need democracy and growth in equal parts—and we need to make sure that the gains in both areas spread to every corner of society.

This was the task before us when Concertación arrived in La Moneda in 1990, and it was a task that Chile is still working toward today: To forge a Chilean way. With the political right intent on growth and the left intent on social justice, it would take all of our strength to carve out a path somewhere in between. I had to go deeper and further than where Aylwin and Frei had left off.

It would have been an impossible task no matter who we were. And when I became president in 2000, I was the first socialist president to occupy La Moneda for nearly 30 years. The right viscerally distrusted me; the left expected me to enact a program of massive social redistribution. Instead, I was going to disappoint every ideology—because it was the only way not to disappoint the Chilean people.

On the day I took office, Chile's economy was in crisis. Between the time I filed my candidacy for the presidency and my inauguration, the Asian tigers collapsed, freezing capital markets and drying up investment. Chile, like much of Latin America, was reeling. That year, our unemployment rate rose by half, up from 6 percent to 9 percent. It would soon touch double digits. The Asian financial crisis had spread.

Worse, the price of oil was rising up and up, becoming prohibitively costly for many Chileans. And at precisely that moment, the price of copper, Chile's most important export, collapsed to just 60 cents a pound—less than half its pre-crisis value. Back then, copper accounted for 50 percent of all Chile's exports as well as a significant portion of the government budget. Our copper revenue dried up at exactly the moment we needed it most.

The downturn was terrible news for our agenda. If we had any hope of lifting Chileans out of poverty, we would have to find a way to pay for it. In other words, my promises of greater equality were staked upon whether we could restore economic growth.

Adding to the difficulty, as the first socialist president, I knew from day one that I would face an uphill battle on economic matters. I would have to go above and beyond the norm to assure Chile's investors that their money would be safe in our country and that our government could manage the budget responsibly. The stakes couldn't have been higher: 80 percent of the investment in Chile comes from the private sector, and a mere 20 percent is governmental. If those private investors fled, it would spell disaster.

It was a crisis in every sense of the word—but also an opportunity, if we could take advantage of it. We had to do something immediate and demonstrable, something that Chileans would benefit from straight away, boosting their confidence in both the economy and our government. We had to create jobs—a lot of them—and fast. I began speaking about the subject on the campaign trail, promising to create 200,000 my first year in office and another 100,000 each year after that, for a total of 700,000 over the course of my term. We would do it with public works programs and economic stimulus. We were still catching up from the two decades in which Pinochet's government did nothing to improve our infrastructure. Two-lane roads from 1973 were still two-lane roads when the junta left power. This was a chance to make up for lost time. Towns got new central squares; highways were paved. We could create thousands of jobs this way with comparatively little money, whereas focusing on rebuilding work in the mining sector, for example, would have been far more expensive. It takes between $1 million and $2 million to create a new job in copper.

I was confident we could do it as I didn't expect the Asian crisis to last. But I broke the first law of politics with the very specific promises that I made, setting precise targets during dire economic times. During my first year of office, the economy grew 4.5 percent, creating 100,000 jobs—not bad but only half of our promised 200,000.

Yet just as I didn't learn that first law of politics, neither did I learn the second: to fudge when results fall short. One must govern truthfully, I believed, so in September of that year, the moment I realized that we were not going to reach the number of jobs I had promised, I spoke frankly on television about why we had missed the goal. The crisis, I explained, had swallowed us completely. Luckily, by 2005, we had created those elusive 700,000 jobs. (Although it is much more difficult to create jobs in the last year of one's administration than in the first.)

If job creation was for our people, macroeconomic reforms were for the investors, whose cash and entrepreneurship we needed. Chile was a serious place, we wanted to remind them. Chile couldn't be a country that expropriated property, that suddenly changed tax rates, that borrowed excessively, or that defaulted on its loans. We had to be as frugal and smart about our cash as a household. The first countries to emerge from recession would be those that were the most dependable and stable, we realized—the ones to which investors could flee when times got tough elsewhere. Chile had to be one of those places.

Much of what this meant was straightforward: We needed to uphold the rule of law, and continue giving our Central Bank—Chile's equivalent to the Federal Reserve—the freedom to operate without political pressure or concerns. We needed clear regulations and we needed to be open to trade. Much of this work had also begun during the administrations of Aylwin and Frei. And before the Asian financial crisis, the investment gains were clear. Chile's per capita income grew at four times the rate of Latin America as a whole during those years. Our economic growth also dwarfed that of other countries in the region; in a mere seven years, we doubled per capita income. Clearly, something we were doing was working.

But what was equally clear was that Chile demonstrated the tell-tale symptoms of a country cursed by its natural wealth. At the whims of the price of copper, we were vulnerable to crisis and unable to stand strong when the global economy was wavering. We were a country that was up when the world markets were up and down when the world was down.

To overcome that fundamental weakness, we needed to be the first country since Norway to beat the so-called resource curse.

To wean an economy from its dependence on natural resources is to overcome one's very humanity. As anyone with a wallet can attest, it's hard not to spend when the fold is stuffed with bills. Why should we have focused on building up other economic sectors when copper—or oil or iron—brought in more than enough wealth for the government? How could we convince citizens that their government should save during good times when the needs for social spending were so incredibly great? How could we keep the Chilean state from bloating when times were good and shrinking when prices sank?

Rarely in history has a country managed to overcome such destructive inclinations brought on by resource wealth. Even in democracy, it has proven difficult. Power changes hands, so even if one government is frugal, another might not be. If one administration is careful to avoid the resource curse, another may not be so inclined.

So we had an idea—one that emerged from listening to academic circles and among the group of Concertación economists and thinkers who had spent time in Europe. There, governments often base their budgets on long-term economic prospects rather than annual ups and downs. My minister of finance and budget director picked up the thread and presented me with a proposal to do the same: We should stabilize our budgets regardless of the copper price. Rather than re-drafting Chile's budget with every commodity price fluctuation, why not make our best guess about what the long-term price would look like and base our spending on that? If prices were down, we could avoid painful cuts to social programs and keep the economy on track. If prices were up, we could start saving for less robust times. Budgets would be written with the long-term price of copper and other exports in mind, rather than the daily whims of the trading floor.

The system would have three advantages: First, it would get Chile's budgets in order and avoid artificial cuts or growth spurts. Second, it would give international investors a clear picture of what to expect from our economy, no matter the commodities markets. Third, it would act as a built-in economic stabilizer in times of crisis. When the economy was down, the budgets themselves would be a stimulus based on the long-term figures rather than the short-term lull. In economic speak, what this amounted to was a countercyclical policy of saving during the booms and borrowing during the busts. We had a built-in response to recession.

It was enough for me just to pronounce that this would be my government's economic principle—one that I resolved to implement. I vowed to follow the new rules during my administration, explaining the benefits to the Chilean people. But when Wall Street heard about the idea, investors were very intrigued. If this could be enshrined as part of Chile's long-term economic policy, it would be a boon to international investment. Particularly since we were kicking off the system during a recession—when we'd be spending more than we had—investors needed to know that we were serious about taking the much harder steps to curb spending when the price of copper bounced back.

To prove our commitments were serious, we institutionalized the promise. The new budgeting system would work this way: One committee would estimate the long-term price of copper and a second would evaluate Chile's broader prospects for growth. The budget had to be written according to those two estimates. During low copper-price swings or economic downturns, we would borrow to spend, since government revenues wouldn't reach the expected amount. When copper was peaking and the economy was strong, the extra money that we brought in would be cordoned off into a fund that no government could be tempted to raid. We imagined saving an annual surplus of 1 percent of GDP—an ambitious but necessary goal. (Bachelet later reduced this from 1 percent to 0.5 percent.)

We set the initial "long-term price" of copper at 89 cents a pound, meaning that anytime it was above that level, Chile was saving money. For the first several years of my term, that was good news; it allowed me to spend more than I would have otherwise been able to. Back then, the price of copper hovered at a mere 60 cents per dollar. In retrospect, that was probably why the policy was accepted; no one—particularly from the political left—had the stomach for cuts, and this offered a responsible way out. So while all of Latin America was cutting back, we kept our economy churning. As a result, even as the rest of the continent's economic growth sank in 2002, we grew by 2.2 percent.

Of course, the real moment of truth came when the global economy began to recover beginning in 2003. The price of copper exploded, hitting an incredible $3 per pound. So dramatic was the shift that our panel of experts raised the benchmark price from 89 cents to $1.10. But we never spent more than that amount, and the difference was stashed away. Tax revenues from 2003 also grew stronger, and what surpassed our long-term forecast was saved for rainier days.

When the markets crashed in September 2008, the wisdom of our policy became immediately clear. As credit dried up and investment retreated the world over, Chile could not only keep spending at its usual rate but was able to drop an economic stimulus package that, relative to the size of our economy, was one of the five largest in the world. Over the eight years that we had followed the rules, our savings fund had reached $20 billion or 15 percent of GDP, and we put a fifth of that into stimulus.

Looking back at 2001 and 2002, I realize how difficult it was to undertake such a policy. Many a government—from Venezuela to Chad—has failed to create a fund for the future without yielding to the temptation of populist policies when times are good.

We couldn't be so short sighted. Chile's copper may well be exhausted by the end of the century, and what we leave behind for our children must be more than a legacy of patronage and rents. The wealth we gain from the earth today must be reinvested in creating another natural resource: an educated people who are able to run a new, modern economy after the copper is gone. Chile stands as an example, perhaps a useful one to any country that has depended heavily on what lies beneath its soil. Oil will run out; coal will be burned. What remains must be more than just an empty mine or a dead petrol drill.

And to those governments wary of abandoning their resource rents, Chile's experience is evidence that the benefits of prudence are far greater. This is a world in which money knows no borders. When Chile proved its economic stability, its seriousness of policy, and its dedication to the rule of law, investors of the world took note. Today, the cost of doing business in Chile is among the lowest in the world precisely because of the trust that the Chilean economy and polity inspires. The premium investors pay to cover political risk in Chile has consistently fallen, even relative to developed markets. Every day, we are strengthening our institutions, our economic policy, our growth, and our social cohesion—all things that tell investors that Chile was a good bet to make.

That's no trivial accomplishment. If our national risk had been that of the rest of Latin America all those years, it would have cost Chilean companies and businesses about $1.36 billion more to borrow money in 2003. Our stability was, in effect, a subsidy of the amount equivalent to the entire annual investment budget of the Ministry of Public Works.

A final factor in all of this was our tax system. Chile's rates are among the world's lowest, and I promised not to raise them, understanding that this would be attractive for businesses looking to operate in our country. I also promised to lower the evasion rate by eliminating loopholes. In September 2000, I sent a law to Congress that would allow us to lower tax evasion from 25 percent to 17 percent. I refused to raise the value-added tax (VAT) on consumption, which was already a drain on our poorest people. Everyone paid that tax at the same rate of 19 percent, which meant that the poor felt by far the most pain from every purchase.

During my legislative battle, I learned an important lesson about taxes: It's nearly impossible to change them. Chile's tax brackets are incredibly unfair. We are one of the very few countries in the world, for example, that has almost exactly the same distribution of income before and after tax returns are filed. In other words, our tax system completely fails to redistribute; it is not a lever for equality so much as a lucky break for our wealthy. To see why, one need only look at the policy for corporations: All over the world, companies are taxed on their profits. But in Chile, our 17 percent tax is collected only on the value of profits that are distributed to shareholders and employees as compensation. All the rest of the profits can be invested tax free.

That's a legacy that we've had to deal with. I remember proposing changes in the tax code to my finance minister, and him responding that, since growth was up, it would be a bad idea to mess with the system. "But no time is ever good," I told him. "When the economy is weak, you can't raise taxes, because that would hurt growth even further. And when economic conditions are improving, the instinct is to say, 'Well, let's not touch anything since we are growing!'"

When I arrived in Bandar Seri Begawan, Brunei, in November 2000, I had one thing on my mind: trade. The obscure island city-state on the tip of the South China Sea had rolled out its red carpet for the leaders of the Pacific Ocean economies, including Chile and, notably, the United States. This would be Bill Clinton's last visit to Asia as president, and I was planning to make a pitch: Chile wanted a free-trade agreement with America, I told Clinton. And I was ready to negotiate.

For Clinton, however, this wouldn't be easy. Just two years after the North American Free Trade Agreement (NAFTA), was passed, it seemed as if the bounds of America's patience for open economic borders had been defined. Blowback from unions and activists decried further openings. And Clinton lacked the so-called "fast track" facility that would have allowed his administration to negotiate trade pacts without fear that Congress would intervene in the details. What that meant in practice was that the negotiations would be long and treacherous, fraught with amendments, backtracking, and partisan wrangling.

But I was determined, and I told Clinton as much. "Let's begin to negotiate," I told him. "And if things fall through, I will come to the United States and address Congress, explaining to them exactly why Chile needs a free trade pact."

Free trade was one of the many ways in which I must have surprised Chile's political right, disproving what they must have expected from their socialist president. These agreements were vital to the economic program for Chile. We were a tiny country, and we simply needed access to bigger markets. When such trade was protected by treaties, it wasn't vulnerable to political whims; firms could be assured that their exports would be allowed to enter the world's biggest markets.

There was another reason for the Chilean economy: Free-trade agreements encourage producers to add value to the goods they export. Without such a pact, tariffs are always higher on finished goods. While raw agricultural goods or crude oil can usually cross borders tax free, clothing, furniture, or electronics garner increasingly steeper tariffs. If we could gain free access to developed markets, our businesses would have an added incentive to export finished goods. Our economy would grow more sophisticated; jobs would open up, staffed by university graduates and skilled workers. In a word, we would develop.

Aylwin and Frei also understood this, and when I assumed the presidency, we had already signed free-trade agreements with Canada, Mexico, and several other Latin American countries too. Still, the U.S. and European markets eluded us. And they also happened to be the most important destinations for our exports.

I decided to begin in Europe, understanding that making our case to the United States would be easier if we already had the European Union (EU) on board. At the time, a larger group of Latin American countries, Mercosur, which included Argentina, Brazil, Paraguay, and Uruguay, was already negotiating a similar pact with Brussels. Geographically and economically similar, we easily added our agreement to the agenda, and our two pacts, for Mercosur and Chile, went through negotiations in tandem.

Being tied to Mercosur had the advantage of getting us in the door, but it soon became clear that the negotiations were fraught with tension, much of it from disagreements over agricultural products. The two giants of Mercosur, Brazil and Argentina, were agricultural economies. And the barriers to entry in the European market were sky-high, given how integral farm subsidies are in the European economic system. For Mercosur countries, those handouts meant that their goods, no matter how efficiently they were produced, would never compete. So for any trade pact to move forward, the countries argued, EU subsidies on farmed goods and livestock would have to go—or at least go down.

This put Chile in something of a bind. Our economy was not agricultural, even if we did produce some farmed goods for export. We weren't interested in holding up negotiations until European farm subsidies came to an end—not least because we knew it was an unachievable demand.

Sensing our divergent position, in early 2001, Pascal Lamy paid me a visit on behalf of the European Commission. We were good friends, having met long ago as fellow socialists; he had been one of the most influential social democrats in France before moving to his new role as chief of staff for Jacques Delors and later as commissioner for European trade. I knew I should heed his advice. We transitioned straight into the business of negotiations. "France is not happy with the way the negotiations are going with Mercosur," he began to explain. The Élysée Palace had no appetite to negotiate agricultural subsidies. Since this mattered little to Chile, Lamy suggested, "Why don't you speak to the government of France and propose that you de-link the negotiations for your agreement from those of Mercosur?"

Weeks later, I arranged to meet with the French government, on April 17 and 18. The evening I arrived, I sat down to dinner with Prime Minister Lionel Jospin, another friend from my days as minister of education.

"This is the finest wine in Paris," he proclaimed at the outset of the meeting, setting an upbeat tone. And indeed, the conversation moved forward smoothly. Trade with Europe, I explained, was vital to our economic growth. I knew that this was a man who would understand our political predicament, so I also explained how important an EU agreement was if we were to convince the United States of the same. Moreover, this was an agreement that would be far easier to sell at home in Chile, since European agreements carry with them promises of cultural and educational exchange. Finally, I explained how, unlike Mercosur, we weren't bothered by the subsidies. I knew that this was really the heart of the issue for the French.

The next day at lunch, I offered the same proposal to President Jacques Chirac. Chirac was a beer drinker—an odd thing for a man so quintessentially French. But he opened wine for me. "This," he said, "is the best wine in all of

Paris," he proclaimed. I chuckled a bit. "Better than the prime minister's?" I asked. "Of course!"

"Don't worry, Mr. President. If you sign a free-trade agreement with Chile, our own wines will never compete with the French wines.

"Mr. President," I continued. "We know that the subsidies issues that Mercosur is raising are complicated. But why not work separately with Chile? We are a small country—and we won't bother with the business of subsidies." As an added advantage for France, I told Chirac, if he signed an agreement with Chile, it would prove that France could negotiate such a pact with a developing country—and that the problem with the Mercosur agreement wasn't a French fear of agricultural and industrial competition from the developing world. Chirac seemed convinced. France was on our side.

But of course, if you want to persuade the EU, you cannot win over France without also convincing Germany. And not long after I left Paris, Lamy called me again in Santiago with those exact words of advice. Germany was less keen on Chile separating its negotiations from Mercosur. The government in Berlin would have liked to see the expensive agricultural subsidies trimmed down; as the largest economy in the EU, Germany paid the bulk of the handouts to countries like France and Spain. Mercosur provided an out. Little Chile was getting in the way.

This was one of the first times that it truly struck me how countries such as Chile figure into the global system—as instruments to be used in the agendas of larger powers. Chile's trade agreement wasn't particularly important to France or Germany—or to the broader EU for that matter. But it suited these two countries for another agenda that had more to do with the French countryside and the German coffers than the Chilean economy. It could easily have been a depressing revelation, to realize that the country I led was, in so many ways, so very small. But it was also the key to understanding how to get what Chile needed—the key to playing our cards right.

I traveled to see the chancellor of Germany, Gerhard Schroeder, not long after, and I was received in his newly renovated quarters in the chancellery. My strategy was to pretend as if I didn't know that Chile was being discussed in the context of the subsidy debate. I understood, I explained to Schroeder, that the subsidies issue was at the heart of negotiations with Mercosur. We in Chile were not a part of that fight. So what loss would it be for Berlin to endorse our tiny country's trade agreement?

Schroeder understood and told me he could "make it work." So it was on to his foreign minister, Joschka Fischer, whom I would also have to convince. Here again, I presented Chile's case for free trade, adding that if Germany signed on with Chile, it would be proof that the EU had no problem negotiating free-trade pacts—and specifically free-trade pacts with Latin America. It was just Mercosur that was making things complicated.

Finally, my persuasion worked. And with both France and Germany convinced, we were able to move speedily from there to sign an agreement in May 2002 with the EU.

Then it was on to the United States, where equal persistence—and even more time—would be required. Chile's copper already came in and out of the United States tariff free, but part of our strategy for defeating the resource curse meant moving away from a two-tiered economic system in which copper was privileged before almost everything else.

We began our negotiations shortly after Brunei despite Clinton's warnings that it could get tough. Our countries' teams were able to lay the groundwork before the change of power in the United States; from there, the real discussions happened under George W. Bush. Luckily for Chile, the new president had won the fast-track facility from Congress. Free trade was a politically popular cause in those first years of the Bush administration, with Republicans in Congress and a politically adept trade negotiator, future World Bank President Robert Zoellick, at the helm. These were times of strong economic growth; they were also times when the United States was eager to win allies for its War on Terror.

Still, that didn't mean getting a free-trade pact was easy. Labor unions in the United States protested at first, and we had to explain our labor laws to allay their concerns. Even more difficult was convincing the U.S. Treasury Department about a rule we had in place to prevent foreign capital flight. In times of crisis, we wanted to have the ability to implement a mechanism wherein every foreign dollar that came to Chile had to stay there for a year. This wouldn't be the norm; during everyday commerce, dollars could come in and out of Chile in a matter of hours with no problem. But in times of crisis, such a facility could prevent speculation and sudden crashes in foreign investment. Fresh in our minds was the Mexican peso crisis of 1994, when capital had fled from that country so fast that the entire economic system almost instantaneously crumbled.

The World Bank and the IMF had both gotten behind exactly this sort of one-year minimum investment mechanism as a way to stave off system collapse. But that didn't matter to the U.S. Congress. To Washington, the policy seemed interventionist and anti–free trade. Our talks with the Treasury were arduous, with neither side terribly eager to cave.

But during the final stages of negotiating with the Treasury in December 2002, I decided it was time to put in a word with Bush so as to explain exactly why the one-year rule was so necessary. I was quite sure he would not be kept in the loop on such a technical—yet important—detail unless I brought it to his attention. I asked National Security Advisor Condoleezza Rice for a phone call with the president. The negotiations were in their final stages, she explained, so the best course was to wait until the following morning. If everything went as planned, Bush would simply call to congratulate me. And if there was some sticking point, we could then discuss it.

The phone rang at 7 A.M. the next morning, a characteristically early call from Bush.

"Condi tells me that there's nothing for us to discuss this morning, Ricardo, because everything is sorted out. All we have to do is applaud!" He was jubilant, throwing in a few Spanish words here and there as we talked. I was pleased too. We'd done what we had set out to do.

What saved the deal in the end was an innovative trick that allowed each side to save face. The United States would protest every time the mechanism was enforced—but Chile would have a year to respond, which in practice meant that we got our one-year rule.

Not long after we signed the trade pact with Europe, a solemn-looking Frenchman arrived at a fruit farm in the south of Chile unannounced. It was a summer day, during what had been a frigid winter in Europe. The farm had recently begun exporting produce to a French pastry shop. The supply was perfect in timing and size; it came just when the frost was chilling the Parisian countryside and the warm sun was growing our strawberries, blueberries, and grapes. But when the Frenchman arrived, he wasn't interested in inspecting the vines. Almost immediately after shaking hands with the Chilean farmer, he began inquiring about the crop's water supply. He wanted to see it. And he wanted to run a water-quality test, right there on the spot. If the water failed, that Chilean farmer would lose his best new client.

Signing Chile's free-trade pacts was, in many ways, the easy part. The real work began when Chilean goods actually had to start to compete. These next obstacles are what you might call "non-trade barriers." In plain language, our standards weren't up to snuff. The hard part was when the French—and the Americans, Germans, Italians, and others—actually came looking for Chilean goods, and we had to make them appealing for Western consumers.

It wasn't just the fruit producers. The day we signed those long-awaited trade agreements with Europe and the United States, not a single one of our meat or dairy producers could have met the standards to sell their products in these newly opened markets. Our refrigerated containers weren't up to par, and our processing wasn't modern enough. Other products also lagged behind as well, not meeting the high quality necessitated by the agreement.

Indeed, what the trade agreements provided was the opportunity—not the market access itself. Chile would have to work for years—we are still working, in fact—to become the modern economy that our trade agreements require. It was a golden chance: All of a sudden, Chile had an incentive not just to produce raw goods, but to make them into products—brandable, marketable, and ready to earn a far more handsome profit.

The government also played a role in this. One of the biggest challenges we have faced in modernization is Chile's energy supply, since we lack any fossil fuels of our own. For years, we had imported natural gas from Argentina, but during the beginning of my term, the supply became less reliable, and we were forced to look elsewhere. We began to buy from the international market instead, building a terminal to receive the stuff on our Pacific coast. We also harnessed the power of Chile's water supplies to boost our hydroelectric capacity, which today provides about half of the electricity for Chile's largest urban areas. It was an example of how the state and the economy are inextricably linked, even in a free-market economy.

Many Chilean entrepreneurs were also up to the task, like the nut farmer I met when I visited his plot just south of Santiago, in a town called Linderos, as president.

"I used to export almonds in bulk," he told me as we toured his farm. "Then one day it occurred to me: Why not visit the United States and see how they packaged their almonds? That's what I did—and I was surprised to find that their methods were so labor-intensive," he continued. "I realized that the cost of labor in Chile was surely much lower than that of the United States. So if I could do what the Americans did, my packaged nuts would sell for less." After reconfiguring his production chain, within just months, he had found a U.S. buyer: hotel chains that used the Chilean almonds and walnuts in the mini-bar.

He handed me a package as I left, offering me a sample. They were far more elegant than the boxes I had seen just moments ago in his packaging shop. The ones he offered me were destined for the five-star hotels, he explained. It had worked, I thought to myself: Our producers were adding value to their goods.

Today, Chile exports gourmet meats, fish, and processed goods to Europe and the United States. We send wine to American grocery stores, and our grapes also stock their shelves. We ship furniture to California. Chile is everywhere.

Surely by now, the skeptics are convinced; this socialist president opened doors to the private sector. I knew that globalization was here to stay. And I knew that meant that the private sector and the government shared a common ambition of economic growth. Firms, companies, and small businesses do the heavy lifting of creating jobs and pushing forward new products and services. But it is the government that provides the context—the investment climate, the management, and the stability to get work done. This is an important characteristic of the Chilean way: cooperation between business and state to make the economy grow. That's how we have been able to achieve so much.

Inequality is the best-kept secret of the last 50 years. Global prosperity has skyrocketed since the 1950s and 1960s. Standards of living have risen exponentially. By every possible economic measure, the world is better off today than ever before in history. Except one: how the riches are spread. As the world's average wealth has climbed higher and higher, the disparities between those who control it and those who don't have grown even wider. In 1976, the richest 1 percent of Americans controlled 8.9 percent of U.S. wealth, for example. By 2007, that same group controlled a massive 23.5 percent. We live in a world today that is vastly unequal. And it's getting worse, not better.

Developed countries like the United States, France, or Canada can afford to grow a bit less evenly. But Chile has no such leeway. By the end of the twentieth century, the disparities between our richest and poorest had reached unsustainable levels. While our elite could compete with the world's top businessmen for wealth and stature, our poorest suffered through substandard schools, could barely afford health care, and sometimes even went hungry. Our cities were still ringed with sprawling shantytowns where men and women scraped by in tin metal-roofed shelters along the river. Concertación constructed a great deal low-cost housing in its first decade of rule, but not nearly enough.

Feigning ignorance or callousness was not an answer; that was what Chile had tried for two decades under Pinochet. Those poor people—whom the dictator had ignored—were the very same Chileans who believed in democracy again and helped us bring it back. For their basic human dignity, and to prove that their belief in democracy was not in vain, we were determined to reduce the number of people living under the poverty line.

The question was how to do it. Should we build housing for them? Hand out cash grants? Lean on charities or churches to provide services? Sometimes our answers came from government advisors and economists; other times, communities, unions, and even whole regions made their case for our attention. Everything was done with a simple intuition: to restore dignity to Chile's poorest members. "Growth with Equality" was what we called it.

There was no more visible problem than housing. One out of every five Chileans was unable to afford a roof over his head. Some were unemployed or held odd jobs; others' salaries simply weren't enough to cover all of their families' needs. To build a country upon such deprivation was to build a skyscraper with no foundation. No matter how fast our GDP or exports grew, we would leave 20 percent of Chileans behind. Without a home, no family could build an economic life for itself. This was perhaps the most basic human need, and we couldn't leave its fulfillment up to chance. But neither did we have ample wealth of money or resources through which to help.

So we had to be strategic. First, we needed to know whom to help, and it was clear that we should focus initially on those who had the least. Next, we realized, Chile was desperately short on affordable housing; we were going to have to build it. We set out to construct 100,000 modest houses per year, about

400 square feet each, equipped with potable water, a bathroom, and a kitchen. Those few square feet felt terribly small, and they were. But as a family got back on its feet again, they could be expanded to about double or even quadruple the size. We intentionally built the houses using an architectural plan that anticipated future growth. The one and only payment required for the houses was just $300.

Our program, Vivienda Social Dinámica sin Deuda (Dynamic Social Housing without Debt), was the subject of much internal debate from the day we began. Some in my cabinet worried that the "Casas Lagos," or Lagos Houses, as people came to call them, would be too small; no one would want to live there. Others worried that we were simply moving the poor from one ghetto to another, relegating them to the same fate by another name in another location. They would build dependency; they would set a bad precedent.

But how wrong we were to be concerned about such things. We should have simply asked the poor. The demand for the Casas Lagos was overwhelming, so much so that our builders couldn't keep up. We added 100,000 houses a year, spread across the country. The logistics involved every piece of the community, which may well be why they worked. The City Council allocated the land and drew up waiting lists. The people themselves helped decide where they wanted a school and other services. Law enforcement was reorganized to ensure that the houses wouldn't be home to crime. We were constructing new communities, not just new buildings. Now, a decade later, Chile can truthfully say that it has almost eliminated slums.

The 2010 earthquake brought tragedy; 150,000 houses, many of them older houses made of adobe, were destroyed, and an equal number would need to be reconstructed. But had we never set out on the housing project in the first place, our loss would have been that much greater. And in many cases, it wasn't the poorest who were hit by the earthquake, but the middle class, who can secure loans to rebuild. With Chile's help, they will.

I arrived in Lautaro on an icy day that froze my every breath as soon as I took it. The town is small and quiet—no more than a village really—located at Chile's southern tip, in a region called Araucanía where our indigenous people, the Mapuche, used to live. This was 1999, when I was traveling the country from top to bottom for my presidential campaign. But on that particular trip,

I decided to make a spontaneous stop, dropping in to see a doctor at the rural medical center. I was curious to see what the conditions were like—what "health care" meant in this village.

When I walked in the doors, a group of villagers had gathered in the waiting room, wrapped in coats to keep warm while they waited to be seen. They looked hearty but worn, tired of the cold beating down their backs. I introduced myself and then asked a simple question. "What could be done to improve your health care? What do you lack or need?"

A woman's voice jumped in to respond. "We need a stove heater to keep us warm while we are waiting."

I had come to Lautaro to discover what it was like to seek health care in a rural clinic, and now I had my answer. So desperate were the conditions that a heater was the first priority—not the health care, not the doctor, not the medicine. So great were their needs that an attitude of resignation prevailed. Health care was a luxury, and so the expectations of the poor were low: just something to warm the room.

Chile's health system in those days was as unequal as the society it served. The richest among us had access to first-class facilities, doctors, and insurance plans. The poorest had access only to the most basic care. In 1990, at least 780 children died each winter in Chile when they caught the flu or another respiratory infection for which they were not treated. By 2005, we would lower that number to just 70. But it took all of our political strength.

The irony when we began is that health care was already enshrined into law as a right of every Chilean. But only a quarter of Chileans had private health insurance, the ticket that allowed them access to the best and most specialized care. The rest, a majority 75 percent, had to depend entirely on the public health facilities. What that meant in practice was that three quarters of Chileans were locked out of a system of private clinics and well-trained doctors. The right to health care existed on paper. In reality, it depended on our fixing the system—and specifically, fixing the national, public system.

Allusions to healthcare reform at that time conjured the foreboding experience of the United States, whose first lady, Hillary Clinton, had tried and failed not long before to amend the system there. In Washington, the push for change had been a devastating failure, for both the administration and the millions of Americans who lacked health insurance. Congress had harpooned the reforms; powerful lobbies got their way. We were determined to learn from America's mistakes and hopefully avoid them ourselves.

As luck would have it, the man in charge of our health reforms, Hernan Sandoval, knew the chief Clinton aide for health care. Throughout the 1980s, Sandoval had worked with the World Health Organization in Mexico, when a young Ph.D. student from the United States came to visit and conduct research. The man, David Michaels, became Sandoval's advisee. They also became friends. And so years later, when Michaels worked for the White House as the assistant secretary for environment, safety, and health in the Department of Energy (today he is the national director of the Occupational Safety and Health Administration), he opened every door to Sandoval. He pulled every expert and interest from the U.S. healthcare fight into a room in Washington to speak to our Chilean health reformer, who then asked them point blank: Why did things go so wrong?

The answer he heard was helpful: Reforms had failed because they had been narrowly focused on the 45 million Americans who lacked health insurance. They had tried to reform a system that included 200 million Americans by thinking of the 45 million who were looking in from the outside—the least politically powerful and most disenfranchised. They didn't represent any political constituency with power or influence. They couldn't push the right levers of pressure to get vested interests on board.

Chile's politics have more in common with the United States than perhaps either country realized. We both have a free-market history and a powerful business class. But we also both have poor who remain largely on the margins of political life. So if fighting for the poor had failed in Washington, it would surely fail in Santiago as well. We decided that our own healthcare reform had to include everyone, both those who were part of the public system and those who used private health care.

We also had to start by defining the pathologies specific to our healthcare system—what exactly was going wrong. It helped me to think of a story I had once heard about Chinese emperors. When the leaders and their families were in good health, the doctors were paid well and regularly. As soon as they fell ill, the doctors would cease to be paid. Those doctors could make no mistakes: They were responsible for the health of the emperor. The incentives behind our modern system in Chile were the polar opposite.

The problem with services started with primary-care physicians, the doctors whom patients seek out for their basic needs—when a woman is pregnant, when a child is sick, or when the elderly have arthritis pain. This is where vaccinations took place, where colds and flus were treated. It was where Chile could prevent or limit the worst outbreaks of disease. But when I took office, only 12 percent of the Ministry of Health's budget was devoted to primary care. (For comparison, that number is around 50 percent in Britain.) I set a new goal of boosting our own share of funding to 30 percent, which we achieved by the time I left office. Back then, too much of our health care was happening in hospitals—which told us that too many people were waiting until the situation became dire.

The problem with "the system" also had to do with entrenched interests in the industry. No matter what reforms we undertook, we could be sure that we would be pitting ourselves against the private insurance firms. Anytime we spoke of expanding services, these companies feared that they would take the hit, suddenly competing with free care from the state, even as their clients had to share their well-trained doctors with a larger share of the population. Doctors also worried about expanding care without expanding the healthcare workforce. Physicians were equally opposed to the kind of protocols and standards that would have to be a part of any reform. We would have to decide what tests and procedures the government would cover, or not—a decision that physicians believed would be best left to them. This wasn't a matter of being stingy or controlling on our side; we just simply couldn't write a budget if we didn't know what services the government would be asked to pay for.

But the supposedly rosy status quo that both the insurance firms and the doctors defended—good health care for patients and high wages for doctors—never existed to begin with. What happened instead was that men and women who paid their insurance premiums for years—decades—would suddenly find their coverage dropped when they were actually diagnosed with a condition. To cover costs, the insurance companies stacked the risks in their favor, preferring to offer plans to the young, the male, and the wealthy. Patients were abandoned for "pre-existing conditions" or treatments that were supposedly uncovered by their original plans. Health insurance contracts were written on a year-to-year basis, and if you developed a condition, you could wake up on January 1 and realize without warning that your contract had not been renewed. It was unjust not only for those without insurance, but even those with it. (All of this may sound familiar to many Americans.)

The flawed system meant that there was a large constituency for change. On our side were the millions of Chileans who had to save for months to afford a doctor office visit or had to borrow to pay for emergency care. On our side were the middle-class citizens who had paid their premiums for health care but received little in return. Confident we could win support for an overhaul, a team of about 20 aides, thinkers, and economists in my administration set about to reimagine the system. And over the course of 2002, we proposed four bills to Congress covering various components of our proposed reform.

Our strategy was to start small. We wanted to give all Chileans access to the specialized care that they needed. But we began with just a few key specialties. We went to Congress with a plan to guarantee Chileans access to 56 medical pathologists, which together constituted 70 percent of all hospital care. For each one, we would guarantee that a patient should be seen at a decent hospital or clinic, that treatment would have to take place within three months, and that if the patient lacked the resources to cover the usual co-payment, the government would pay the full cost. We planned to pay for all this through a public-private healthcare fund—although in the end a political battle with the opposition in Congress forced us to settle for something much simpler: a tax on alcohol and cigarettes.

Our plan also promised to increase the number of cases that the health care system would have to support, so we had to think hard about whether we had the capacity we needed. Guaranteeing access to care was never going to be enough; a guarantee of care would translate into long lines if there was a shortage of doctors or hospital beds. Luckily, capacity wasn't the problem; it was allocation. We had enough doctors and hospitals, but they were just clustered in the private sector.

The answer, then, was to make the system more efficient. We planned to decentralize control of Chile's public hospitals, putting control in the hands of the medical teams that ran them. Rather than working in private clinics all day, the doctors would do their surgeries and hospital rounds in the morning, retiring to private clinics in the afternoon for private appointments. If there was not enough space in the morning rounds for patients from the public system, the state would extend the hours in the hospitals in the afternoon and send patients there. In extreme cases, the state could "buy" surgery appointments from within the private sector.

Making sure that these reforms happened freely and equally for all required appointing a superintendent—an office within the government meant to settle disputes and make sure that our guarantees for care were happening on the ground. In the extreme case, citizens who felt that they were denied care could turn to the courts to oblige the state to pay for their care at a private clinic.

We crafted our reforms to meet as many demands as possible, while improving the chances that all Chileans would receive quality care. Every citizen would now be able to make and pay for a medical appointment. Doctors would expand their patient base while still retaining their lucrative private clients as well. Those who preferred health insurance could keep it, but everyone had access to the state system. These reforms weren't outside our reach, nor were they more costly than the country could afford. We increased the Ministry of Health's budget by a mere 20 percent—very small relative to the increase in coverage that we provided to our people.

Still, it was a hard fight, as fighting entrenched interests always is. We didn't have a majority in the Senate, and the proposals met hard opposition there. So I called on the Chilean people to stand behind me: I spoke about the numbers of patients who were excluded from care. I spoke about the real people who had a real interest in reforming health care—but who lacked both the political power and the voice to speak on behalf of their demands. The doctors had a political voice, so did the nurses, the lobbyists, and certainly the insurance companies. But the majority of patients had none.

Inevitably, our law was held up in Congress. But I wasn't willing to wait, so we began a pilot program through the Ministry of Health—guaranteeing access to a small number of pathologists in order to demonstrate how our larger system would function. We started with just three specialties and later five, giving a hint of how beneficial the new system could be and how it could economically function.

It was around this time that the battle got nasty—when the opposition went from voicing concerns to making accusations. They were annoyed that I had begun my pilot program without their say. My administration had also begun to advertise the new services, putting up banners and signs in favor of the change. The parties of the right put forth a complaint to the comptroller general against me, claiming that both these moves were illegal. They also started their own public information campaign of sorts, picturing me as Pinocchio in public ads and decrying my conduct.

But public opinion decided the contest. The pilot program was popular—so popular that the people demanded more and more medical specialties be added to it. Resistance slowly faded, even among the private sector, after we demonstrated that the approach could work. And at the end of the debate, we finally walked away with a new healthcare system, the Acceso Universal con Garantías Explícitas (AUGE).

Having the people on board was the key to making Chile's healthcare reform move forward. If they hadn't supported us, no one would. And if we tinkered with something so dear and so personal without explaining why it would help, we would lose not only our legislative battle but the people's trust in our policies across the board. Knowing this motivated me to travel the length of the country, explaining our plan. Making the case for change was just as important as doing it.

To be sure, we made sacrifices along the way, of the sort that political compromise always necessitates. We had to raise the alcohol and cigarette tax to cover the costs, instead of using the fund I had proposed, for example. But what we achieved is far greater than anything we lost.

Since AUGE came into effect in 2005, thousands upon thousands of procedures and operations have been performed under its purview—some 17,000 cataract removals and 10,000 cesarean sections, for example. But more importantly, ours was and is a healthcare experiment in offering explicit guarantees of care on a level never before undertaken. In addition to the mere services this has yielded, AUGE has transformed the mentality of Chileans toward health care. Every citizen today is an active, empowered consumer. They understand what their rights are and when they will have to pay from their pockets. And for all the Chileans now covered by the system, that has made for very healthy change.

I t would have been easy to stop there. Our old healthcare system was the biggest piece of Chile's warped social structure. It was among the most fundamental causes of inequality. But it wasn't the only one.

Next in line was the pension system, long ago privatized by the Chicago Boys under Augusto Pinochet. But Pinochet never had the reams of elderly that Chile does today. As recently as 2003, about 11 percent of Chileans were over the age of 65. By 2020, that percentage will double. Across the Western world this is increasingly the case, exacerbating budget crunches and increasing state welfare burdens. Britain, France, Germany, and the United States have all toyed with the idea of raising the retirement age, shaving a few years off the benefit system. Back in 2004, we considered the same idea. Our answer was to scale the pensions by age, paying less to the youngest and more with each year after age 75. The system remains privatized, with a key caveat: if your private funding runs out in your lifetime, the state will supplement those funds up to the minimum standard pension level.

Another piece was unemployment insurance, which Chile lacked altogether just a decade ago. If you lost your job, there was no aid from the state and no temporary assistance to fall back upon. This seemed incredibly unfair, particularly as we promoted exports and trade. Global commerce often rises and falls at the whims of the market, leaving workers hired or fired as well. It was normal for the marketplace to adjust—but there was no market that was going to take care of the jobless. One of my first moves in office was to introduce unemployment insurance for a short, six-month maximum, although this has been extended over time. Like most countries, we had an extensive debate about the knock-on effects that unemployment insurance could have on our labor market—about whether it would deter workers from looking for jobs or make them complacent. But at least so far, there is no evidence that anything close to the excesses that can be seen in places like Europe have come to affect Chile. And during the most recent financial crisis, unemployment insurance has served as vital life support for the 5 percent of workers who lost their jobs with the crash.

Poverty is such a sticky thing. It was depressing to realize: After all our social policies, and after all we had done to expand the services available to the poorest of the poor in Chile, the bulk were still entrenched in desperation. Overall rates of poverty had been cut in half since the 1990s. But these drops were largely from the middle, not the most desperately poor. To be destitute, we realized, is not just to be without resources and money. It's a form of severe social isolation. And nothing we could do from La Moneda would help puncture it. We needed an intervention much deeper within poor communities to finally reach those most distant Chileans.

So in 2002, I decided that we needed new ideas. How could we reach the poorest of the poor? I asked a group of political scientists and analysts from both Concertación and the opposition. Cash transfers were suggested by some, but others objected for fear of the clientelistic dependence this could produce or the impact such a handout could have on the dignity of the recipients.

Then we stumbled upon a very different possibility: Chile's poorest probably weren't aware of all the services that we had put in place for their use. They would have no way of knowing, for example, about the stipends for students who stay in school or the extent of our healthcare reforms. So isolated were these communities that they would not be reading the news; their social networks wouldn't necessarily provide them with this civic information. And so our services were likely underutilized by those who most needed them. If the poorest weren't coming to us for services, we would have to go to them. Our idea was to send a social worker, a "family helper" (*apoyo familiar*), to visit every one of Chile's poorest areas and explain their rights and their access to state facilities. The family helpers would be members of these very communities, trained to offer support to their peers as they worked to transcend extreme poverty. We knew exactly who these families—earning $200 a month or less—were, making it possible and vital that we target them. Many of them were registered with the Chilean equivalent of a Social Security number, so we had their names and addresses.

Our community outreach program grew from this simple idea and soon became Chile Solidario (Chile Solidarity), through which we visited the 225,000 families living in extreme poverty—more than 800,000 Chileans. Those family helpers helped explain the state benefits and scholarships that we had created for students who completed high school. We helped parents learn to read and write and encouraged kids to stay in school. We helped the handicapped get their state stipends and those who were over 65 to receive their pensions. We helped the homeless to enter the Casas Lagos program. Chile Solidarity was about bringing the families in the most extreme poverty under the state's umbrella—from which they had long been isolated by their inhumane living conditions.

The program was a great success for the many Chileans who would never have been reached by any market or any service program. As a result of our policies, by 2006, poverty was just 13.6 percent, down from 20 percent in 2000. It was a smaller drop in percentage terms than what we'd experienced before; poverty had dropped by 50 percent between 1990 and 2000. But the lower the rates of destitution got, the harder they were to dent. Incredibly, the population living in extreme poverty, once hovering at 6.7 percent, was cut in half—a big drop for such a short time period. Our progress represented a monumental social change. By the end of my administration, in 2006, almost all of the 225,000 families we had sought had passed through Chile Solidario. A testament to its success is the frequency with which the program has now been copied and repeated—by the World Bank, the United Nations, and other countries.

But the most incredible part of Chile Solidario was what it did for the dignity of the human person. Take the case of Carmen Vera, a widow with two children who lived with her entire family in a single room in 2002, when she entered Chile Solidario. Not long after, she wrote me a letter to tell me that before the program, she could neither read nor write. "Today, I can write for the first time. I was able to collect my thoughts on paper, saying all the things that I wanted to say to you."

Another modest woman in Santiago, who spoke to me at a meeting for Chile Solidario, told me that she had been incredibly ashamed to be poor. "I couldn't bring myself to go to the local government and ask for help," she said. "But after the family helper came, I knew that even though I am poor I have rights. You have taught me how to have dignity precisely because I am poor."

One evening during my presidential campaign, when Luisa and I returned to our hotel for the night, she pointed out something striking that she had noticed during our travels. Many of the poorest women, she remarked, had lost some of their teeth, leaving haphazard gaps in their smiles. For these women, going to a dentist was prohibitively costly. So when they felt pain come on, the cheapest treatment was simply to remove the tooth.

Luisa was struck by what this must have meant for the women—the social shame and physical disability they would have to endure. So my wife began a campaign called Sonrisa de Mujer (Women's Smiles) with the aim of giving these impoverished women dental care. She investigated how much it would cost to replace a woman's teeth—$180 on average, or half a month's salary for a poor family. Luisa reached out to dentists and made her case for a lower rate, convincing them to participate in the program.

Sonrisa de Mujer captured the imagination of the country and touched the most profound soul of Chile. Thousands of people mobilized, and the results began pouring in: More than 25,000 women who had lost their teeth regained their smiles through the program. Luisa received hundreds of cards and letters from women who had benefited. There were women whose husbands had invited them to the movies for the first time in many years, now with their new teeth; women recounted how they had been embarrassed to speak in meetings or smile when it wasn't necessary for fear of showing their empty mouths.

Sometimes, very modest things produce unbelievable results. Now when I go out campaigning, there are men who ask when their own chance for a program will come, since the women have had their opportunity. We still have work to do.

For Chile, there is one monumental challenge that remains as we enter our next decade. We reduced poverty tremendously during the last 20 years. But what we have been unable to do is make our country more equal. Even as the lives of the poor incrementally improved, the lives of the wealthy were made exponentially better. Chile, like all countries in Latin America, still has one of the worst inequality rates in the world. The average income of the top quintile of Chileans is still 14 times that of the lowest quintile. Part of this is still a relic of how wealth was first distributed in colonial times, when the wealthiest of Spaniards had large plots of land. Part of it is simply because elites tend to reproduce themselves—through education, opportunities, and the inheritance of wealth. Our tax system makes matters worse, as distribution of income remains the same before and after taxes are collected. So our only lever for change is social spending, most of which goes to the poorest people. And indeed, when such spending is taken into account, the difference in income between our richest and poorest quintiles drops from 14 to 7.8 percent. That figure represents success—but it also signals that much of the rest of the gains will have to come elsewhere, for example, from the tax system.

It's a long-term battle, not as simple as growing the economy or providing services to the poor. Combating inequality is a game that we have to play because we might win tomorrow, if not today. It means giving the most to those who have the least themselves. It means creating incentives for the private sector to invest, deepening liberties so that innovation and creativity flourish, and opening opportunities for those without a voice to speak and be heard. That is the Chilean way.

When I look back, I feel like we have come a long distance. We made mistakes along the way; we never did as much as we wanted to do. But it was far better than if we had sat, arms crossed, and done nothing to rethink the injustices of our country. Progress is impossible where there is social conflict, and nothing is a recipe for conflict like a system that is unfair. Social policies are not only about improving the material conditions of life; they are also about creating a set of values that drive progress. A society that is more conscious of its weaknesses is better prepared to tackle them.

Little Chile, our small, far-flung country at the end of the world, reminds me every day what great hope there is for the progress of humanity. We have made many mistakes; we have lived through tyranny. But we have learned and moved forward. We have struggled to build a strong country, and we will never give up that fight. The Chilean way—the guiding principles that we follow—requires perseverance and conviction in new ideas, realizing that there is no one path to development and there are many perils. But there is an answer—and we have come a little bit closer to finding it in Chile during these years of democracy.

NINE

BUSH, SADDAM, AND ME*

G eorge W. Bush liked to open conversations in Spanish whenever he called me—which he did often in the first few months of 2003. The Iraq war was looking increasingly imminent, and Chile had just taken a seat on the U.N. Security Council. We were more than just an ordinary member, in fact: Chile controlled the swing vote—informally leading the group of "undecided six" members who weren't sure, or at least weren't saying, how they would vote on a resolution that could lead to war. In a pattern that settled into a routine, Bush tried to sway me to his side during those several months, through regular phone calls. "Hello, Ricardo. *Vamos a ganar!*" he

---

* The title of this chapter is by no means intended to inflate my role in these events; it so happened that Chile became a key player during the run-up to the Iraq war. A funny story puts things in perspective: A year after the conflict started, I got a call from a friend who was just returning from London. "Ricardo, I've just come from Britain, and you won't believe it: You've got a starring role in the theater." I'd heard about the play, a comedy called "Stuff Happens" by the British playwright David Hare, but this was the first I'd known that I was featured in it. "Well, tell me more," I inquired. "The actor who plays your part has to memorize just one line," he replied. "All you say to Bush is 'no.'"

would begin, repeating a phrase he had used at rallies in Hispanic areas during his 2000 campaign. "We're going to win!"

Chile would provide no end of frustration for the American president in the coming weeks. Ours was a sincere effort to stop a rush to war that we thought would prove disastrous, not a bid to thwart American power. But we didn't prevail, and for that I am deeply sorry.

I actually liked Bush personally. He came across as just a guy from Texas who had suddenly been thrust into the White House. Charming, confident, and personable, Bush liked to think that we were friends—and I'd like to think the same. We developed an odd and amiable relationship even when we were disagreeing about his march to Baghdad.

I knew through it all that Bush had come to office expecting things to go differently. He was going to be the president of free trade and education. Had it not been for September 11, he also expected to be the Spanish-speaking president who revived U.S. relations with Latin America. His first trip abroad was to Mexico, a meeting that the American press dubbed the "cowboy summit." He was proud of his Spanish vocabulary. He wanted America's backyard to be open to trade, to cooperation. Most of us in the region weren't entirely opposed to the idea—with a few notable exceptions, most vocally the Venezuelan president, Hugo Chávez.

In fact, it was Chávez who first brought Bush and me together.

"Hugo, come join us," I beckoned. There was a short coffee break during the April 2001 Summit of the Americas in Quebec, Canada—Bush's first summit—and I had been enjoying his company. He had arrived triumphantly, ready to dominate the discussions as the leader of the free world. It was as if we were all governors of remote Roman provinces—and he was the emperor.

As we chatted, I had caught Chávez's broad figure pass by out of the corner of my eye. I knew that the two hadn't yet met, and their two countries' diplomatic relationship was wary. Even then Chávez was noisier than most world leaders, but at that point it really was just bluster. Still, I knew that Bush was nervous about the meeting; he had told me as much a few days earlier. It seemed the perfect opportunity to introduce them casually.

"I want to introduce President Bush," I told Chávez. The Venezuelan leader turned toward us and approached, extending his hand. His left arm reached around Bush's back in the half-embrace that is Chávez's trademark greeting. Back then, before Iraq or September 11 or the 2002 coup attempt that Chávez blamed on the CIA, they were just two leaders shaking hands for the first time. I served as their translator, as neither man's foreign-language skills were up to the task. Both were clearly a bit on edge.

Earlier that week, I had held my first meeting with Bush in Washington, late in the afternoon on April 17, 2001. We were members of roughly the same "class" of newly elected leaders: Bush had been elected not long after I came to office and was inaugurated a year into my term.

From the moment I stepped into the White House, I found him both pleasant and disarming. He slapped me on the back, shook my hand, and called me Ricardo. He threw in Spanish words here and there (although rarely in full sentences) and liked to leave every meeting with all parties feeling they were walking away good friends. It worked; I also felt comfortable when we met, and we developed a warm relationship over the years, despite more than one disagreement. We could speak openly. It also wasn't just me who found Bush so amiable. My fellow Latin American president and close personal friend, Brazil's Fernando Henrique Cardoso, met with Bush just after he had famously told the world that he had looked into Vladimir Putin's eyes and seen his soul—seen that he was a good man. Cardoso began their meeting by opening his eyes wide, lowering his glasses, and asking Bush, "Mr. President, do you need to see my eyes before we begin?"

In my first meeting on that April day, Bush was accompanied by his secretary of state, Colin Powell, and the national security advisor, Condoleezza Rice. I also had a delegation, including my foreign minister and ambassador. But the aides were nearly invisible, never saying a word—during that meeting or any other between myself and Bush—aside from the occasional request to clarify something or remind their boss of a point.

Before September 11 and everything that followed, Latin America was supposed to be a priority, I opened our conversation by bringing up our interest in a free-trade agreement with the United States. Bush was receptive; he was seeking "fast-track" authority from Congress—allowing his team to negotiate without having to haggle endlessly on Capitol Hill—and seemed open to continuing the preliminary work that we had begun under the Clinton administration. (I once teased Bush about his steel tariffs, saying that he should perhaps convert the mills into cultural centers, as Mexico had done. And he replied, "You'll remember my steel tariffs when I get fast-track approval in Congress." He was correct.)

But Bush also had something else on his mind. His first international summit was around the corner—the Montréal summit. And like anyone, he wanted to make a good impression. Chávez was the known unknown.

"Ricardo, what do you think Chávez will say at the summit?" Bush asked me.

"Well," I replied blandly, "I suppose he will give a presentation of some of the work that he has done lately." Bush persisted—what specifically? I could see the concern on his face. Don't worry, I tried to assure him. There was really nothing to be concerned so much about. What was the worst that could happen? Bush still seemed unsatisfied.

"Would you like me to try and find out what President Chávez intends to do at the summit?" I asked, thinking it was a rather absurd question.

"Yes," Bush replied, "I would appreciate it very much."

I was struck by his concern. Chávez back then was not as polarizing as he is today. I believe that I understood—and still understand—where he comes from: widespread popular disaffection with a profoundly unequal political system. For decade upon decade, Venezuelan politics took place isolated from the needs of the people. To many Venezuelans, it seemed that elitist parties simply rotated power like it was a spoil to be portioned off, with little regard for the rest of the country. Chávez was the manifestation of the people's frustration. He was born of a desire for something—anything—else. And he embodied it 100 percent. For the first time in Venezuelan history, the poor rather than the upper class held the political power. Chávez's policies were disruptive and radical. But that's what Venezuelans seemed to want.

It is only in recent years that Chávez's revolution became so ideological. When Chávez turned to Cuba, seeing Fidel Castro as his intellectual godfather, his radical agenda at home became a caustic one in the region, too.

In a way, however—and even back then—I understood Bush's fears. I had felt the wrath of Chávez, and it was not something I would wish upon anyone. Despite our common socialist background, we had spats of our own: First, Chávez visited Bolivia and publically asked when Chile would return the country its access to the sea (which formally became Chilean territory after a peace treaty was signed in 1904, ending the War of the Pacific). Then, it was my turn to anger Chávez: At the high point of the guerrilla war in Colombia, I announced at a summit that Chile would support President Álvaro Uribe's counterinsurgency drive against the leftist Revolutionary Armed Forces of Colombia (FARC), which were thought to be backed by Venezuela. We would even send troops if needed, I said, because we weren't about to let Colombia become Latin America's Kosovo.

Chávez was fuming. He launched into a tirade, vowing never to take the Venezuelan army outside the country's borders. It was preposterous and against tradition! How could I say such a thing? Matters only worsened when I reminded Chávez that his intellectual icon, the Latin American independence hero Simón Bolívar, had led the Venezuelan army into battle in Colombia, Ecuador, and Peru. If there is one thing Hugo Chávez hates, it is being told he is wrong.

Still, we always managed to patch things up, and when I visited Caracas in 2005, I was greeted with the red banners of the political left in a ceremony that harkened back to the Cold War. (Indeed, it was only in Vietnam and Venezuela that I was ever treated as a comrade.) At the beginning of his term at least, Chávez was also grateful for my healthy relationship with the White House. For, as things devolved between the United States and Venezuela over the coming years, I remained neutral ground. He would often phone me in La Moneda and ask me to transmit a message to Washington, hoping to avoid a fight with Bush. When the State Department worried that Chávez was using his weight in OPEC to push up oil prices, for example, Chávez tried to explain—through me—that he just needed the cash to keep his government moving. It wasn't terribly persuasive, but at least the exchange avoided a diplomatic incident.

As time went on, however, Chávez grew more and more fervent in his anti-Bush rhetoric, and he used me less and less to communicate with the White House. And at the same time, the Bush administration wisely learned that it was better simply to ignore him. He is a man who needs an enemy. Better not to give him one.

During these (at times absurd) go-betweens, I often tried to give him advice, for example, on how to get his point across without appearing so erratic and making global headlines as a result. But I was always much more middle-of-the-road than the Venezuelan president, and, as such, Chávez never fully trusted me. I realize looking back that he likely never listened to me either—or if he did, it didn't last long. We simply operated on different planes. I made decisions based on numbers and ideas. Chávez made decisions that drew on a rigid ideology. We were like a mathematician and a philosopher trying to agree upon the meaning of life. We didn't even speak with the same vocabulary.

There was one leader in Latin America back then, however, who seemed to have Chávez's full trust. And luckily for all of us, he also had a more moderate approach to international politics. Whenever we met as a region, Chávez would begin by recognizing that Cardoso—Brazil's academic-turned-president—was, as he put it, "our professor." Chávez looked to Cardoso as a model and a source of wisdom, a sort of senior statesman of the region. I, of course, knew Cardoso well; he had lived and worked in Chile while Brazil was ruled by a military dictatorship. And so when Bush asked me to surmise what Chávez would say in Quebec, I immediately called Brasilia.

Cardoso planned to have lunch with Chávez before the summit, he told me, and could take the opportunity to ask him about his plans for Montréal. He assured me that there would be nothing to worry about, confirming my own suspicions. And at the beginning of the summit, when I passed Condoleezza Rice in the hallway, I told her as much.

"I don't think that there will be any trouble," I promised. That would come much later.

A year and a half after the Twin Towers fell in New York City, Colin Powell edged toward the microphone from his seat around the U.N. Security Council's famous U-shaped table. His voice had a tenor of gravitas, and his posture was regal, if perhaps not totally confident. "This is an important day for us all," he began, after greeting the council, explaining that his presentation would help "review the situation with respect to Iraq and its disarmament." The room was silent and anxious, with only the occasional clipping sound from the camera men filming Powell's speech—which was broadcast live around the world.

On that February day in 2003, I was one of the many viewers worldwide who had tuned in. There was a small television in the private chamber of my office, and in between phone calls and daily business, I slipped inside to watch Powell's presentation. My ambassador to the Security Council, Juan Gabriel

Valdés, was there in person; Chile had joined the council as a rotating member just a month earlier.

By then, it was more than clear what Bush was hoping to accomplish with Powell's speech. America was going to war; if the world could be convinced to play along, it would simply be a bonus. The Pentagon had already dispatched the first U.S. troops to the Iraqi border, and they were holding vigil in Kuwait until the moment was right. Months earlier, the U.S. State Department had invited Valdés to Foggy Bottom to become acquainted with the U.S. positions in the council—including on Iraq. On top of it all, I'd started receiving calls from Bush himself. We were, Bush knew, leading the swing votes on the council. Bush had personally asked me to watch Powell's presentation. He seemed confident that I would find it convincing.

I didn't. Superficially, Powell's speech, his movements, his low-pitched tone, and his argument all recalled an iconic moment in U.N. history: Adlai Stevenson, the U.S. ambassador under President John F. Kennedy, embarrassing the Soviet Union with clear evidence of its treachery in sending nuclear weapons to Cuba. In contrast, Powell's evidence could not have been less convincing. "What you will see is an accumulation of facts and disturbing patterns of behavior," Powell warned the council. But we never got to that punch line.

As soon as Powell finished and a rising din of earnest conversation filled the council chamber, I received a call in my office at La Moneda. It was Bush, asking to speak with me about an urgent matter, an aide informed me.

The American president's voice was upbeat as I answered the call. "Ricardo, how are you? *Vamos a ganar!*" His overconfidence was brash, echoing almost comically over the phone. "Did you watch, Ricardo?" Bush asked eagerly.

Yes, I told him, I'd seen it all.

And?

"There were interesting moments . . ." I hedged. It wasn't the time to tell Bush that I was unconvinced.

What was racing through my mind was the eerie contrast between Powell's and Stevenson's remarks. America's incredible impatience struck me most of all. How long were "we" willing to wait, Powell asked, for Iraq to disarm? The answer of course, was obvious: The Bush administration wasn't willing to wait at all.

Months earlier, on September 12, 2002, Bush had addressed the United Nations. He vowed to work with the Security Council—kind of. He argued that the body's past resolutions made the case that Saddam's Iraq was a dangerous rogue state. "Are Security Council resolutions to be honored and enforced, or cast aside without consequence?" he asked in challenge. "Will the U.N. serve the purpose of its founding or will it be irrelevant?" It was extremely clear language: I've come to solicit your approval, but if you don't give it, we will go ahead all the same.

At this time, Chile was still running for a seat on the Security Council, hoping to fill one of the rotating regional seats that were up for election. We hadn't put in our bid with any thought to Iraq; we had started campaigning for the seat a full two years earlier. The council, I thought, was a chance to showcase how far Chile had come, from a mismanaged dictatorship to an exemplar of economic growth and freedom. Our ambassador for the run would be Juan Gabriel Valdés, an esteemed political scientist who had cut his teeth as a professor at Catholic University in Chile. He was a well-spoken man, with the matted, slightly longer hair—unusual for a Chilean diplomat—of a man who had spent time in Spain as our ambassador and picked up a bit of European style. I knew him well by then; he had spoken in our television promotions for the No campaign. He had served as the undersecretary for international economic relations and then the minister of foreign affairs under my predecessor Eduardo Frei, and he handled a tricky situation during the uproar over Pinochet's conviction. Valdés was the one who had to defend, to the entire Socialist Party, the unpopular idea of bringing Pinochet back to Santiago from London. So he was no stranger to difficult political times—good training, it turned out, for the Security Council term.

We got the votes we needed in September and would take our seat at the turn of the new year. In those days, Iraq was far from our minds; we were too focused on domestic policy. But as the next several months unfolded, we watched in anticipation, knowing that our vote would soon matter urgently on the council.

The intervening months saw a frenzy of diplomatic activity. Throughout October, the United States pushed and pushed for a resolution that would authorize war if Saddam didn't cooperate. France and others stood firm against it (that's when some geniuses in the U.S. Congress invented "freedom fries").

Again and again, draft language was floated and turned down. It was not until the French and the American delegation hashed out language together that something amenable was agreed upon, I was later told by diplomat friends involved. Resolution 1441 finally passed on November 8, 2002, calling out Saddam as a violator of U.N. sanctions imposed after the Gulf War, demanding his "active, immediate, and unconditional cooperation" with U.N. weapons inspectors, and warning of "serious consequences" should he fail to comply.

In essence, 1441 passed because everyone at the council could interpret it exactly as they wished. For the Americans, it was enough to promise consequences for Saddam's lack of compliance, albeit with no firm timeline. What further language could they possibly need before going to war? In international diplomacy, everyone knows what "consequences" means, right? For the French, it merely said that Saddam needed to comply—but since it laid forth neither firm consequences nor a timeline, going to war would clearly require another resolution. The resolution was conveniently malleable. Everyone could get behind it because it meant everything—and nothing.

This was all very ominous as we watched in anticipation, understanding what dilemmas would await us when we joined the council in January 2003. The question on the table would be deceptively simple: Did the United States need another resolution before it launched an unprovoked war? The answer wouldn't come easy, and it carried troubling implications for a small country like Chile, which relied on a rules-bound world order.

As someone who had lived, studied, and worked in the United States, I was hardly immune to the trauma the events of September 11 held for Americans. It wasn't just a territorial assault; it was a visceral attack on what it meant to be free—to live in the United States of America. It was one of those awful days in history when time seemed to stand still—when the global order tilts 180 degrees as the whole world watches, uncertain.

When the planes hit the Twin Towers, I was across the Atlantic in Europe, on a visit to Portugal before heading to London that evening to meet with Prime Minister Blair. My lunch in Lisbon began as planned. About 20 of us, our Chilean delegation and that of Portuguese prime minister, António Guterres, were enjoying a lovely meal. I had been looking forward to the visit, expecting what was always very rewarding conversation. Guterres was a very well-spoken, intellectual man, someone who thought deeply about politics and listened with equal seriousness to others. The meal would mark the end of our two days of meetings in Lisbon, where we had been discussing our pursuit of a free-trade agreement with the EU.

About midway through our main course, one of the prime minister's aides approached him. Guterres leaned over from his seated position to listen. The aide slipped away out of sight, and Guterres told us the news. "I have just been informed that a small plane has hit a skyscraper in New York City," he said. About ten minutes later, the aide returned, a look of deep concern now on his face. Guterres again listened, but this time he too was alarmed. "A commercial plane seems to have hit the Twin Towers," he said. No one touched the dessert that had just been served.

We still had no idea of the extent of what was unfolding. But it was clear that we needed to finish our meeting in a hurry. Several members from both our delegations excused themselves, and the prime minister and I hurried through the end of our final discussions. We couldn't focus. We had to find out exactly what was happening. By this point, I knew in my gut that this was no accident—that there was more behind this tragedy.

I left directly to the last place the rest of the world was thinking of going: the airport. I had come to Portugal with Luisa, and she planned to return to Santiago after Lisbon while I continued on with my European tour to London. Her flight was through Madrid on a commercial airline. (Some minutes after she caught the connection to Chile, the pilot told her: "Madame, we are the only flight over the Atlantic tonight.")

It was in that airport that I realized we were now living in a different world. As we awaited the news of Luisa's flight in the lounge reserved for visiting officials, those horrible pictures of the planes crashing into the Twin Towers were being broadcast around the world. Then, we saw the towers come crashing down. And along with them, the world order.

My colleagues began discussing whether we should even continue with our trip. Perhaps we should return directly to Chile. Yet the worst kind of victory for these terrorists, we also thought, would be for all of us to let their assault have its intended impact: to change everything. We would stick with our plans.

On the plane, my mind raced. I picked up a pen and began writing, trying to make sense of the paradigmatic shift that was unfolding before us. I thought about what this would mean for the free countries of the world, Chile included. I had plenty of time to ponder. The pilot informed us that we would have to circle for about an hour before landing, following a very specific flight pattern that had been designated for all air travel that night. No one could fly over the city of London.

As our plane touched down, the mood was somber. It was still just midday in New York City, and the horror there was still unfolding as frantic rescuers attempted to sift through the rubble. The immediate injuries and traumas of the day were still in the making. I was the only head of state who arrived in London that night, and the press took advantage, meeting me at the airport to ask what I was thinking. "It is a great tragedy for humanity," I told them. "What's important now is that all the governments of the world maintain a united front against terrorism, fighting it in a manner that is serious and effective. The American people will rise to their traditions and they will pass through this difficult test."

Our delegation's first meeting was a dinner introducing several important British business leaders to the CEOs and entrepreneurs in the Chilean delegation. We held our conversation as planned, but of course the subject matter changed. We could hardly keep our minds on bilateral business ties when the world around us was becoming a different one from which any of us knew. The next day, I also continued with my planned schedule to meet with Blair at 5 P.M.

It was only the second time that I had met him, but as soon as I saw Blair, I could tell that he was worried. The gravity of the global shift we were witnessing was weighing on the prime minister. He felt a profound sense of history—this was the first time that the biggest international security threat was not a country or a person, but a nebulous group of actors over whom no sovereign entity wielded control. It clearly wasn't lost on Blair, either, how similar the September 11 attacks were to the Nazis' air assaults during World War II. When London was bombed, it was the first time that England felt vulnerable—the first time the homeland itself had come under attack. Now, the target was New York, and nobody knew how Americans would react.

Despite his evident concern, Blair greeted me warmly, leading me into one of the tiny meeting rooms in 10 Downing Street. The cozy quarters put one immediately at ease; as if in a personal household, there are no formalities or flacks sitting in on the conversation. Blair himself is also very direct, speaking intelligently and clearly, in a way that charms and relaxes his interlocutor.

We found it difficult to speak about much other than what had happened the day before. But I broached the topic we had come to discuss: our free-trade agreement with Europe, explaining our goals and our rationale. It was a matter of minutes before we returned to discussing the attacks on the Twin Towers.

I asked the prime minister what was on his mind. Had he spoken to Bush? What was his government thinking? Blair had already conveyed his country's support and condolences to President Bush, he told me. Maintaining the transatlantic alliance was Blair's top priority, and he had said as much to the U.S. president. His critics later ripped Blair—unfairly, I thought—as "Bush's poodle." But the British leader saw his role as something of a translator, he told me, explaining Bush's message and goals to European ears. Britain, in other words, was the bridge between the United States and Europe. It was the same role that Churchill had so successfully navigated during World War II. In the left-leaning Parliament, Blair didn't find his position very comfortable. But in those early hours after the attacks, we didn't talk about politics. We didn't talk about next steps—about a U.S. strike in Afghanistan or the global war on terror. We spoke only in terms of solidarity. This may well have been the moment when the United States enjoyed its greatest international support.

To be a head of state in September 2001 was to witness firsthand a clear "before and after" in international affairs. Before September 11, the main agenda items for any international discussion were economics, trade, and perhaps humanitarian issues. Afterward, security became priority number one. Prior to September 11, conflicts had been defined between states and governments; the world had a set of mechanisms and protocols with which to address these disputes. But in this new world, it was non-state actors we were fighting. How could we deal with such an ephemeral threat? Almost overnight, the world came to know the names al Qaeda and Osama bin Laden. It was the first time since Pearl Harbor that anyone had successfully attacked the world's overwhelming superpower on its own soil. Fortress America was under assault.

I t is difficult to push for peace when troops are already skulking on the border, positioned and ready to invade. And indeed, when Valdés sat down in the U.N. Security Council chamber for the first time in January 2003, we were already feeling the pressure. The United States was bracing for war. America was already dictating the use of global airspace. When I crossed the Pacific that January, on my way to Japan and South Korea, we were forbidden from refueling in Guam, where the United States has a base, and were redirected to the Marshall Islands. (On the upside, my relationship with the president of the Marshall Islands became far closer.)

When Chile took up its place on the Security Council that same month, it was as if the fate of the questions before us were already decided. We were debating a new resolution on Iraq's supposed weapons of mass destruction (WMDs). But Bush had already decided to go to war. We were fighting to stop a conflict that Bush believed was inevitable. And in the end, maybe he was right—war couldn't have been avoided, because Bush was the one pulling the strings. American conviction was a self-fulfilling prophecy about which we could do little.

The first diplomatic scuffle came just after the New Year. Sanctions that had been imposed on Iraq back in 1999 stipulated that U.N. weapons inspectors should report to the Security Council three times a year, which put their next briefing in March 2003. That was too late for the United States, which would have to launch an assault that month if it was to avoid the deadly desert heat of the Iraqi summer.

U.S. Ambassador John Negroponte raised the issue with our delegation on a number of occasions, explaining again and again that there was no time for the council to wait until March to move forward. Officially, he was only talking about weapons inspections, but it was obvious that the United States was hell-bent on getting boots on the ground.

Then came the heart of the matter: Did the United States need another U.N. resolution? As far as I was concerned, it did. Chile is a small country— one that relies upon an international system that treats it, and all members, equitably. While a big country such as the United States could afford to break the rules—or not have them in the first place—we could not. The agglomeration of international rules and informal understandings that had been built since World War II protected Chile and countless other middle and small powers within the system. If the United States went to war without U.N. backing, it would break all those promises and accords, both spoken and unspoken. If any single country held itself above the system, all the rest of us would cease to be protected by it.

On top of that, I was stuck by the incredible one-sidedness of all the resolutions that the United States had been proposing. These were resolutions written with the singular purpose of justifying a war. My philosophy is that, when one is making the case for conflict, there must also be a path toward peace. If a U.S. invasion would result from one set of choices, a separate set of choices should, in theory, prevent it. The road to peace that Washington was offering was booby-trapped with impossible conditions and sacrifices that no government—least of all the hubristic Iraqi regime—could accept.

And of course, even if we accepted the premise of the resolutions, I couldn't help but question the facts that were supposedly justifying a U.S. attack. I hadn't seen any convincing evidence that the infamous WMDs actually did exist. And at this time, Bush wasn't really talking about bringing democracy to Iraq; he was focused on the supposed threat Saddam's weapons posed to the international community.

Both Bush and Blair have said repeatedly that if they had known there were no WMDs in Iraq, they would still have invaded. But launching a war to bring democracy to a dictatorship would have been a far more difficult case to sell. How do you single out one dictator in a world replete with tyranny? Chileans had suffered under one ourselves—but I knew that Pinochet was far from the worst. Had the United States truly wanted to unseat tyranny, that's a conversation I would have welcomed. Let's make a list of the top dictators in the world—in Burma, in North Korea, and so forth. We would quickly realize that unseating a dictator is rarely a good *casus belli*.

I n the 1970s in Denver, Colorado, one of Condoleezza Rice's good friends was a former militant from the socialist youth in Chile, my friend and colleague Heraldo Muñoz. The two were earning their Ph.D.s at the University of Denver, an urban campus nestled in the southern half of the mile-high city. Back then, they were ideological allies. Condi was a Democrat until 1982, when she switched parties. Muñoz had fled Pinochet's regime to study abroad.

Their friendship was solidified when they both spent a year working for different congressmen's offices in Denver.

Years later, in January 1999, Muñoz introduced me to Rice at the World Economic Forum in Davos. I had been speaking on a panel about the so-called political Third Way; Rice was there in an academic capacity. She had already had a distinguished career as a scholar when we shook hands for the first time. I had always thought of her in friendly terms, perhaps because Muñoz always spoke highly of her.

Their paths later intersected in a very different way. By 2003, Muñoz was secretary-general of my government, a position akin to the White House chief of staff. Rice was the U.S. national security advisor. And one day in January, she called up her old friend with a question: What was Chile thinking about Iraq?

Rice laid out the by then familiar case for a Yes vote from Chile on any upcoming resolution on Iraq. We didn't have a veto in the Security Council, of course, but if any permanent members abstained, as some were almost certain to do, the United States would have to get more Yes votes from the rotating members. Abstention, she reminded Muñoz, was tantamount to voting No.

Washington wasn't the only one banging on our door those days. The prime minister of Japan called, as did the presidents of the Philippines and Indonesia. Leader after Latin American leader rang my private line. Everyone wanted Chile's answer to the same question: How were we going to vote on Iraq? Not one of them pressured me; they just wanted to know. The leaders of Japan and the Philippines, for example, simply thanked me for my honest opinion, and that was that. Blair was ringing my line most of all.

And Bush began calling too.

When the American president rang the first time, on January 22, 2003, he got straight to the point; this was not a man to waste time with pleasantries. "You know, Ricardo, the issue of security and terrorism is so important for the United States," he began to explain, clearly referring to Iraq. The United States, he continued, had gotten one resolution from the Security Council, "and I think it's enough," he told me. But Blair had his Parliament to worry about, and he wanted one more push. Bush was willing to give it a try, and he was hoping for Chile's support.

I was sympathetic to Bush's security concerns; indeed, they were global concerns by that time. But I didn't see the connection to Iraq. "Mr. President," I asked him, "Do you think that Saddam Hussein was involved in September 11?"

No, Bush replied. But his rogue regime . . . it was all tied to the support of terror.

I tried another way of asking. "Are you sure that there are WMDs? How good is your intelligence?"

He didn't answer; he stuck to his script. But my question would begin a long buildup of tensions that culminated in Powell's presentation, which was supposed to prove to doubters like me that there were indeed WMDs in Iraq.

My relationship with Blair was different, if equally warm. We shared our embrace of the Third Way. I remember how eagerly I had anticipated our first meeting at the United Nations in 2000. To be a Third Way proponent in those days and to meet Tony Blair was to be inducted into a club of young pragmatists who believed—and were proving—that hard divisions between the political right and the political left were an anachronism. One could embrace the free-market openness of globalization even while working for social justice at home.

On Iraq, you might also say that we also sought an alternative. Chile was unhappy with the resolution that the United States was after—one that seemed to lead unconditionally to war. But nor were we happy with the positions of France and Russia, whose preferred text would have meant that the outcome would have been the same whether Hussein complied or not. The biggest point of diversion was the timetable imposed upon Iraq for compliance with weapons inspections. The Americans would have listed "tomorrow" if they'd had their way; the Europeans and the Russians wanted no schedule at all.

So in February, Blair and I began negotiating an independent version of the Iraq resolution in secret—one that, we hoped, would appease all sides. These were sensitive days, and our discussions would surely have been of great interest to any number of parties. So one day as we were speaking, Blair asked me to let the British embassy install a device in my phone to ensure that it was a secure line. "Who are you worried will listen?" I asked him. "Because Tony, I'm not so important—I'm not worried about these things." He laughed. This was a measure to prevent American snooping. We waited to tell the Americans about our work on the alternative text—until what I realize now was too late. They would later react with the ire of a superpower kept out of the loop (which indeed they were). We weren't trying to irritate the Americans, however; we were simply trying to buy more time for diplomacy, and we believed that these negotiations—if they could produce something concrete—had a chance of stopping a war. And that was very much worth doing.

Blair and I began our work by speaking with Hans Blix, the Swedish weapons inspector who had emerged as Bush's biggest obstacle to war. Whenever the United States wanted to accelerate the timeframe, it seemed, there was Blix pushing back, demanding more time. Bush's impatience didn't faze him; he remained calmly insistent on a timeframe of weeks, not days.

When Blair rang Blix, the U.N. diplomat had already mapped out an ideal resolution: It had to include five specific conditions that would determine whether Iraq was or was not in compliance with the United Nations. They were "precise, concrete goals," Blix wrote later in his memoir.

Blair and I took those five points from Blix and turned them into diplomatic language. Our resolution was built on five conditions for Iraq. If they were met, war could be avoided:

1. Put 30 [Iraqi] scientists, identified by the U.N. weapons inspectors, at the disposition of the United Nations to be interviewed outside of Iraq. If they wished, they could be accompanied by their families.

2. Turn over all nerve gas weapons or aerial bombs containing nerve gas, which had gone missing since 1998, or if they had been destroyed, reveal the necessary documentation.

3. Turn over the 10,000 missing liters of anthrax or hand over evidence that proves their destruction.

4. Destroy all Al Samoud II missiles and all of their components.

5. Prove that the unmanned aerial vehicles are not carrying portable biological weapons systems.

By the end of February, Blair and I had agreed on the principles, the language, and the details of the resolution. We had reached a point in our negotiations where the agreement was nearly ready, and he rang me in La

Moneda. "I'm coming to Santiago so we can sign the resolution jointly," Blair
told me.

"It's a good idea," I replied. "Why don't you stop first in Moscow to
get Putin's signature?" I suggested, only half joking. In some ways, our
counter-resolution had to follow the same logic the American resolution
would: Win the French to get the Germans, and win the Russians to bring
on board the Chinese. (China in 2003 was not China today; back then,
Moscow took the lead.)

But Blair never came to Santiago. We agreed on every detail when it came
to the conditions upon Iraq, but diverged almost completely when it came to
the consequences should Baghdad fail to act. Blair wanted a failure to comply
to trigger automatic Security Council approval to attack. I felt that such a decision should be in the hands of the council members themselves—not in the
hands of one man in Washington.

Perhaps Blair thought that I just didn't absorb the gravity of it all—so
rather than coming to La Moneda, he dispatched two special guests.

"Ricardo, I want to send two people to meet with you," he told me over the
phone. He told me he was sending two of his top experts on Britain's Iraq intelligence. The secret envoys were meant to convince me what Powell's presentation hadn't: that Saddam was hiding WMDs. They would arrive on a Sunday
morning, February 24.

On the day of our meeting, I was hurrying back from my weekend home
in the mountains outside Santiago. I sped back to the capital, going directly to
the Defense Ministry. We entered through a side driveway that led straight to a
secure room with no windows, where we knew we could speak freely—no one
would be listening.

The two envoys walked in. Blair had sent me David Manning, the second
in charge of the Foreign Office, and John Scarlett, a former intelligence official
who had worked in Moscow until Blair brought him back to London to serve
in his government. (He would later become director general of MI6, the fabled
British spy agency, from 2004 to 2009. Manning was named ambassador to the
United States in the middle of 2003.)

We greeted one another amiably, and the conversation began. It was a
businesslike meeting, incredibly formal and equally indirect. Manning started

the presentation, followed by Scarlett, who was meant to show me a smoking gun on Iraq's WMDs.

The more they spoke, however, the more I realized that I was not learning a thing. The visit, which was supposed to dispel any doubts left by Powell's presentation, in fact only left me convinced of one thing: British intelligence had no idea if and where the WMDs existed.

Several times during the presentation, I kindly stopped my British guests. "Sir, I want to ask you straight: Do you know where the weapons are?"

They mumbled in reply. "Mr. President, that's a secret; we really can't answer that question."

"I'm not asking you tell *me* where they are," I replied. "I'm asking if you know—and if you do, why don't you tell Hans Blix," the top U.N. weapons inspector.

Silence. They continued with their rehearsed points. I asked again. If I were going to war—with the supposed rationale of destroying the WMDs—the location of the weapons would be pretty high on my list of things to know. I asked again. But the only assurance I got was my assumption that perhaps if they *did* know where the weapons were, they were afraid to tell Blix for fear that he would say something in public—and Saddam would simply relocate his stocks before an air assault. It was plausible, but the intelligence officers gave me no reason to believe they had such evidence in the first place.

By the time they stood up to leave, the words of another intelligence briefing were echoing in my ears. When I spoke with Jacques Chirac by phone just days earlier, I had asked him the same question point blank. And the French president answered it equally bluntly. "President, with all certainty, I can say that my intelligence services have found no evidence of nuclear weapons in Iraq," he told me. "And neither have they found any elements of WMDs. We cannot of course say for certain that they don't exist. But we have no proof that they do."

Manning and Scarlett packed their briefcases and shook my hand, thanking me for listening. I showed them out, knowing that they were on something of a tour. After our discussion, they would travel to Mexico to offer their "proof" to President Vicente Fox. But when Fox and I later exchanged notes, we found ourselves reaching the same conclusion: The presentation was an utter failure. We had yet to see any reason for the Iraq war.

B y mid-February, it was clear that we were far from the only members of the Security Council who were not persuaded.

During that month, I had begun speaking with Fox more often, hoping to persuade him that our ambassadors should join forces at the United Nations. Our respective diplomats were close personal friends, and it was soon clear that our countries were both on the same page.

That month, the Pakistani ambassador to the United Nations asked for a meeting with Valdés in New York. He had watched Chile navigate the negotiations, he explained, and was impressed. He wanted to forge a sort of alliance, joining the de facto partnership we already had with Mexico.

After Powell's presentation, more countries approached our delegation. The three African countries on the council wanted to join. Everyone, it seemed, was feeling what Chile felt: that there wasn't enough evidence, that the United States was bent on war, and that in such an environment we didn't yet know where we would end up.

That unlikely group of countries—Angola, Cameroon, Guinea, Mexico, Pakistan, and Chile—became the "Uncommitted Six," or simply the "U-6." We were the swing votes. And in our solidarity, we created a block of indecision that would decide the resolution—despite the fact that not a single one of us had a veto. Bush, by that time, had truly secured just four votes: Britain, Bulgaria, Spain, and his own. He needed the U-6, and Chile most of all.

We later learned just how serious the Bush administration took that challenge. That winter, our mission's phone lines at the United Nations were tapped, as were those of Pakistan and several other countries. Chile found out like everybody else in February, when the U.S. press reported the story. Luckily, we knew the rules of the game we were playing. Rule No. 1 at the United Nations is that everyone assumes that someone is listening to their calls. Rule No. 2 is that when you find out, you have to protest. And rule No. 3 is that whoever is guilty will deny it. It's all part of the diplomatic game.

But the pressure was bearing down in more visible ways as well. Chile never felt threatened by the United States to vote one way or another, but neither were we naive about what it could mean for our country.

This was always difficult for the veto-wielding powers to understand. During one of my phone calls with Chirac in February, he asked me how I planned to vote on a resolution, should it come to the floor. The French also needed allies, and Chirac tried to convince us to vote No by summoning the righteousness of French values of equality, multilateralism, and human dignity. These were values that necessitated the U.N. system, he explained. (The French always did like to remind their allies that they were the true founders of democracy.)

I understood all that, I explained to Chirac. And Chile too needed a multilateral system. But on the question of how we'd vote, matters were more complicated.

"Mr. President, you want to know how Chile will vote?" I replied. "Chile will vote in favor of a resolution that establishes a clear set of steps that Hussein must comply with. And if he does not comply, we will have to decide whether to use force."

Chirac protested, but I stopped him before he could go further. "Mr. President," I replied, "Do you know what the difference is between you and me?"

He seemed very surprised and momentarily lapsed into an uncomfortable silence. "The difference is that you have both a vote and a veto," I told him. "If you abstain, Bush will call and thank you the next day. As president of Chile, I have only a vote. If I abstain, Bush won't get the nine votes that he needs." I didn't need to say any more. Bush wouldn't be calling to thank me if I abstained.

I continued, turning the question on Chirac. "But since you have asked me how we will vote, I think, sir, that I must also ask you how France plans to use its veto. Because if you veto a resolution, we can adopt another type of resolution"—the sort that Blair and I were agreeing upon.

Apparently one doesn't speak to the French president that way. The next morning, Valdés called. "Mr. President, what you told President Chirac last night. . . . Chirac told my French colleague, Ambassador Jean David Levitte, that you had challenged him rather energetically." No, I explained, Chile had done no such thing. Chirac had asked me how we would vote; it was only fair that I ask him how the French would vote as well.

The pressure from the bigger countries came down harder on some of our colleagues in the U-6. The French foreign minister, Dominique de Villepin, warned three African countries not to support Bush. We could also tell that some were feeling pressure from the Americans. I knew that it would be particularly difficult for Mexico to stand up to its largest trading partner. And so when Vicente Fox and I first discussed Iraq, I always gave him an out, understanding he might need to take it. Just give me 24 hours' notice, I told him, before you leave the U-6. Others were under the gun too. They wouldn't say it; their diplomats were too proud—as well they should have been. But here and there, they would disappear from discussions or excuse themselves when sensitive matters arose. We all understood quite clearly what was going on.

On February 16, I took a call from Felipe González, the former Spanish prime minister. He had just returned from the United States, he told me, where he had met an old friend, James Baker. González had been a pivotal player in the first Gulf War under George H.W. Bush, arranging matters such that the U.S. military could land its planes and supply its troops on Spanish soil.

Baker, of course, was the secretary of state in the first Bush administration, and he had been instrumental in the diplomacy leading up to the first Iraq War. He had seen the inside of the Hussein regime in Iraq, and he understood, at least a bit, what a hold it had on Iraqi society.

Unlike Brent Scowcroft, the former national security advisor, Baker didn't speak out against the war. But Baker had seen enough, González relayed, to believe that this Iraq War would be a disaster.

During his conversation with Baker, it became clear to González that the former statesmen of the George H.W. Bush administration—perhaps including the former president himself—were opposed to the war. Toppling Hussein would unleash the sort of chaos on Baghdad that no one could predict. It would destabilize the region. This was much bigger than Bush Jr. was ready for. I don't know whether these views were ever conveyed to the president himself, but one assumes that the father and son at least discussed the matter on occasion.

Baker was hardly the first person to remark about how poorly prepared the Bush administration appeared to be for what would come immediately after the invasion. During one of my discussions with Chirac in February, he raised the point as well. Chirac believed that the assault on Baghdad would open up a floodgate of crises that the United States would be unable to man-age. "They will win the war, but to win the peace, they will need the United Nations once again," he told me forebodingly. "And that will be the moment in which we will have to return to action. If they try to win the peace without the United Nations, it will be a complete disaster."

With everything I learned about the U.S. position, I grew more torn about where Chile should stand. So at last I called the one man I thought would truly know the whole story on Iraq: Blix. I wondered if the Americans or British were sharing more with him than they were with me. I wondered if there was a way that we could move forward, as he saw it from his seat. I wondered if—should he have more time for inspections—we could avoid war.

"We need 45 more days," he told me, to verify whether or not Iraq has WMDs.

"Mr. Blix, I think 30 days are the most we can ask," I told him. It was enough, I thought. We could get another resolution; we could push back Washington's immovable timetable.

I wasn't the only one who thought this—that another resolution was still possible. Bill Clinton did as well.

Toward the end of February, the former American president traveled to Chequers, the traditional retreat of the British prime minister, to meet with Blair. The two had discussed Iraq, and Clinton left with the impression that Blair still wanted and needed a resolution.

Not long after Clinton left Britain, he asked a friend and former White House chief of staff, Thomas "Mack" MacLarty, to get in touch with my interior minister. He was using back-channel diplomacy to relay that he wanted to speak with me—but that I should be the one to call. Clinton was smart; he knew that he couldn't be seen as intervening. He wanted me to ring and simply ask how he was doing. And matters would proceed from there. And so I did; I telephoned Clinton unassumingly. "How are you, Bill?"

Clinton told me about his recent time with Blair. "Look Ricardo, I think it might be useful to know," he said, "that there is one last opportunity for a resolution, it seems." Blair was willing to try to float a draft similar to the text that he and I had been working on. There was a chance that this could yield a consensus on the council. Blair could win over Bush, he seemed to believe. It was our last chance at stopping war.

By this time, I had in fact already told President Bush that Blair and I were working out a resolution on the sidelines. Bush rang La Moneda on February 22, a sort of usual routine that we had fallen into by then, wherein he would ask how I was thinking about Iraq, and I would explain that I still needed to be convinced.

I thought the moment was opportune—mostly because I believed that it was fast fading. But Bush was in no mood for another resolution. There wasn't enough time, he argued.

"I asked Blair to convince you! But sometimes Blair is more like your lawyer at the White House than my partner in fighting terror," Bush replied when I told him of our final attempt. It wasn't a resolution born out of spite, I told him. I just wanted to prevent a war.

As we entered March, it was becoming clearer by the day that there was a deep split on the council. On March 5, France, Germany, and Russia issued a joint statement of dissent from the U.S. position. Just two days later, Russian President Vladimir Putin announced that he planned to veto any resolution put forward by the United States that would lead to war in Iraq. The United States—and Britain even more so—was being backed into a corner.

So Blair began a frantic series of phone calls—and one of them was to Blix on March 10.

Blair saw a chance to get the last resolution that he so desperately needed in Parliament, and he decided to make one final go. He took Blix's points—the same ones that he and I had agreed upon—and added to them just one more: that Saddam Hussein would have to admit publically, in a televised address, that he had WMDs, that he planned to give them up, and that he would comply with the Security Council. Blair wanted the six conditions met—and the speech given—by March 17. One week.

I wanted to work with Blair—but this was too fast and too much. These were conditions that, even under the most ideal circumstances, Saddam would never accept. Especially not in a mere seven days. The other council members clearly felt the same, and Blair's proposed resolution flopped.

Bush wasn't about to support Blair's resolution, either. On Saturday, March 8, Bush and I spoke in one of our now-usual conversations. Time was already up, he said. He had more than 100,000 soldiers in place along the Iraqi border, and they were not going to simply wait there forever. I tried to convince him that there was still time to pursue a new resolution. He told me, in a friendly tone, that he didn't want to have that conversation; he hoped we would have another week. But now, Ricardo, he told me, was "the moment for action."

Bush called again on March 12—his last call, which would last a mere 14 minutes. He had eight votes for the U.S. resolution, he said, and he wanted to know if he could count on mine.

"Are you sure it's time to bring up the vote?" I asked him. I wanted more time—I needed more time to offer an alternative resolution that was more feasible than what Blair had put on the table.

"It's time to bring up the vote, Ricardo. We've had this debate too long."

"But we're making progress."

My arguments weren't going to win the president over. "That's only because we've got a couple of hundred thousand troops [on the border]. If those troops weren't there, there'd be even less progress diplomatically. And Saddam Hussein could care less. Any progress you think is being made is illusory." He continued, "And I'm not going to leave our troops there. They're either going to go in and remove him or they're coming home, Ricardo.

"If I don't have your vote, I'm not going to a second resolution," Bush said. "And if I don't have your vote, then there is a new question: I want to know if you will participate in the coalition of the willing."

It was happening too fast. "Mr. President," I said, "Chile and the United States have a strong friendship. But if you form a coalition outside of the Security Council, Chile can't participate."

Bush ended the conversation politely. "Thank you, Mr. President. I appreciate your frankness." With equal formality, I replied, "Mr. President, friends are supposed to be frank."

At that moment, I ceased to be just Ricardo.

During those weeks of frantic diplomacy, I tried on more than one occasion to ask Bush to just slow down. I don't mean the resolutions—although this was true as well. I wanted him to think hard about what he was doing and about the weight that he was placing on Iraq when the conflict between Israel and the Palestinians was the Middle East issue that needed his urgent attention.

Bush always found my prodding a bit strange. "Why do you care so much about the Palestinians?" he asked me. He became even more certain I had some hidden agenda when he learned that Palestinians are the largest diaspora community living in Chile. "You must just want to please your people," he would tell me.

In fact, domestic politics had little to do with my thinking. I was genuinely worried about where this was all going. There wasn't going to be a democratic revolution in Iraq. There was going to be a divided country with a leadership vacuum—and a great deal of destruction and bloodshed. There was going to be an American war against Iraq, a Muslim country. At the same time, the United States was—and would certainly remain—a close ally of Israel. It didn't add up to a Middle East peace policy.

"If you are going to war against Iraq, why don't you make some overtures toward the Palestinians so as to balance the idea that the United States is pitted against the Muslim people?" I used to tell Bush.

By March, I knew that I had to make one last effort. The Americans were walking away from the Security Council. The British proposal looked destined to fail. But we had one more chance. I phoned Valdés with the news, asking him to convene a meeting of the U-6 countries on March 14 to go over the text of a new resolution. In the back of my mind, I kept thinking about the call I'd had with Clinton days before: There was still a window.

We looked over the British proposal—the one that Blair had worked together from our previous negotiations and his new conditions. It would have to be made more feasible, more likely to be passed, and more likely to bring Saddam around. We lengthened the time for Iraq to comply from 7 to 30 days. And we made the drive to war conditional on approval and consensus of the entire Security Council, not any one member, when the deadline was up.

The U-6 insisted that Chile present the resolution in public. So on March 14, I held a press conference announcing that we would be circulating a new resolution. I had six votes—the entire swing vote of the Security Council.

The moment our new resolution was made available, the United States denounced it. Even before the U-6 could gather to review the final text, U.S. officials had put in calls to the capitals of all our countries. Their message? The United States was going to war. Leave Washington alone. Don't go to the meeting. The African ambassadors got word from their leaders back home. And they politely excused themselves from the discussions. Blair, by this point, also gave up. Bush had clearly spoken with him after our last call, and now Blair knew that he had no more room to maneuver.

In retrospect, you could argue that our last-ditch attempt at a resolution actually accelerated the timeline for war. The United States had to make clear that it was not interested in another resolution. And the easiest way to do that was to go to war. I regret not warning the U.S. delegation at the United Nations earlier of our forthcoming resolution. After being caught off guard, White House spokesman Ari Fleischer called our resolution a "nonstarter." The war would start the following week.

Saddam Hussein wasn't fond of our resolution either, proclaiming in an Iraqi newspaper that "either Chile knew nothing of the situation in Iraq or is at the service of the diabolical U.S. government position." The fact that we won friends on neither side of the argument may have meant that our resolution was just about right.

I tried all day on March 14 to reach Blair but couldn't get through. I left a message asking him to call immediately the next day, which he did, ringing my line at 6 or 7 in the morning. I didn't want this debate to end; I didn't want Blair to give up on the United Nations. I wanted to keep talking when we arrived in the Azores for an emergency summit on Iraq later that day. "I don't want to interfere in the decision that you have taken to go to war," I told him. "And as I told Bush, we didn't release the new text out of spite. It's just that I will work until the last minute to avoid war."

"It's true that the Chilean proposals are very close to our position now," Blair replied. "There could have been more time. This could all have been very different."

As if a surreal omen, I began to hear a military band in the background as we spoke. My god, I thought. "What happened? Has the war started?"

"I'm sorry, Ricardo," he replied. It was just a band playing. "We haven't started the martial music already!" It lightened the mood ever so briefly. He added, "The United States does not want to be tricked into compromise. Yes, maybe we can speak again tomorrow. Maybe there's just a chance of squeezing through to some suitable position. There may be some time left, but it's a squeeze now. I'll keep trying right to the end."

We both knew by the time our conversation finished, however, that Bush was going to war—and there was nothing we could do about it.

L ooking back now almost a decade later, I realize that Bush never understood my reasons for saying no on Iraq. In his memoirs, he attributes my stubbornness to Chilean public opinion; I must have been saying no because my electorate wouldn't have it. I wonder if Bush was listening (or if he heard) when I tried to explain the real reasons for our dissent: Small countries such as Chile needed the international system's institutions intact. And diplomacy aside, the Iraq war seemed like a terrible idea for which the United States was ill-prepared.

Of course, the Iraq war was tricky for me at home—Bush was right in that regard. Before I released our new resolution on March 13, I made the rounds in Chile, calling every political faction of the country, trying to explain what I was planning to do. I wasn't asking their permission so much as ensuring that no one was caught off guard. It was rare that Chile held so much sway in global affairs.

Five days later, I had a reception with Queen Beatriz of Holland as part of her state visit to Chile. Around 10:30 in the evening, one of the queen's military aides approached her and told her something. Two minutes later, my own military aide entered and informed me of the news: the Iraq war had begun. "Your majesty, you have heard, right?" I asked. "Yes," she said.

After the official reception, around 11 P.M., I thought it was necessary to speak to the country. I urged Chileans to be calm: We did everything we could to prevent the war—everything that a small nation could have done in that situation. Our conscience was clear. "Now let's go to sleep," I said, "and tomorrow when your children wake up, tell them that there is a war going on very far away, but that we Chileans have nothing to worry about because we did everything we could to stop it."

I nternational politics, I found during my time in office, has much to do with who you know. During the lead-up to the Iraq war, it was my relationships with Bush and with Blair that allowed us such a pivotal role in the Security Council. In fact, whether it's climate change or human rights, trade or currency, what policies often boil down to is the relationship between two world leaders. Longtime friends have been lost this way, and longtime enemies have reconciled. The shake of a hand in politics really can be an act of statecraft.

No one has understood this more in recent years than an enigma of a leader: Brazil's Lula. Luiz Inácio Lula de Silva, a former union leader, became president in 2003 amid as much popular fervor and hope as did Chávez, but he governed with as much wisdom as Cardoso. If his predecessor laid the groundwork for Brazil's rise, it was only when Lula came that we all suddenly knew that Brasilia would be playing in the big leagues from then on.

Lula has become emblematic of the rise-of-the-rest diplomacy that is increasingly shaping our world. Brazil today is perhaps the most coveted example of a middle power. Its markets are booming, its people are diverse and cosmopolitan, and its government is the exemplar of multilateralism. In diplomatic circles, Brazil is the most wanted representative on every panel or commission—allies of the West and also friends of the Global South. In short, Brazil is objectionable to no one. The appeal extends to developing countries' capitals, where it is often Brazil's example that is held up as a path to progress. If you are Malawi or Bolivia, the U.S. or Swedish models are simply too far away to emulate with any practical utility. But if you look to Brazil, there is something useful to work toward.

In truth, Brazil was always exceptional, even in its own region. The country's national psyche never considered itself Latin American, having Portuguese colonial roots and a population far more diverse than the rest of the region. But while its people believed Brazil was an outlier, its foreign ministry, Itamaraty, knew that Latin America would be the perfect theater in which to take the lead. They understood Brazil's promise as a Latin American giant. It also helped that there were really no candidates stepping up. Argentina had once been our continent's best-developed economy (it would have easily made the G–7 had the body existed at the turn of the twentieth century), but in the early 2000s, the country was tied up in financial crisis; Mexico was too closely allied with the United States, many Latin Americans believed, to truly lead. Colombia, Venezuela, Chile, Peru, and all the others were too small or too consumed by internal matters. But Brazil—which has borders with 10 countries on the continent—was booming.

The rise truly began with Cardoso. As an economist who had lived and traveled in every corner of the continent, Cardoso was the first Brazilian leader who *knew* Spanish-speaking Latin America. He knew the people, and, more importantly, he knew the politicians. And he grasped the chance for Brazil to grow into its role as a natural leader. He focused first at home, introducing sound economic policies, trying out anti-poverty schemes such as the now famous *Bolsa Familia* that offers financial support to the poorest if their children are vaccinated and stay in school. Cardoso was business friendly but also a social democrat at heart. And with each passing year, he garnered more and more respect in the region from a core of regional leaders who were impressed by the Brazilian president's very real results.

Then came Lula, who would epitomize the outward-looking gaze of Itamaraty, setting out to construct his identity as a global power broker.

We all knew immediately just how serious Lula was about taking Brazil's foreign policy to the next level. It was unmissable. When the president of a small country wants to meet, say, the president of the United States, he often finds himself booked in for a sideline meeting or a coffee; the leader of the free world has little time to spare. When Lula was inaugurated, he instituted the same protocol. Heads of state who arrived in Brasilia for his inauguration were rushed in and out of meetings; no one came for dinner. Lula had too much work to do for such pleasantries. He was sending a signal to the rest of Latin America: It's show time.

There were other signs too. Brazil was far from pleased with Chile's free-trade agreement with the United States, which came into force a year after Lula took office. Any such agreement with the north, the country protested, should come only after our region had fully integrated in terms of trade. Brazil wanted to negotiate trade agreements as a bloc. (I replied that our moving ahead hadn't been a question of politics—it was all about economics. Trade is trade, and we weren't going to wait.)

The most pressing foreign-policy issue for Lula's Brazil, however, was to win a seat on the Security Council. Not long after he took office, I met Lula for lunch at his private home. And sure enough, in that meeting—as in many other meetings with Brazil—Lula wanted our final communiqué to raise the issue of Security Council reform. It was trickier than you might imagine for

Chile; while we fully supported expanding the council, we also knew that Argentina also coveted a seat. On that visit in particular, I had to protest. "Mr. President, I cannot sign this today," I told Lula, "because tomorrow I am going to Buenos Aires."

Indeed, Lula's rise was not altogether uncontested. Long the economic giant, Argentina resisted most of all. Chile, having good relations with both countries, became the swing vote—which put me in more than one awkward position during my tenure.

Brazil and Argentina were savvy to power politics, however, and they were eager to be friendly competitors. Argentina always had to come first by protocol when it came to relations with Chile; we shared a border with that country but not with Brazil. After receiving invitations to my inauguration, for example, the two country's presidents consulted about the timing of their replies. At 9 A.M. the day following the invitation, Argentinean president Fernando De La Rúa called to accept the invitation. Cardoso called at 9:15.

For the same reason, I chose to travel to Argentina for my first abroad visit as president—followed by Brazil. I addressed the legislature there and told them that I hoped to work even more closely than before—now 200 years after we had worked together to obtain our independence from Spain. We accomplished exactly what I had in mind during the rest of my term: real, tangible ties. When I walked into La Moneda, Chile had never spoken with its neighbors about building infrastructure on the border. We each had our own highways, and when you continued over the border, what was once a paved freeway might immediately turn to dirt road. By the time I left office, Argentina and Chile had agreed upon 13 passes between us, most of which are now open—and paved.

When it came to Brazil, we often liked to joke that our friendship knew no boundaries—because indeed, we didn't have a land border with Brazil. That's how we had operated for decades, Chile and Brazil, until Lula made it clear that even borderless friendships have a pecking order.

Long before September 11—long before security dominated the agenda and Blair was caricatured for following Bush to war—the British prime minister was iconic for leaders such as me, who sought to follow the principles of his famous Third Way. Beginning with my administration, Chile began to attend the Summit of Progressive Leaders, which met that year in Germany. It was a group of pragmatist leaders who saw the conflict between right and left as a useless simplification. They were Tony Blair of Britain, Bill Clinton of the United States, Gerard Schröder of Germany, Göran Persson of Sweden, Giuliano Amato of Italy, and Lionel Jospin of France. From South America came Fernando de la Rúa of Argentina, Fernando Henrique Cardoso of Brazil, and myself from Chile. The list continued with such incredible leaders as Antonio Guterres of Portugal, South Africa President Thabo Mbeki, and New Zealand President Helen Clark.

We were the upstart leaders, in many ways—set upon changing their home countries and seizing the world stage. So it wasn't surprising that the topic headlining every meeting was Security Council reform. The council, made up of 15 members—5 of whom are permanent and wield a veto—is an anachronism. Even the great powers will admit as much. But it's one thing to understand the contradictions and quite another to change them, particularly when doing so involves taking away power from those who hold it today.

During those meetings, we cobbled together a variety of proposals to make the council more representative of the new multipolar world. We tried to be as realistic as possible about how much change could be achieved, and so we honed in upon one rather simple idea: Instead of one veto, a resolution should require two vetoes to be defeated. Even this, however, has proven too drastic for the many powers around the table—our table—which was already made up of ideological allies.

The trouble is, several of the powers that sit on the Security Council really don't deserve a veto anymore. France and Britain were great powers at the end of World War II. These days, they are still powerful, but certainly not the players they were. When they were given the veto, it was because they were strong. Today, it's the veto itself, and often only that, that makes them relevant in international affairs. For example, during one of those summits, I pitched the idea of two vetoes to Blair, and he replied, with unintended irony, "If that were ever brought up in the council, I would veto the resolution before it was even discussed."

Meetings of the Asia-Pacific Economies Cooperation (APEC) offered a similar sort of openness and frank discussion. To be sure, some of the meetings were pomp and circumstance—often a chance for hosting nations to show off their latest big development projects. The government of Brunei, for example, welcomed leaders in 2000 with newly constructed private homes, specially built for the visiting heads of state and complete with private swimming pools and lawns.

But beyond the showboating, there was a real and constructive summit at APEC, one that had a great impact on Chile's foreign policy during my six years as president. In the most immediate sense, APEC was vital to Chile's economic future. The center of world trade had started shifting toward Asia in the 1980s, and today, some 50 percent of all global exchange takes place across the Pacific. Three decades ago, just 15 percent of Chile's exports were destined for Asia. Now that number has more than doubled—both in tonnage and in value.

But there was something else about the summit that made it particularly useful: It was technically economic—which in fact meant that political questions could more easily be brought to bear. Economics were a mutual, common interest—one that could serve as a pretext to address political concerns. Under no other umbrella or framing could Taiwan and Hong Kong both be present in a forum where China was a leading member, for example. The trick was simply that neither government was represented politically at the meetings. Only finance and economic ministers and functionaries came. In the case of Taiwan, it was represented by Yuan Tseh Lee, a Nobel Prize winner for the inarguably apolitical topic of chemistry.

Chile hosted the APEC summit in 2004, and I welcomed this now familiar group of leaders to La Moneda. That first day, early in the afternoon, I began things with a proposal: Why not approve the final declaration prepared by our sherpas right then and there, so that we could spend the rest of the meeting setting our own agenda? The consensus was unanimous, and we used the rest of our two days together to sort out issues and concerns, ask one another the many questions on our minds, and simply discuss the world.

During lunch the following day, the discussions took a particularly interesting turn. There were 21 heads of state and government in the dining room of the palace, a long but modest space, no bigger than the living area that a wealthy family might have in a country home. The walls are a gentle green color, decorated with paintings from Chile's historical ascent. My favorite depicts a nineteenth-century president talking with his wife in the living room, called Salón Rojo. They both hold a book, so you can't tell exactly who is lecturing whom.

Bush was among the leaders around the table that day. And he had a way of asking loaded or complex questions—but in a way that felt honest and curious, even naïve. At midday during our lunch, Bush turned to China's President Hu Jintao.

"Where is China's economy headed?" he asked, tapping into a debate about the sustainability of China's sprinting growth rates. All of us around the table that day knew the implications, not just of the question—coming from an American president and asked candidly to the Chinese leader—but of the answer. If China's red-hot economy suddenly froze, the rest of our economies, and world trade—in fact the entire world order—would be sent into shock. But if China could cool down slowly, sinking to a sustainable rate, we would all be better off.

Hu could easily have dodged the question. He could have claimed the privacy of sovereignty, and no one would have thought the less of him. But he didn't; instead, in the privacy of those halls, he answered with great candor. Yes, China's growth needed to slow, he admitted to Bush. But his government would do all it could to ensure that the change would impact neither China's own social stability nor the pace of world trade.

Bush seemed pleased with the answer. "I wish you luck," he replied earnestly. These sorts of discussions were APEC at its best.

This is particularly true in the one-on-one meetings, where candor is exactly what produces political progress. There are no sherpas, no functionaries, and no aides present during these bilaterals—only a translator, if needed. It was in such a setting that I first raised the question of a free-trade agreement with the United States in 2000, for example.

I held other fascinating meetings that year as well. One evening on the sidelines, I spoke with Putin, who at the time was the Russian president. We had a very specific and somewhat niche agenda to discuss: There was a fair

amount of Russian credit available to Chile that businessmen were not making full use of. From the moment we sat down, I could tell that Putin hadn't
just read the briefing documents—he had completely absorbed and analyzed
them. The extent to which he understood the issue took me by surprise, particularly given that the issue was truly a detail in our bilateral relations, and in
the scope of issues that Putin must have had on his mind at that summit. This
was a man who meant business.

In the course of sorting out our specific concerns, our conversation veered
into Russian politics. Things had become quite lax and inefficient under his
predecessor, Boris Yeltsin, Putin explained. The country needed a strong hand
to pick up the economy, clean up the bureaucracy, and revive hope in the post-
Soviet project. Putin wasn't asking my opinion on all this; he was telling me
what was coming.

Nothing could have been in more contrast to that direct, down-to-busi-
ness approach than a meeting that I held one year later with Japanese Prime
Minister Junichiro Koizumi, who had just been elected. I had planned to raise
economic issues. But instead, we spent the majority of our time discussing the
prime minister's recent trip to the *Buque Escuela Esmeralda,* a majestic Chilean
sailing ship that has been in our fleet since the 1950s. The trip had obviously
made a deep impression on him. No matter how I tried, I simply couldn't
shift our conversation to more practical matters. We spoke only very generally
about maintaining good ties, and I left feeling a bit puzzled and disappointed.
Until afterward, when an aide explained to me that the prime minister only
discussed these more serious themes once he felt he had gotten to know his
counterpart properly. We were clearly still in that opening phase. I learned a
bit more with each occasion how best to negotiate with the Japanese leader:
never at dinner or any other event that might be construed as a social occasion.
In such moments, Koizumi preferred another topic: his exploits with various
female companions.

Luckily, my relationship with another Asian giant, South Korea, was
rather more productive. Over the course of my term, our two countries negotiated and signed a free-trade agreement. It was the first such agreement with
Korea that any American country had signed, and, as such, the accord was
scrutinized across the region—for how it balanced agricultural interests and
protected manufacturing, for example. Perhaps Barack Obama should have

taken closer notes before he attempted to finalize the U.S.-Korea deal during his fall 2010 trip to Asia.

I n 1879, the Chilean military fought its way into Antofagasta, taking over the small port city that caps the world's driest desert, Atacama. This was the thick of the War of the Pacific, a conflict that lasted half a decade and bruised relations among Chile, Peru, and Bolivia for more than 100 years. The Bolivians were pushed out of Antofagasta, and they haven't ever come back. In 1904, a peace agreement granted Bolivia access to the city's ports for traded goods, mandating the construction of a rail system from the capital of La Paz to Arica in Chile's north. Despite the agreement, however, Bolivia continues to dream of getting permanent access to the sea. And so long as Bolivia remains a landlocked country, it's unlikely we'll be able to have official diplomatic relations. As the Bolivians see it, their predicament is Chile's fault.

Unofficially, however, Bolivia was one of the most fascinating cases of my presidency. The president in those days was General Hugo Banzer, a man who had ruled once before as a military autocrat in the late 1970s and returned to power democratically in 1997. He was a tough, right-wing leader who had led a military uprising in 1971, against then-President Juan José Torres. Banzer never lost his tough image, or his disciplined posture, even when he was resurrected as a democrat—which is precisely why he was able to talk to Chile. It was like Nixon going to China; a softy on communism never could have done it.

Before I took office, I traveled to the inauguration of the new president of Uruguay, where Bolivian President Banzer would also be. Despite his having held power years earlier, we had never met.

As I walked into the small hall, where the heads of state of Latin American countries were gathered, I saw Banzer tucked in a corner by himself. I greeted the packs of diplomats and then gracefully excused myself, making my way over to the Bolivian leader to introduce myself. I was struck by his affinity for open and frank conversation. There was no couching of words or overly restrictive diplomatic formalities.

In the dinner that followed, protocol mandated that I not join the other leaders. But as chance would have it, the woman I sat next to was Banzer's wife, and we spent the evening talking. I hoped to make a good impression so that she would tell her husband: This Ricardo Lagos is a good guy.

A few months later in Asunción, Paraguay, I found myself in the same hotel as Banzer during a summit of the South American Common Market, Mercado Común del Sur (MERCOSUR). The hotel was a fair distance from the presidential palace where an official dinner would take place, so that night we hopped onto a shuttle that took us back and forth during the summit. I took my seat next to Banzer. "We have much to speak about, Mr. President," I told him.

"Yes, we do," he replied, not wasting a moment. "I want to explain the two problems that consume my administration." Banzer launched: "The first problem is that I need to halt the cultivation of coca," something that he had begun in collaboration with a White House then increasingly concerned about the drug trade heading north. "This is difficult, because I have to find alternative crops for so many farmers to grow.

"But my second problem—as you can imagine—is access to the sea," he told me. "And in particular, access to the sea so that we can sell our natural gas."

Bolivia has a lot of natural gas—the second largest reserve of any country in Latin America—and the profits from that natural bounty represent one of the greatest sources of hope for the country's development. Protests over how the revenues have been spread through society have broken out several times in the last decade, and nearly every contract and extraction deal signed has sent demonstrators to the streets. Back then, most of the gas left the country through a pipeline to Brazil. Selling it on the Pacific coast as well would be a huge boon to the Bolivian economy. But the problem, without a coastline of Bolivia's own, was where—and how.

Banzer had a clear understanding of what was holding them back. If the gas was exported through Chile, it would have to be liquefied before it left. And because the port would be Chilean, that liquefaction would have to take place in Chile, not Bolivia. "I could export Bolivian gas for some $400 million a year to Chile," he explained. "But Chile, after liquefying it, could sell that gas on the global market for $1.5 billion. How can I possibly explain to the Bolivian people that this is a good deal for our country?"

His explanation impressed me. And I immediately replied, "President, if that is the problem, why don't we refer back to the peace treaty?" I continued, "Chile can offer you that land that you need for a liquefaction plant free of charge on a contract of 99 years. You can begin soliciting offers from international companies to liquefy the gas. And hence, all of the taxes and royalties from the processing can go to Bolivia. The gas will be defined as a product "in transit," and it will be Bolivia that receives the $1.5 billion, since the gas is yours." Banzer was intrigued.

On face value, the offer I made to Banzer could have been political suicide for me at home. Giving away land to Bolivia was not going to be possible at first. The land was government owned, so there were not concerns about concessions or rights. But on principle, even though the war had ended more than 100 years ago, this land was Chile's.

I have always believed that when you speak to the people—no matter the issue—with the dignity and transparency that they deserve, you'll be able to win public support on your side. If we made enough progress, I thought at the time, I would explain to the people why such a deal was necessary—why we needed to end our spat and why the solution we were working toward was the best possible option. Time and time again, Chileans proved to me that they were mature enough to accept difficult politics—if I made the effort to explain what I was doing and why.

And so that short bus-ride conversation became regional statecraft—and it would have advanced further if Banzer had not suddenly fallen ill. Our respective negotiators had barely laid the groundwork before word came from La Paz that the Bolivian president was not well. It was lung and liver cancer, and by August 2001, he had resigned power to his vice president, Jorge Quiroga—who also happened to be the one charged with negotiating Bolivia's use of the land.

Several months after Quiroga took over, it became clear that Banzer was likely to die. If the ex-president did pass away, I told Quiroga, I would like to attend his funeral and offer personal testimony, despite our lacking official diplomatic relations. One Sunday morning not long thereafter, I got the call. The funeral would be held the following morning. I flew to Santa Cruz very early that day on a small Air Force plane. The foreign minister awaited my landing, informing me that we would have to proceed directly to the ceremonies.

At first, as I entered the public ceremony, a wave of silence—perhaps stupefaction at seeing a Chilean president—overcame the air, giving way, however, to applause. I walked forward, by now seeing that it was clear that I would face the color guard of the Bolivian flag. We were not on diplomatic speaking terms, our two countries. So should I simply stare forward? Should I salute? Should I bow? I hadn't the slightest idea. I nodded my head slightly in respect. And luckily, the applause continued. I kept walking in the procession to greet Quiroga and then Banzer's widow, who was touched by my presence there. When I spoke to the press, I lauded the progress we had made toward bringing our two countries back together on good terms.

Our negotiations continued under Quiroga, who was in office for only a few months, until the next elections, which were won by Gonzalo Sánchez de Lozada. It was the beginning of a downward spiral that saw president after Bolivian president, administration after administration, drowned by political chaos. Lozada was replaced by his vice president, Carlos Mesa Guisbert, who was then unseated and replaced again by the head of the Supreme Court, Eduardo Rodríguez. In the six years that I was president, I had to deal with six different Bolivian heads of state.

The most difficult partner I found was Carlos Mesa, who had assumed the presidency after Lozada was removed from power. Just two weeks after the new Bolivian president was inaugurated, he hosted the Ibero-American summit and didn't waste a moment in approaching me about Bolivia's landlocked territory. I told him he would have to approach not just me, but also Peru's president, since any coastal land we gave to Bolivia would have to be cut out of both of our territories, not just Chile's. Mesa wasn't appeased, however, and by the time Mexico hosted the Summit of the Americas that summer, I got wind that he planned to publically confront me about the issue.

Bush was also at that summit, and I felt it was important for him to know about the confrontation that Mesa intended to provoke. I requested a side meeting with him and Condoleezza Rice, who took notes while I was speaking. They thanked me for the information and seemed unconcerned, although happy to be kept in the loop.

After our dinner, I approached Mesa and tried to dissuade him from turning our private negotiations into a public *j'accuse*. It was 1 A.M. by the time we finished the evening's activities and our sideline meeting began. "I know that you plan to raise the issue of access to the sea," I told him. "Please don't. Because if you raise the issue, I will have to respond. And that will be the end of our negotiations. We'll have to wait another 20 years to have the same fresh start."

Mesa didn't take my advice, and in the final session, he brought it up, demanding that Chile grant his country access to the sea. I, of course, had to reply. I explained in detail the efforts we had made toward resolving the crisis; I made it clear that Chile was ready to talk. My speech grew impassioned. And at the end, I proclaimed to Bolivia: "I offer diplomatic relations here and now." The crowd was clapping by the time I finished. And Mesa looked like the uncooperative one.

After the speech, Bush approached me. He had been listening to my address—in Spanish—through a translator. But together with my body language, what had just happened was very clear. "Ricardo, I want to make sure that next time you are on my side," Bush told me. "Because I don't want to be the target of a speech like that!"

When I returned home to Chile from the summit, a humor magazine found my remarks less serious and more amusing. On the cover of *The Clinic* that week was a beautiful, bikini-clad woman, her arms open as if to embrace. "I offer relations—here and now," the cover read.

But my overtures didn't sway Mesa, and anyway, he was gone from the presidency not long thereafter. Bolivian politics was a rotating door, I began to think.

Until finally, there came Evo Morales.

Morales, like Chávez, was truly a product of his people's aspirations. In the years I had been in the government, I had come across the indigenous peoples of Bolivia on several occasions, and it was always clear that there were leaders—and then there was Morales, The Leader. He spoke modestly and softly as president, a contrast from his impassioned speeches in his native Quechua language.

I met Morales in his personal home, just prior to his inauguration ceremony in January 2006. And those modest rooms told me everything about this man, who had risen from the depths of Bolivian inequality to become the leader of a nation. It was a tiny abode, and every conceivable nook and cranny was crammed with books—every imaginable type of book. There was a small kitchen leading into a combined living-dining room so small that the dining table had been pushed into a corner to make room for a few people to meet on the couch. Even then, the room could seat only a couple of bodies. Although I'd come with a delegation of diplomats and ministers, I was able to attend the meeting with just one colleague—my son, Ricardo, who was by then a member of the incoming administration of Michele Bachelet. Journalists would follow the same ritual to speak with the new Bolivian president, waiting in the small kitchen to the side until someone else left that room and there was space for another visitor to enter and greet him.

Our intimate conversation gave me a chance to tell Morales a bit more about what progress the negotiations between Chile and Bolivia had made. "Mr. President, I know that you must have the important subject of gas on your mind," I began. "I want to tell you that Chile will continue to welcome you if you want to run your export business into the Pacific."

I continued with what I thought would be good news for Morales: He could raise the price in coming years to equal the level of the international market. "Chile, as you know, needs to import gas. And we have been doing so from Argentina until recently; the Argentine economy requires more and more energy and they are exporting less and less." What that meant, I told him, was that Chile had decided to build a processing plant at home, through which we can re-gasify the liquid natural gas bought from abroad. "Since Chile now refines its own natural gas, you can also begin to sell your unrefined gas at the price that Chile pays. You can tell your gas-buying clients that you will begin charging the same price that Chile has to pay, between 10 and 15 cents." It was an amount three times the price that Bolivia was currently charging.

Morales looked at me quietly, his brow slightly curved with an expression of contemplation. He turned to his vice president, Alvaro García Linera, with an inquiring expression, as if unsure as to what I'd just said. "I believe the president of Chile is correct," Garcia told him.

In October 2010, in the same Atacama desert, Morales joined Chilean President Sebastian Piñera to great fanfare. The two men were celebrating. Nearly 70 days earlier, 33 miners had found themselves trapped almost half a mile below the ground. For the first few days, the searches seemed hopeless; they were lost to the crevices of the mine. But then something amazing happened: The miners were found alive. And after 69 days underground, they were all brought up safely.

What the world saw of Chile in that moment was a triumphant country, finding hope and being vindicated after a terrible crisis. I wish that the world could see more of this Chile—because it extends far beyond the tales of these individual miners. We are a country that has overcome its past, not without hiccups, and not without vestiges that still require attention. But Chile keeps trying. The entire country invested in getting those miners out safely, aided and inspired by international cooperation that came from every corner of the world. If there's one word that explains why an almost impossible task was performed so well, its perseverance.

That's Chile—ready and eager. And we know that the world will be as pleased to discover Chile as we were to see the miners again after 69 days underground. When each one of the men was pulled up in fresh clothes to the cheers of camera crews and a worldwide audience of viewers, they saw the real hope that is Chile.

EPILOGUE

On November 28, 1998, the former president of Colombia leaned toward me from his dinner seat in Guadalajara, Mexico, where we were both attending a conference with such other dignitaries as the authors Gabriel García Márquez and Carlos Fuentes. Belisario Betancourt's voice was always dignified—he spoke like an intellectual, not a politician, his grammar ornate and his thoughts perfectly articulated. But this time there was something else there too—a childlike joy animating his words. He was like a schoolboy sharing a secret. "Ricardo, I have made a great discovery that I want to share with you: There is a life after the presidency."

I laughed and turned back to him, surprised by his sudden segue. "But I also have bad news, Mr. Lagos. The life after the presidency—it's a good life. The bad news is that first, you have to be the president." We laughed again.

More than two decades later, I can confirm Betancourt's wisdom, of which I have thought often: There is a life after the presidency. Politics, as they say, is a profession from which you can never retire, even long after you leave office. If you choose to embrace it, the destiny of ex-presidents is more and greater public service.

There are, of course, several discreet tasks that tend to accompany presidents out of office. We are called upon to act in diplomatic roles. I served in many such posts, for example, working on high-level commissions (although I've never heard of any commissions calling themselves low or medium level) for the United Nations, the World Health Organization, and the International

Monetary Fund, or serving as the chairman of the Club de Madrid, an advisory group made up of former heads of state. I always found this kind of work compelling. Most recently, I was asked to work as U.N. Secretary General Ban Ki-Moon's special envoy for climate change for the 2009 Copenhagen conference, which yielded the unexpected last-minute deal between the United States and the emerging economies.

Beyond these sorts of ad hoc missions, there is a truly greater task that befalls an ex-president: to reflect. When you're in office, there is never enough time to simply sit and think. Presidential terms are always too short, and decisions are made with that urgency in mind—knowing that no matter how hard one tries, all of the things you set out to accomplish will never fit into just four or six years of office.

Perhaps the most miraculous change as a former statesman is the timeline. Only after leaving office do you have the luxury—indeed, the responsibility—of taking the long view, of thinking about the challenges that transcend term limits. You think about the path that your country will take, not in a few years but over the course of generations. We ex-presidents are no longer the decision makers, but that's exactly why we can and should encourage our societies to think outside the sometimes narrow confines of partisan politics.

The kinds of questions we can ask out of office are profound, and they are changing as quickly as the world itself. We have to consider the mistakes that we made, from the projects we didn't finish to the things that weren't executed quite as we hoped. We have to consider the structures of government we took for granted in office—was there something about the system itself that was thwarting change? And we have to consider the world and the role we play in it. Never before in history has my country—and many like it in Latin America and the so-called Global South—had the opportunity to play such an important role on the global stage. After years of playing supporting roles in the world economy, after years of suffering financial crises of our own making, we are now the powerhouses, the growth engines, and the emerging centers of innovation. Much of the future depends on how the rising powers rise—and on the world we create.

The challenges to Chile and its peers are mirrored across the developing and developed worlds. In fact, many of the greatest questions facing us cannot be answered by any one country alone. Whether it's combating inequality or protecting democracy, promoting human rights or stopping climate change, the challenges of our time carry consequences in every corner of the globe and require action from all. No one president or congress can prevent the planet from warming; no one trading bloc can define international exchange. Even the United States is beginning to recognize this emerging reality—that while Washington cannot solve the world's problems, neither will the world's problems be solved without Americans. We all need each other to progress in this new age.

W hen Pedro de Valdivia conquered Chile in 1541, founding Santiago, the Spanish conquistador could never have imagined that his new city would someday swell into a buzzing metropolis of 6 million, packed tightly among mountains in every direction. His colonial town was built for horses, not masses of cars spewing emissions and fogging the sky with grey smog in the winter. The main avenues had space enough for busy days back then, but nowhere near the capacity for bus after bus of workers coming into the heart of the city each morning and leaving each night.

This legacy (how could Valdivia have known?) is something we have been fighting in Chile for the last century in our transportation system. And my first regret is that we were unable to do more.

Since we couldn't rebuild the city, we had to try to make it more humane for those who rely on public transportation for their daily survival. We succeeded in extending the metro lines in Santiago from just 25 miles in 2000 to 55 miles in 2006; we also added some 45 miles of highway. But the second half of our reforms proved more complicated. Through the so-called Transantiago program, we planned to cordon off one lane of highway exclusively for bus traffic and upgrade the buses themselves, which would have cut commuting time by 25 percent. But along the way, the program stalled. Too many bus drivers weren't running their lines on off-peak hours, and we had no way—technologically speaking—to ensure that the vehicles followed a schedule. The bus program was fully implemented by my successor, Michele Bachelet, but to this day, the technology is not ideal. We've paid a high price for waiting. And the poorest, as the group that relies heaviest on public transit, suffered the most.

There are other areas, too, where we could have done better. We made good progress in preserving the environment, but the task of creating a minister of environment would fall to Bachelet. Nor were we able to approve a new water code that would have returned outdated or unused water concessions to the state. There is also a much-needed bridge that we were never able to build, which would have linked together two isolated parts of the country. A feat of engineering, the structure was meant to connect the Isla Grandes de Chiloe with continental Chile and with the southern city of Puerto Montt. It was a costly and daring project, but I never had any doubts that it could be completed if work were allowed to continue. After all, the same company that had successfully built a bridge between Denmark and Sweden was ready to undertake the building. After I left office, however, the project stalled. The upfront costs were just too politically daunting, even though I believed that private concessions combined with a toll no higher than the cost of the existing ferry could raise the funds.

There were political failures too. Even after a decade of democracy had passed since Pinochet, we were still unable to push through the kind of constitutional reforms that would have finally normalized our democracy. We were unable to change the undemocratic voting system that gives an advantage to minority parties. Nor were we able to lift a very odd, neoliberal rule that prohibited the state from doing business in any sector where private businesses operate. To this day, the Chilean government can't build solar power plants or craft an updated electrical grid; it's illegal for us to do business anywhere we might compete with a non-state company.

All of these shortcomings are merely details—albeit important ones to many people's daily lives—in a broader story about the failings of government. Humans, of course, err, but systems abet mistakes. And here, I believe there are four main narratives about where democratic systems around the world fail and need to be rethought.

The first is the influence of technocrats within a government. Look at governments across the globe today—from Latin America to Europe—and you'll often find that many of the internationally lauded governments are stacked thick with technocrats: men and women who have the academic training and expertise to keep the macroeconomy sound and budgets under control. These sorts of cabinets are designed to prove our countries' seriousness to investors around the world. And in our case, it has worked: Chile is today the recipient of billions of dollars in foreign investment every year, and our macroeconomic performance is top rate.

Yet while this strategy has had success in attracting money from abroad, it has also caused problems at home. Eager to prove that public projects can be self-funded and bear little cost to taxpayers, technocrats are not likely to take political risks—particularly on behalf of those citizens who have the least. What economist would submit a proposal for transportation or electricity subsidies targeted toward the poor? This is not to say that financial considerations are unimportant. But nor should they be the only concerns of a government. We have to think about the numbers—and then we have to think beyond them. As global inequality grows, it should be a priority of every society to strengthen the safety net for its poorest constituents.

A second systematic failure of government, in Chile in particular, stems from its organization, which is at once too centralized at the top and too chaotic at the local level. Take the city of Santiago, for example: Every district has its own mayor despite the deep interconnectedness of the entire city. When we built a trans-city highway during my term, I had to ask some 12 separate mayors for their permission. Given such fractured local power, members of the central government, such as the ministers of health or education, find themselves overstretched in managing it. This institutional architecture is anachronistic, dating back to a time when our country, and the world, was far less intertwined. Today, our cities need strong, metropolis-wide governments. And our regional government needs to yield more autonomy to those authorities at the local level.

Third is the ever-vexing question of how to ensure some continuity in policy from one administration to another. There are two cases in which this tends to happen by itself—when the subsequent administration is of the same political affiliation as the first, and when public policies are enormously popular. Still, even in the best of circumstances, it is only human for each new president to feel as if he or she is somehow starting with a blank slate. Coming into office, the new leader will have a new agenda, new ideas, and new programs all his own. That's healthy. But the history of a country doesn't begin when someone new is elected to office. For public policy to truly be institutionalized, it is vital that there is continuity from one administration to another.

I experienced firsthand both how difficult this could be and how important it was for the nation's future. Toward the end of Frei's term in 1998, he began to reform the judicial system, transforming it from an onerous written procedure into an oral one. Before the reforms, our courts operated a bit like the Spanish Inquisition—one judge served as prosecutor and adjudicator. The new rules brought our justice system up to date, instituting prosecution and defense lawyers. The difference was enormous; trial times were effectively cut from years to months. But these reforms were also expensive, and there was some doubt during the presidential election about whether the new president—either I or my opponent—would continue them. The new code was written in 1997 and 1998, when Chile was growing at 6 percent annually—when no one imagined that the Asian financial crisis would so devastate our growth. By 2000, our fiscal system looked much different, and we had to think hard about how to keep the momentum of reform going without breaking the bank. It took courage and determination to make the case that judicial reform was just too important to let die, and I am very proud that we succeeded.

Imagine if we had not, and it becomes clear why continuity is so important. Chile's sound judicial system is today vital to our ability to offer justice to our citizens and also convince businesses and investors that any legal action they should face will be just and speedy. Before the changes we made, cases could literally drag on for years, and the entire fate of the proceedings would be in the hands of just one judge. No modern society or economy could be built upon such a shaky pillar of justice.

I am grateful and proud that many of my own administration's policies have continued uninterrupted to this day, despite the fact that Chile's president is not currently from Concertación. I have watched Chile Solidario and our healthcare reforms become institutions, not just one-off programs. These policies have been kept in place because Chileans wanted them. It is only a truly successful political system that can judge its policies in this way—based on their merit and not on the affiliation or party of their creators.

A final structural concern in all counties is corruption, a hot global topic in recent years. Its ubiquity and ever-changing face make it a theory problem: Corruption can penetrate every corner of society and cloud every transition; it can hide in unexpected sectors and ruin the most promising projects in unexpected ways. Governments that are opaque can never truly be democratic, just as economies tarnished by illegitimate gains will never rise above a certain level of development. Put simply, transparency is vital to modernity. And as I look at how Chile operates, I see this as one of the most striking areas where we must improve, as is the case with many countries in the developing world.

Taking just the figures alone, on Transparency International's annual corruption index, Chile ranks best in Latin America and twenty-first in the world, on par with the United States and Britain. We can be proud of that relative accountability, but we also have to do much better. We must never grow complacent or deny the intimate relationship between money and politics.

We are always vulnerable to the temptations of the human spirit. A good government is one that puts in place systems and institutions to prevent the temptations from arising in the first place. Donations to political campaigns, for example, must be regulated, as they are in the United States. Resource-rich countries might find it useful to institutionalize a means of saving their mineral revenues, as Chile has done with its fiscal stabilization fund. At the ground level, public servants need competitive salaries so they aren't tempted to earn their keep in other ways. There must be consequences for dishonesty and investigations into misdeeds. And all this must be done in a way that is nonpartisan. Anti-corruption campaigns mustn't become witch hunts for members of one party or another.

In my experience, the press is also vital—and not just in Chile. Governments need a free and vibrant fourth estate to ask questions and keep them honest. These days, there is also an emerging fifth estate—the Internet—through which any citizen can report abuses and grievances. It is up to us to build the mechanisms and the institutions to listen.

But we are still discussing details. To take the long view means to examine what the challenges of future generations will be—what will make or break our societies in the years to come. On the horizon, I see the challenges of inequality, changing technology, and environmental degradation as paramount. These are the narratives that our children and grandchildren will spend their lives writing; we can set them up for success or leave them to grapple with our failures.

Perhaps the most pressing social problem is inequality. When Pinochet left office in 1989, the average income in Chile was $5,000 per capita, a bit behind our neighbors Argentina and Uruguay. Growing that number, we knew, was vital to Chile's economic future—every successful country since the end of World War II had done so. Without growth, there could be no progress. And progress was exactly what we achieved: By 2010, we had tripled our per capita income to $15,000. If we continue at our current growth rate, the IMF expects the average Chilean will earn $20,000 by 2016 (other estimates suggest we may reach this level by 2020). Meanwhile, Chile has also progressed on nearly every indicator you can measure—from child mortality to women's health to life expectancy. We are better off today than at any other time in our history.

It's a story that has been repeated all over the world: Growth is like magic. But because its benefits are so undisputed, the world also worries less about how these gains are distributed; the assumption tends to be that progress in one sector of the economy will be contagious, triggering a self-perpetuating cycle. We now know, having learned the hard way, that this isn't necessarily, or even usually, the case. Our world has grown vastly more unequal as the average person has grown more prosperous.

Behind the statistics are real lives at stake. To accept an unequal society means that whole sectors of the population lack the opportunity to make better lives for themselves. They lack access to education; they cannot obtain credit or think beyond their next meal. In the language of the United States, an unequal world is one in which the American dream doesn't exist. It simply isn't possible for a poor father's son to rise beyond his own economic status at birth.

In Chile, our inequality has nearly reached the tipping point where global growth no longer improves the average quality of life. Recent studies indicate that once a country passes $20,000 in annual income per capita, social indicators scarcely improve from further gains in growth alone. Something else has to happen—something that addresses inequality. We have to ensure a minimum standard of living for every person in our society. Latin America scores particularly poorly with regard to inequality. And within the region, Chile has the particular dishonor of being among the most unequal, despite our efforts to combat poverty.

In the late summer of 2011, the consequences of continued inequality were on vivid display, when students flooded the streets of Santiago to call for access to better and more equal education. These are the children of Chile's democracy, born after the fall of the dictator and raised in a country that has come to expect and demand responsive and responsible government. These are young men and women who know Chile as an economic leader in its region—but still an imperfect one.

Under the dictatorship, we found Chile's inequality tragic. In our new democracy, the students have found it intolerable. And in many ways, this should make us proud: That so many students have come to the streets to demand their rights is both an indication of how far we have come and how far we have left to go. This new generation has taken advantage of the opportunities they have under democracy—to learn and think freely, and to build their own lives. Very rightly, they have been frustrated by the obstacles in their way, from the continued income gaps and differences in the quality of public services among Chilean communities to the sad reality that it remains all too difficult to break out of class boundaries. The protests have reminded us that we must never waver in our quest for social justice.

Luckily, we have tools at our disposal to fix this problem in the short, medium, and long terms.

In the short term, any government can reduce imbalances almost immediately with social spending. Here, Chile has done quite well. We have helped the poor with housing and health care, offered them grants and scholarships to stay in school, and worked to combat the social stigma that often follows from being destitute. After you account for these government subsidies to the less fortunate, income inequality between the richest and poorest parts of Chilean society dramatically shrinks.

It's the other half of the short-term solution, taxation, where Chile falls short. In every other country in the Organisation for Economic Co-operation and Development (OECD) group of developed economies, inequality improves a bit after taxation because the government collects more revenue from the wealthiest than from its poorest citizens. But in our own case, the distribution of income remains the same before and after the collection of taxes.

Further down the line, one of the keys to equitable growth is a country's labor laws. Minimum wages can ensure that firms offer competitive salaries. But more importantly, workers must have the ability to organize and demand fair working conditions and compensation linked to better productivity. It's no coincidence that the world's most equal countries, for example, those in Scandinavia, also have the most developed labor unions, which are adept at negotiating without pushing their demands to confrontation.

And of course, there is also education, the building block of all social change. Ensuring that every child has access to the same high-quality teachers, facilities, and curriculum is the antidote to inequality for generations to come. Elites will always tend to reproduce themselves, but it's in those early formative years of growth that talents can rise above the social structures that constrain them.

This is the first challenge of our coming decades—not just in Chile but across the world. In the United States, for example, the problem is increasingly acute. In the 1970s, the top 1 percent of society earned 9 percent of the country's income. Today, that number is more than 20 percent. Inequality has more than doubled just in the past 40 years. I'm certain that this stems from the very tendency that is often cited as America's strength: a reliance on free markets. A society that is built on neoliberal economic ideas will indeed foster GDP growth and innovation. But unless it is complemented with public policy aimed at promoting equality, a free-market society will always be inherently unfair.

The challenge for countries seeking to join the developed world is to prove that we can be prosperous without exacerbating the gap between rich and poor. So far, our track record augurs well. We have followed the same combination of economic opening and social policy that Scandinavian countries used to prosper after the end of World War II, when they became real players in the European economy. If we can do the same in Latin America and on the world stage, we will consider ourselves successful. We must never forget that the stakes are high—because they're measured in the dignity of human lives.

I like to think of democracy as the permanent process of expanding the boundaries of what is humanly possible. Never has this been more true than in a world of fast-changing technology. I lived much of my life in a world of Democracy 1.0. Today, we are living in Democracy 2.0—a world in which the Internet has transformed the relationship between citizens and their government. What was once an onerous exchange of ideas between the two—the government making declarations and citizens reacting with their votes—has been transformed into an ongoing dialogue. It's as if democracy were returning to the days of ancient Athens, when all the citizens would gather in one plaza to discuss politics. Everyone can share his or her opinion; the government can capture the public mood instantaneously. The Internet has created a new plaza of governance, the capacity of which is infinite.

This is the second theme of our coming century—one that is already omnipresent in our daily lives. The possibilities for using these new tools in government are truly infinite. In countries where the media is consolidated in the hands of a few or where the government discourages dissent, the Internet provides an alternative forum to discuss what's on people's minds. In open societies, there's no doubt that the Internet will be used to cast votes or perhaps even craft legislation. Governments themselves can also run more efficiently using the Web, mirroring the gains that the private sector is pioneering. Like anywhere, governing in the Internet age will be about building institutions that facilitate what takes place online.

There are, of course, also challenges in navigating this new system. The Internet would surely be the worst nightmare of Alexis de Tocqueville, who feared that the "tyranny of the majority" would render politicians too responsive to the whims of the people, who didn't necessarily know what was best. And indeed, if every notion expressed on the Internet were heeded, the quality of government would surely suffer. Even responding to the constant dialogue online can drain a government's political capital. Scandal is the online media's stock in trade, hyping stories that might otherwise be only minor controversies.

But the way to deal with this risk is to accept it and understand it in the context of all your government or administration hopes to do. If your short-term goal is criticized online, perhaps it should be placed in the context of a broader plan. I have always believed that the most effective administrations are those that are coherent to their voters; your vision of the future must be clearly articulated, and every move must fit into that broader story. There's no reason a conversation with the online community should follow any other model.

When we looked at a country in the twentieth century, the first questions we asked were about the health of its economy: How big is the market, and what is the average income per capita? In the coming decades, the question on our lips will change: What are the greenhouse gas emissions per capita?

There is simply no denying it: Our existence on this planet in unsustainable if our economy continues to grow as it has. The environment is bearing the costs of our rapid industrialization and urbanization, our rising population, our growing appetite for material wealth, and our ballooning carbon emissions. Climate change is already happening; more dangerous global warming looks inevitable if *we* do not begin to change. And the sooner the better.

Countries like Chile, which today contribute only a tiny proportion of global emissions, still have a vital role to play. Our emissions per capita are less than a fourth of those of the United States. But as our economy grows, so too do our emissions. And emerging economies, today the engine of global growth, will contribute markedly to climate change in the coming years.

This also means that we have the greatest opportunity to prove that there is another way. We will have to couple our economic growth with advances in green technology. Technologies already exist that allow us to grow in a more energy efficient way. We can use more efficient light bulbs and build our houses so as to guard the heat in winter and keep cool in the warmer months. The small individual gains of, say, driving more efficient cars or buying low-electricity appliances will certainly add up.

As a special envoy to the U.N. secretary general on climate negotiations, I have had the opportunity to participate in many discussions on this theme, and I understand the challenges that exist. I understand the political complications of fighting climate change, particularly in the United States. But Chile must be an example to the other Latin American countries in the next round of negotiations, indicating that we are ready for a new set of international norms for developing countries that would ensure the lowering of emissions by 2020.

So great is the magnitude of this final challenge that I believe that in the twenty-first century, those countries that fail to control their emissions will be marginalized from the community of civilized nations.

There is much talk today about the new rising world order, defined by the emergence of Asia and the burgeoning diplomatic clout of the global south, where the world's population and economic growth are increasingly centered. There is also much talk about American and European decline—the idea that amid the rise of new powers the old powers must inevitably fade.

I don't believe either side has the full story. In years to come, our world will be built on the institutions of the old powers, the dynamism of the new-comers, and the moral compulsion that all global leaders feel to work with one another. No country can rise without the help of others; no country will fall without the global community being complicit. In an interconnected world, the realists and the idealists all have to agree: There are more partners than rivals and more alliances than estranged friends.

In March 2011, U.S. President Barack Obama traveled to Latin America and spoke of this very subject. In his trip to Chile, he spoke about the need to understand that the relationship between the United States and Latin America was a relationship among equals, one in which there were many common themes to discuss. He defined an agenda of security and commercial cooperation, as well as a need to work together to reform the international financial system in light of the latest international crisis. He spoke about immigration, drug trafficking, and climate change. This is the agenda that all countries of the world face in the twenty-first century. It's an agenda that the world's greatest power, the United States, is increasingly conscious that it cannot tackle alone.

As members of this global conversation, we—just one country in Latin America—can contribute our ideas. We can contribute to creating a constructive global debate. We can put our misgivings on the table with transparency. We can share our values and push toward common goals. We can take the long view and realize that there are going to be hard discussions, difficult decisions, and sacrifices along a path that we, humanity, know we must take—for greater justice, sustainability, and dignity in every life.

In my own small way, this is what I have tried to do in these days since I left the office. I've done what I can to look at the horizon, and I've tried to look backward and learn enough that our children don't suffer the burdens of the past.

My friend Belisario Betancourt was right: There is life after the presidency.

INDEX

ABC News, 67
Abrams, Elliot, 65, 67
Acceso Universal conGarantías
    Explícitas (AUGE), 194
Acuña, Lionel, 80, 86–7, 98
AD, See Democratic Alliance
Ahumada, Jaime, 53
al Qaeda, 211
Alessandri, Jorge, 23–4, 40, 44
Alfonsín, Argentina, 101
Alfonsín, Raúl, 59, 84, 87
Allende, Isabelle, 135, 148
Allende, Salvador, viii, 3–4, 16, 23–32,
    37, 40–2, 44, 47–8, 51–2, 54,
    63, 65, 120–1, 127, 135–6, 148,
    160–1, 169–72 and coup d'état,
    26–8; and economic collapse,
    25–6, 37, 42, 172; final address
    of, 29; friendship with Lagos,
    23–6; and land redistribution,
    41; presidency of, 23–9; suicide
    of, 29, 52, 170–1
Allende, Tencha, 51–2, 171
Almeyda, Clodomiro, 24, 51–4, 67, 73,
    90–1, 93, 114, 120
Altamirano, Carlos, 51–2
Alvayay, Rodrigo, 47, 53
Alzamora, Angélica, xii, 89
Amato, Giuliano, 230–1
Análisis, 63–4, 74
APEC, See Asia-Pacific Economies
    Cooperation
Arevalo, Juan José, 23
Árbenz Guzmán, Jacobo, 23
Argentina, 2, 30, 33–6, 41–2, 50, 59–60,
    84, 87, 90, 101, 138, 147, 180,
    185, 228–31, 240, 248
Arriagada, Genaro, 98, 101–2, 107
Article 8, 108–9
Asia-Pacific Economies Cooperation
    (APEC), 231–3
Asian financial crisis (1997), 172–5, 247
assassinations, vii, 2, 33–4, 41–2, 44,
    54, 60, 68–9, 71–2, 74–6, 81–2,
    87, 153
AUGE, See Acceso Universal
    conGarantías Explícitas
Aylwin, Patricio, 3–4, 6, 13, 76, 99,
    102–3, 109, 111–12, 114–15,
    118–20, 128, 133–7, 139, 152,
    154, 158, 166, 173, 175, 180

Bachelet, Michelle, 81, 168–9, 177,
    239, 244–5
Baeza, Ernesto, 79
Baker, James, 221
Balmaceda, Jose Manuel, 16, 95
Baltra, Alberto, 19
Baltra, Mirella, 93
Ban Ki-Moon, 243
Bañados, Patricio, 95
Bandung Conference (1955), 20
Banzer, Hugo, 235–7
Barnes, Jr., Harry G., 66, 100, 109
Barrios, Gracia, 106
"Bases del Diálogo para un Gran
    Acuerdo Nacional" (Principles
    of Dialogue for a Grand
    National Accord), 57

Batlle, Jorge, 65
Beltrán, Gonzalo, 9–10
Berlin Wall, 19
Bernstein, Enrique, 80
Betancourt, Belisario, 242, 254
Bill and Melinda Gates Foundation, 130
bin Laden, Osama, 211
Blair, Tony, 135, 146–7, 208, 210–11,
    213–17, 220, 222–7, 230–1
Blix, Hans, 216, 218, 222–3
Bolívar, Simón, 204
Bolivia, 67, 130, 203, 228, 234–40
Brazil, 24, 34–5, 47, 138, 180, 202, 205,
    228–31, 236
Brazilian Center of Planning
    (CEBRAP), 34–5
Bretton Woods, 25
Buenos Aires, 30, 33–6, 75, 229
Bush, George H. W., 24, 221
Bush, George W., 183–4, 200–41

Cambodia, 166
Cáceres, Carlos, 109
Campusano, Julieta, 93
Capitalism and Freedom (Friedman),
    39
Cardemil, Alberto, 84–5, 103
Cardoso, Fernando Henrique, 24, 34–5,
    47, 202, 205, 228–31
Carrasco, José, 74–5
Carter, Jimmy, 42–3, 84, 87
"Casas Lagos," 188, 196
Castro, Fidel, 24, 203
Catholic Church, 61–2, 131–2, 155
Catholic University in Chile, 39–41,
    46, 94, 207
CEBRAP, See Brazilian Center of
    Planning
Central Bank, 37, 175
Central Intelligence Agency (CIA), 25,
    27–8, 32, 42, 63, 66, 201
Central Nacional de Informaciones
    (CNI), 43, 54, 74, 78
Cerda, Pedro Aguirre, 17, 23
Chad, 177
Chávez, Hugo, 201–5, 228, 239
Cheyre, Juan Emilio, 166
"Chicago Boys," 20, 39–49, 92, 123–4,
    138, 147, 150, 195
"Chile, la alegría ya viene (Chile, joy is
    coming)," 96
"Chile: The Grand Themes of the
    Reconstruction" (conference),
    60
Chile Chico, 90–1
Chile Solidario (Chile Solidarity),
    196–7, 247
Chilean miners (2010), 241
"Chilean miracle," 42
China, 19, 24, 142–5, 217, 232–3, 235
Cimma, Enrique Silva, 114
Chirac, Jacques, 181–2, 219–21
Christian Democratic Party, 3–4, 10,
    13, 18, 24, 35, 40, 133, 145
Churchill, Winston, 121
Clark, Helen, 231
climate change, 227, 243–4, 252–4
Clinton, Bill, viii-x, 144, 167, 179, 183,
    189–90, 202, 222, 225, 230

Clinton, Hillary, 189–90
CNI, See Central Nacional de
    Informaciones
CNN interview, 105–6
Cold War, 16–17, 23, 204
colonization, 17, 170, 198, 228, 244
"Committee for Free Elections," 88
Committee for Peace, 62
Communist Party, 51, 57, 65–7, 81,
    89, 100
communists, 7–8, 19–20, 24–5, 27, 39,
    42–4, 48, 51, 57, 63, 65–7, 73,
    81, 83, 89, 93, 100, 235
Concertación, 90, 102, 106–12, 114–18,
    123, 136–7, 145, 153, 164, 167,
    172–3, 176, 187, 196, 247
Concertación of Political Parties for
    Democracy, 107
Conservative party, 18, 23–4, 40
constitution of Chile, vii, 2–3, 8–9,
    27–8, 44–5, 55, 57, 71, 67, 83,
    87–9, 93–4, 103, 107–11, 114,
    117, 121, 169–70, 245
Coordinadora Nacional Sindical (CNI),
    54 See secret police
Copenhagen climate conference
    (2009), 243
copper, ix, 18, 23, 46, 55, 173–8, 183
Correa, Germán, 73
Correa, Raquel, vii, 1, 3, 6, 10–11, 73,
    113–14
Cosas magazine interview, 46
coup d'état (1973) (Chile), 2, 4, 26–35,
    40–5, 47, 49, 51–2, 59, 62, 90,
    108, 135, 154–5, 157, 160–1,
    166, 168–72, 201 and mindset
    changes, 32; and opposition
    parties, 43–4; roundups, 30–1;
    and the U.S., 27–8, 31–2. See
    Augusto Pinochet; human
    rights abuses; junta "way of life"
coup de serviette (napkin revolt),
    155–6
CPU, See Permanent Committee for
    Socialist Unity
Cuba, 24, 67, 203, 206
currency, 26, 46

Dawson Island prison, 30–1, 33, 151
De Castro, Sergio, 41–3, 45–6
De Gasperi, Alcide, 7
De Gaulle, Charles, 7, 25, 104
De La Rúa, Fernando, 230–1
De Negri, Verónica, 66
De Silva, Luiz Inácio ("Lula"), 228–30
De Solano, Alicia, 72
De Villepin, Dominique, 220
Democratic Alliance (AD), 10–11,
    57–64, 66–7, 88
"Democratic Manifesto,"55
democracy, vii, xi, 3–7, 10, 23, 25, 28,
    31, 35, 40–3, 45, 48, 52, 59–61,
    64–5, 89–90, 94, 103, 107, 111,
    117, 130, 132, 135, 137, 147,
    154–5, 158–9, 165, 169–70,
    172–3, 176, 187, 199, 213, 220,
    244–5, 249–51
Dependency and Development in Latin
    America (Faletto), 47

diamonds, 178
dictatorship, See Augusto Pinochet; junta "way of life"
DINA, See Dirección de Inteligencia Nacional
Dirección de Inteligencia Nacional (DINA), 43 See secret police
disappeared persons, 61, 151–60
Dodd, Christopher, 65
Domeyko, 141–2
Duke University, 15, 19
Dupont Circle, 42
Durán, Hernán (brother-in-law), 35
Durán, Hernan (father-in-law), 28–9
Durán, Pedro (brother-in-law), 35, 72, 90, 160
Durán, Pedro (son-in-law), 90

Earlbaum, Joaquín, 82
earthquake of 2010, 188
Economic Commission for Latin America and the Caribbean Countries, 37
economic liberalism, 39–50, 121, 245, 251 See "Chicago Boys"
economics, 21, 25–6, 35–49, 55, 134, 142–5, 172–89, 207, 231–3, 248–53 and crises, 38, 46, 173See Asian financial crisis; and currency, 26, 46; and exports, See exports; and finance, 37; and free market, See "Chicago boys"; free market economics; privatization; and free trade agreements, See free trade agreements; and growth, See economic growth; and inflation, See inflation; and the informal economy, See informal economy; job creation, See job creation; and Lagos's presidency, 172–89; and long-term policy, 175–8; and mining, See mining; and natural resources, 175–8; and "non-trade barriers," 185; recession, See recession; redefining, 48; and regulation, 47; and U.S. sanctions, 27; and "shock therapy," See shock therapy; and stimulus, 177; and sustainability, 26; and taxes, 178–9, 198; trade with China, 142–5; and unemployment, See unemployment
economic growth, 21, 25–6, 46–7, 55, 172–5, 177, 181, 183, 186, 207, 248–53 and sustainability, 25–6
"Economic Growth and Income Inequality" (Kuznets), 21
education system, 122–33, 140, 249 and dropouts, 129; and high school, 128–9; and inequality, 130; and Internet, 130–1; and libraries, 129–30; and pregnancies, 131–3; and teachers, 125–8. See Program of the 900
elections, viii, 1–8, 19, 22–7, 32, 43–7, 52–3, 65–7, 87–103, 107–18, 120, 124, 127, 136–7, 145, 163–4, 169, 207, 227, 247
Electoral Commission, 169
El Mercurio, 1, 27, 63, 113, 145
Enke, Stephen, 21
Errázuriz, Federico, 170–1
Estate Defense Council, 150
European Commission, 181
European Union (EU), 181–3, 208
exiles, 2, 14, 30, 32–6, 41–2, 44–5, 48–9, 51, 88, 90, 93, 100, 108, 146, 159–62

exports, 18, 114–15, 130, 138, 140–1, 173, 176, 180–6 See copper; diamonds; grapes

Face of the Nation interview, 1–14, 94
Faletto, Enzo, 47, 50, 53
Falkland Islands, 147
FARC, Revolutionary Armed Forces of Colombia
Faynzilber, Fernando, 37
Fernández, Mario, 168
Fernández, Sergio, 92–3, 103, 109
FLACSO, See Latin American Faculty of Social Sciences
14th Arrondissement (Paris), 72
Fischer, Joschka, 183
Fleischer, Ari, 226
Fox, Vicente, 220
Foxley, Alejandro, 37, 119, 125, 134
France, 7–8, 35, 48, 101, 140, 156, 181–3, 187, 195, 207, 215, 220, 223, 231
free market economics, 20, 39–42, 48, 147, 185, 190, 215, 251 See "Chicago Boys"
free trade agreements, 179–86, 208, 211
"freedom riders," 15
Frei Montalva, Eduardo, viii, 23–5, 40, 45, 63, 76, 88, 118–19, 136–7, 142, 145, 147, 154, 162, 173, 175, 180, 207, 246–7
Fresno, Francisco, 63
Friedman, Milton, 20, 39, 41
Fuentes, Carlos, 242
future of Chile, 242–54

Gandhi, Mahatma, 20, 64–5
García Márquez, Gabriel, 242
Garzón, Baltazar, 146, 151
Germany, 62, 88–9, 182–3, 195, 223, 230
Gil, Federico, 34
global economic recession (1980), 46
global financial crisis (2007–present), 177
Global South, 228, 243
globalization, 186, 215
gold standard, 25
González, Felipe, 84, 221
grapes (Chilean), 114–15, 140–1
Great Britain, 17, 19, 28, 42, 48–9, 147–8, 151, 191, 195, 210–11, 215, 217–19, 222–3, 225, 230–1, 248
Great Depression, 18, 39
Group of 24, 55
"Growth with Equality," 187
Guadalajara, Mexico, 242
Guastavino, Luis, 93
Guatemalan coup d'état (1954), 23
Guillier, Alejandro, 14
Guterres, António, 208–9, 231
Guzmán, Jaime, 117–18

Hales, Alejandro, 76, 99, 114
Harberger, Arnold, 39–40
Hart, Judith, 49
health care, 41, 63, 187–94, 196, 247, 250
Helms, Richard, 27
Henríquez (former student), 74
highway expansion, 139–40
Hoover, Calvin B., 20
housing, 187–8, 196 See "Casas Lagos"
human rights abuses, vii, 2, 10, 31–2, 42–3, 61–2, 74–6, 85, 88, 93, 95, 99, 119, 127, 135, 143–4, 146, 148, 150–69, 227, 244 See disappeared persons; kidnappings; torture; Valech Report

Hussein, Saddam, 206–8, 213–15, 217–18, 220–1, 223–6

IBM, 144
independence day (Chilean), 135
Independent Democratic Union Party (UDI), 108
inequality, viii, 7, 15, 17–18, 21, 124–5, 129, 172, 186–7, 194, 198–9, 239, 243–51
inflation, 19, 26, 127, 134
informal economy, 35–7
infrastructure, ix–x, 7, 37–8, 60, 119, 123, 137–40, 143, 174, 230
Insulza, José Miguel, 146
Inter-American College of Defense, 168
Inter-American Development Bank, 31, 65, 168
International Labor Organization (ILO), 35–6
International Monetary Fund (IMF), 37, 184, 242–3, 249
International Red Cross, 31
Internet, 130–1, 248, 251–2
Iraq war (2003–present), 200–1, 205–8, 211–27
Izurieta, Ricardo, 156

Japan, 212, 214, 234
Jaramillo, Armando, 3, 11–12
Jarpa, Sergio Onofre, 61, 63, 102, 109, 112
Jiang Zemin, 143–4
Jim Crow laws, 15
Jiménez, Tucapel, 54–5
job creation, 174–5, 180
John Paul II, 93, 162
Johnson, Lyndon, 21
Jospin, Lionel, 135, 181, 231
junta "way of life," viii, x, 1–2, 6, 9, 12, 28–34, 40–5, 48, 54, 61, 63, 87, 93, 99, 103, 106–9, 150, 161, 166, 174

Kennedy, John F., 206
Keynes, John Maynard, 20–1, 39
kidnapping, 62, 152, 155
Kissinger, Henry, 24, 31–2
Koizumi, Junichiro, 234
Korry, Edward, 25
Krauss, Enrique, 119
Kuznets, Simón, 21

La Celebración del Triunfo del No (The Celebration of the Triumph of the No) (painting), 106
La Comedia (Santiago), 65
la cueca, 81, 95
La Moneda, viii, 2, 12, 28–30, 40, 45–7, 63, 89, 92, 106, 120–1, 135, 137, 145, 169–71, 173, 195, 204, 206, 216–17, 222, 230, 232
La Nación newspaper, 74
La Paz, 235, 237
La Reina, 28, 55, 70
La Serena, 4–6, 63, 91
labor unions, 54, 63, 88, 116, 183, 250
Lacalle, Luis Alberto, 65
Lagos, Alejandro (son), xii, 59–60, 69
Lagos, Carmen Weber (first wife), 19, 22
Lagos, Emma Escobar Morales (mother), 16–17, 28, 76–7, 87
Lagos, Francisca (daughter), 13, 36
Lagos, Froilán (father), 16–17
Lagos, Hernán (son), xii, 59–60, 72–3
Lagos, Panchita (daughter), xii, 59–60, 70
Lagos, Luisa Durán de la Fuente (second wife), xii, 22–3, 26, 28,

30, 34–6, 50, 59, 69–70, 73, 76,
  84–5, 108, 118, 197–8, 209
Lagos, Ricardo academic career of,
  22, 24, 34–5, 49–50; arrest
  of, 69–86; childhood of,
  16–17; diplomatic career of,
  24–5, 35–6, 50–1; education
  of, 15–23; political career of,
  See political career; and self-
  imposed exile, 33–6
Lagos, Ricardo (son), xii, 22, 33,
  59–60, 81
Lagos, Ximena (daughter), xii, 22,
  59–60, 118
Lamy, Pascal, 181–2
Latin American Faculty of Social
  Sciences (FLACSO), 24, 32–5
Latin American Social Sciences
  Council, 34–5
Lavin, Joaquín, 145, 148
Lee, Yuan Tseh, 232
leftist ideology, 4–5, 17, 29–32, 37,
  44, 48–52, 58, 68, 73–4, 82–3,
  87–9, 108, 113, 115, 127, 148,
  160–1, 164, 173, 177, 203–4,
  211, 215, 250
Leigh, Gustavo, 29, 43
Leighton, Bernardo, 42
Letelier, Orlando, 42–3, 146
Levitte, Jean David, 220
Li Peng, 143–4
Lipset, Seymour, 22
Luengo, Luis Fernando, 4
Lugar, Richard, 65

MacLarty, Thomas ("Mack"), 222
Maluenda, Maria, 62
Manning, David, 217–18
Marotto, Rafael, 73–4
Marshall Islands, 212
Martinez, Reynaldo, 161
Marxism, 25, 29, 32
Massachusetts Institute of Technology,
  21
Matte Valdés, Luis ("Lucho"), 47
Matthei, Fernando, 93, 99, 103
Mauroy, Pierre, 101
Mbeki, Thabo, 231
MDP, See Popular Democratic
  Movement
MERCOSUR, See South American
  Common Market (Mercado
  Común del Sur)
Merino, José Toribio, 12, 93, 103
Mesa de Diálogo (Table for Dialogue),
  154–8, 167
Mesa Guisbert, Carlos, 238–9
Mexican peso crisis of 1994, 183
Mexico, 19, 35, 51, 180, 190, 201–2,
  218–20, 228, 238, 242
Michaels, David Michaels, 190
Military Academy, 30, 136
Military of Chile, 28, 155–7, 166
mining, 41, 67, 96–7, 141–2, 144,
  174, 178
Ministry of Defense, 93, 100, 102, 168
Ministry of Education, xi, 106, 120,
  123, 126, 136, 145, 153, 155,
  157, 181
Ministry of Finance, 37, 41, 43, 46, 88,
  109, 119–20, 134, 176, 179, 232
Ministry of Foreign Affairs, 80, 105–6,
  120, 146, 207
Ministry of Health, 168, 191, 193, 246
Ministry of Interior, 4, 9, 12–13, 27, 61,
  85, 92, 108–9, 119–20, 222
Ministry of Justice, 119
Ministry of Labor, 41
Ministry of Public Works, ix, xi, 119,
  137, 141–3, 178

Mizzala, Alejandra, 50
modernization, 21, 41, 141, 185, 247–8
Molina, Gustavo, 160–1
Molina, Sergio, 88
Morales, Evo, 239–40
Muñoz, Heraldo, 47, 53, 100, 213–14

Nasser, Gamal Abdel, 20
National Congress of Chile, 23, 26, 28,
  44, 87, 112, 121, 128, 133, 149,
  168, 178–80
National Institute, 17
National Renewal (RN) Party, 3, 108–9,
  111–12
National Security Council, 109, 169
natural resources, 175–8
Nazi Germany, 210
Negroponte, John, 212
Nehru, Jawaharlal, 20
Neruda, Pablo, viii, 122–3, 125
New Deal, 21, 39
Newsweek interview, 82
Nixon, Richard, ix, 24–5, 27, 31–2, 235
"No" campaign, 3, 9, 13–14, 45, 88,
  90–103, 106–7, 207
Norway, 175
Núñez, Ricardo, 52, 114, 120

O'Higgins, Bernardo, 5, 58–9
Obama, Barack, 234, 254
OECD, See Organisation for Economic
  Co-operation and Development
oil, 46, 173, 175, 178, 180, 204
Ono, Yoko, 148
OPEC, See Organization of Petroleum
  Exporting Countries
Organization of Petroleum Exporting
  Countries (OPEC), 204
"Operation Colombo," 150
Operation Condor, 41–2, 146
opposition to Pinochet, 50–68, 69–77,
  87–104, 105–15 and church,
  62–3; and comedy, 65; and
  European support, 87–9; and
  human rights abuses, See
  human rights abuses; post-
  referendum period, 105–15
  See Concertación; and Rodrigo
  Rojas de Negri, 66–7; and
  torture, See torture; and U.S.
  support, 65–6; and victory, 105;
  and violence, 51–2, 67–8, 71, 87;
  See "No" campaign; protests
Organization of American States, 32
Organisation for Economic Cooperation and Development
  (OECD), 250
Ortiz, Eduardo, 47, 53
Oviedo, Carlos, 131–3

Palestinians, 224–5
Parada, José Manuel, 62
Parada, Roberto, 62
Party for Democracy (PPD), vii, 1–3,
  8, 11, 89–92, 98, 102–3, 113–15,
  118–19, 168 creating, 89–92
pensions, 8, 41, 63, 195
Perez Yoma, Edmundo, 155, 168
Permanent Committee for Socialist
  Unity (CPU), 52
Perón, Juan, 33
Persson, Göran, 230–1
Peru, 67, 160, 204, 228, 234, 238
Piñera, José, 41
Piñera, Sebastian, 240
Pinochet, Augusto, vii-viii, 1–14, 20,
  23, 28–9, 31–2, 34–5, 37–8,
  40–52, 54–61, 63–71, 73–4,
  76–9, 82–90, 92–104, 105–21,
  123, 125, 127–8, 133–6, 142–3,

145, 146–64, 166–72, 174,
  187, 195, 207, 213, 245, 248
  abdicating power, 103–4, 133–4;
  as Army chief, 28; arrests of,
  146–51; assassination attempt
  on, 68, 69–70, 74, 87; and
  "cabinet of projection," 92–3;
  and corruption, 150–1; and
  economics, 37–8, 40–8, 134,
  172; and education reform, 127;
  and elections, 43–5; and human
  rights abuses, See human rights
  abuses; legacy of, 150–1, 167–9;
  opposition to, See opposition;
  referendum against, See "No"
  campaign; and secret police,
  See secret police; and security
  alliances, 41–2; senator, 149–50;
  U.S. support of, 31
Plan Z, 161
plebiscites, vii-viii, 2–3, 6, 8–11, 13, 28,
  43–5, 67, 87–93, 97–8, 100–1,
  106, 108, 110, 112–13
Policía de Investigaciones, 69–71,
  74–5, 78–9
political career ambassador to Soviet
  Union, 25, 32; campaigning for
  Concertación, 115–18, 164–5;
  informal advisor to Allende, 24;
  and Kissinger, 31–2; meeting
  Pinochet, 135–6; minister
  of education, xi, 106, 120–1,
  122–8, 134–6, 145, 157, 181;
  minister of justice, 119; minister
  of public works, 137, 145; and
  "No" campaign, 90–106; post-
  referendum period, 105–13;
  and presidency, See presidency;
  and the senate, 115–19; and tear
  gas, 116–17; and tripod theory
  of government, 172–3
Popular Action Front party, 24
Popular Democratic Movement
  (MDP), 67
poverty, 8, 15–17, 19, 36, 54, 114,
  173–4, 186–7, 195–8, 229,
  246, 249
Powell, Colin, 202, 205–6, 215, 217, 219
Prats González, Carlos, 27–8, 30, 33–4,
  41–2, 146, 166 assassination of,
  34, 41, 166
PREALC, See Regional Program for
  Employment in Latin America
  and the Caribbean
presidency (Lagos's), 16, 31–2,
  47, 113–14, 130, 135–7,
  147–8, 155–6, 164, 167, 172–99,
  201–41 campaigning for, 147–8,
  155–6, 188–9, 197; and the
  economy, 172–89; first run
  for, 136–7; and health care,
  187–94; inauguration for, 148,
  155; and job creation, 174–5,
  180; and pension system, 195;
  and poverty, 195–6; and tripod
  theory of government, 172–3.
  See Iraq war; September 11,
  2001
prisons, 140
privatization, viii, ix, 40–2, 46, 48, 121,
  123–4, 134, 139–40, 142, 151–2,
  163, 174, 186, 189–95, 199, 231,
  238, 245, 252
Program of the 900, 125–9
protests, 10–11, 47, 50–1, 53, 55–7,
  61, 66–7, 74, 79, 93, 102, 107,
  108, 128, 130–1, 135, 219, 236
  250 anti-Pinochet, 10–11, 47,
  50–1, 53, 55–7, 61, 66–7, 74,
  79, 93, 102, 107, 108, 128; and

education, 130–1, 135, 219, 236 250
Puerto Montt, 116–17, 139, 245
Putin, Vladimir, 202, 223, 233–4

Radical Party, 17, 23–4, 55, 88, 98, 152

PPD, See Party for Democracy

Quintana, Carmen, 66
Quiroga, Jorge, 237–8

Radio Cooperativa, 56, 85, 92
Radio Escolar, 126
Radio Magallanes, 29
Radio Nacional, 26–7
Reagan, Ronald, 42, 48, 65, 67
recession (1982–1983), 46–7, 50–4
Regional Program for Employment in Latin America and the Caribbean (PREALC), 35–7
Rettig Report, 151–4, 167
Revolution in Liberty, 24–5
Revolutionary Armed Forces of Colombia (FARC), 203–4
Rice, Condoleezza, 184, 202, 205, 213–14, 238
Riggs Bank, 150
RN, See National Renewal Party
Rodríguez, Aniceto, 116
Rodríguez, Eduardo, 238
Rojas de Negri, Rodrigo, 66
Roosevelt, Franklin Delano, 21
Rostow, Walt, 21
Russia, 215–17, 223, 233
Rwanda, 166

Sandoval, Hernan, 190
Scarlett, John, 217–18
Schaulsohn, Jorge, 4
Schnake, Erich, 93
Schroeder, Gerhard, 182–3, 230–1
Scowcroft, Brent, 221
Shultz, George, 66–7
secret police, 41–3, 50, 64, 74, 78–9, 98, 116, 150, 158
Seers, Dudley, 48
Seguel, Rodolfo, 55–7
September 11, 2001, 201–2, 205, 208–11, 214, 230
Sepúlveda, María Luisa, 162
Serra, José, 24
Sherping, Guillermo, 73, 81
"shock therapy," 37, 41–3
Sierra Leone, 166
Solimano, Giorgio, 161
Silva Cimma, Enrique, 58–9, 114, 119
Silva Henríquez, Raúl, 28, 62–3
Smith, Robert S., 19
socialists, viii-ix, 2, 5–6, 18, 23, 25, 27, 29–30, 32, 35, 37, 40, 44, 47–9, 51–5, 57–61, 67, 71, 73, 85, 87–91, 93, 111, 114, 118, 120, 139, 147, 169, 173–4, 180–1, 186, 203, 207, 213

Socialist Party, 5–6, 44, 51–3, 58–9, 67, 71, 73, 88–9, 91, 114, 118, 120, 147, 207
Solano, Alicia de, 72
Solano, Miguel, 84–5
Sonrisa de Mujer (Women's Smiles), 197–8
Soto, Akin, 53–4
Soto, Alicia, 29
Soto, Oscar, 29
South American Common Market, Mercado Común del Sur (MERCOSUR), 180–3, 235
Soviet Union, 18–20, 25, 32, 206
Spain, 5, 48, 88–9, 146–8, 169, 182, 207, 219, 230
Spengler, Joseph J., 20
Sputnik, 18
The Stages of Economic Growth (1960) (Rostow), 21
Stange, Rodolfo, 99
Stevenson, Adlai, 206
Stiglitz, Joseph, 37
Straw, Jack, 148
Stuardo, Julio, 53–4
Summit of the Americas, 201
Summit of Progressive Leaders, 230–1
Supreme Court, 109, 149–50, 166, 169, 238
Sweden, 88, 116, 160, 230–1, 245

Taiwan, 24, 42, 232
taxes, 178–9, 198
"Teachers Statute," 128
Tejas Verdes, 161
Telteilboin, Volodia, 100
Thatcher, Margaret, 42, 48, 147
Third Way, 215, 230
Tito, Marshal, 20
Tocqueville, Alex de, 252
Tohá, Carolina, 4
Tohá, José, 4, 33
Tohá, Moy de, 33
Tokman, Victor Tokman, 36
Tomkins, Douglas, 75–6
Torres, Juan José, 234
Torres, Miguel, 140–1
torture, vii, 2, 30–1, 52, 60, 66, 108, 134, 151–2, 161–9
Townley, Michael, 43
Trabucco, Eduardo, 47, 53
Transantiago program, 244
transperancy, 237, 247, 254

UDI, See Independent Democratic Union Party
"Uncommitted Six" ("U-6"), 219, 225
unemployment, ix, 26, 36–7, 42, 54, 173, 187, 195. See informal economy
United Nations, 24–5, 28, 30, 35–6, 43, 50–1, 55, 59, 82, 85, 134, 143, 197, 200, 205–8, 211–12, 215–16, 218–19, 221, 226, 242–3, 253

U.N. Educational, Scientific and Cultural Organization (UNESCO), 35, 134
U.N. General Assembly, 24, 85
U.N. Human Rights Commission, 24, 143
U.N. Security Council, 24, 200, 205, 207, 212, 214, 217–18, 223–5, 227, 229, 231
U.S. AFL-CIO, 55
U.S. Congress, 27, 32, 42, 183–4, 189–90
U.S. Embassy, 75–6, 100, 114
U.S. Food and Drug Administration, 114
U.S. trade deficit, 25
U.S. Treasury Department, 183–4
University of Chicago, 39–49 See "Chicago Boys"
University of Chile, 17, 22, 49–50
University of North Carolina, Chapel Hill, 34–5
University of Texas, Austin, 35
Uribe, Álvaro, 204
Uruguay, 65, 72, 180, 235, 248

Valdés, Gabriel, 57–9, 61, 63, 205–7, 211, 219–20, 225
Valdivia, Pedro de, 96, 157, 164–5, 244
Valech Aldunate, Sergio, 162–7
Valech Report, 162–7
value added tax (VAT), 178
Vanguardia interview, 81
Vector institute, 47–53
Venezuela, 177, 201, 203–4, 228
Venice, 137–8
Vicariate de la Solidaridad, 61–2, 152, 159, 162
Viera-Gallo, José Antonio, 111
Vivienda Social Dinámica sin Deuda (Dynamic Social Housing without Debt), 187–8

War College, 33
War in Afghanistan (2001–present), 211
War of the Pacific (1879–1883), 203, 234
War on Terror, 183, 211
"Washington Consensus," 37
water industry, 141–2
wine industry, 140–1
Winter, Augusto, 123
Women for Democracy, 63
Woodrow Wilson Center for Scholars, 65
World Bank, ix, 125, 129, 183–4, 197
World Economic Forum (1999), 213–14
World Health Organization, 35, 190, 242
World War II, 7, 19, 25, 104, 210–12, 231, 248–9, 251

Yohe, William P., 20

Zaldivar, Andrés, 118, 145
Zoellick, Robert, 183